Contents

Pumpkin Brownies

Prep: 20 mins **Cook:** 40 mins **Total:** 1 hr **Servings:** 16 **Yield:** 1 - 8x8 inch pan of brownies

Ingredients

- ¾ cup all-purpose flour
- ½ teaspoon baking powder
- ½ teaspoon salt
- ¾ cup butter, melted
- 1 ½ cups white sugar
- 2 teaspoons vanilla extract
- 3 large eggs eggs

- ¼ cup cocoa powder
- ½ cup semi-sweet chocolate chips
- ½ cup pumpkin puree
- ½ cup chopped walnuts
- ¾ teaspoon ground cinnamon
- ½ teaspoon ground cloves
- ½ teaspoon ground nutmeg

Directions

Step 1

Preheat oven to 350 degrees F (175 degrees C). Grease an 8x8 inch baking pan. Stir the flour, baking powder, and salt together in a bowl.

Step 2

In another bowl, stir together the melted butter, sugar, and vanilla extract; beat in the eggs one at a time with a spoon. Gradually add the flour mixture, and stir the batter until it's evenly moistened. Divide the batter in half in two separate bowls.

Step 3

Into one bowl of batter, blend the cocoa powder and chocolate chips. In the second bowl of batter, stir in the pumpkin puree, walnuts, cinnamon, cloves, and nutmeg.

Step 4

Spread 1/2 of the chocolate batter into the bottom of the prepared baking pan, and follow with 1/2 of the pumpkin batter. Repeat the layers, ending with a pumpkin layer, and drag a kitchen knife or small spatula gently through the layers in a swirling motion, to create a marbled appearance.

Step 5

Bake in the preheated oven until the brownies begin to pull away from the sides of the pan, and a toothpick inserted into the center comes out clean, 40 to 45 minutes. Cool in the pan, cut into squares, and serve.

Nutrition Facts

Per Serving:

241.5 calories; protein 3g 6% DV; carbohydrates 28.8g 9% DV; fat 13.9g 21% DV; cholesterol 57.8mg 19% DV; sodium 182mg 7% DV.

Spooky Witches' Fingers

Prep: 35 mins **Cook:** 20 mins **Additional:** 20 mins **Total:** 1 hr 15 mins **Servings:** 60 **Yield:** 60 cookies

Ingredients

- 1 cup butter, softened
- 1 cup confectioners' sugar
- 1 egg
- 1 teaspoon almond extract
- 1 teaspoon vanilla extract

- 2 ⅔ cups all-purpose flour
- 1 teaspoon baking powder
- 1 teaspoon salt
- ¾ cup whole almonds
- 1 (.75 ounce) tube red decorating gel

Directions

Step 1

Combine the butter, sugar, egg, almond extract, and vanilla extract in a mixing bowl. Beat together with an electric mixer; gradually add the flour, baking powder, and salt, continually beating; refrigerate 20 to 30 minutes.

Step 2

Preheat oven to 325 degrees F (165 degrees C). Lightly grease baking sheets.

Step 3

Remove dough from refrigerator in small amounts. Scoop 1 heaping teaspoon at a time onto a piece of waxed paper. Use the waxed paper to roll the dough into a thin finger-shaped cookie. Press one almond into one end of each cookie to give the appearance of a long fingernail. Squeeze cookie near the tip and again near the center of each to give the impression of knuckles. You can also cut into the dough with a sharp knife at the same points to help give a more finger-like appearance. Arrange the shaped cookies on the baking sheets.

Step 4

Bake in the preheated oven until the cookies are slightly golden in color, 20 to 25 minutes.

Step 5

Remove the almond from the end of each cookie; squeeze a small amount of red decorating gel into the cavity; replace the almond to cause the gel to ooze out around the tip of the cookie.

Nutrition Facts

Per Serving:

68.3 calories; protein 1.1g 2% DV; carbohydrates 6.9g 2% DV; fat 4.1g 6% DV; cholesterol 11.2mg 4% DV; sodium 75.7mg 3% DV.

Halloween Chocolate Chip Cookies with Spiders

Prep: 30 mins **Cook:** 11 mins **Additional:** 1 min **Total:** 42 mins **Servings:** 48 **Yield:** 4 dozen

Ingredients

- 2 ½ cups all-purpose flour
- 1 teaspoon baking soda
- 1 teaspoon salt
- ½ teaspoon baking powder
- 1 cup unsalted butter, at room temperature
- ¾ cup white sugar
- ¾ cup packed brown sugar
- 2 large eggs eggs
- 1 teaspoon vanilla extract
- 2 ½ cups semisweet chocolate chips, divided

Directions

Step 1

Preheat oven to 350 degrees F (175 degrees C).

Step 2

Combine flour, baking soda, salt, and baking powder in a large bowl and stir with a fork to mix ingredients well.

Step 3

Combine butter, white sugar, and brown sugar in a large bowl; beat with an electric mixer until smooth and creamy. Add eggs and vanilla extract and beat until smooth and fluffy. Add in flour mixture, 1 cup at a time, and mix in with a spatula until well incorporated. Fold in 1 1/2 cups chocolate chips until well combined.

Step 4

Drop cookies onto ungreased baking sheets. Pour 1/2 cup chocolate chips into a bowl. Push about 3 to 4 chocolate chips onto each cookie, tip-side down, to make the spider bodies.

Step 5

Bake in the the preheated oven until edges are golden, 10 to 15 minutes. Cool on the baking sheet for 1 minute before removing to a wire rack.

Step 6

Melt remaining 1/2 cup chocolate in a microwave-safe glass or ceramic bowl in 15-second intervals, stirring after each melting, 1 to 3 minutes. Spoon melted chocolate into a piping bag with a small tip and draw little legs on each side of the spider bodies to create spider legs.

Nutrition Facts

Per Serving:

127.9 calories; protein 1.3g 3% DV; carbohydrates 17g 6% DV; fat 6.7g 10% DV; cholesterol 17.9mg 6% DV; sodium 112mg 5% DV.

Witches' Hats

Prep: 1 hr **Total:** 1 hr **Servings:** 32 **Yield:** 32 servings

Ingredients

- 2 (16 ounce) packages fudge stripe cookies
- ¼ cup honey, or as needed
- 1 (9 ounce) bag milk chocolate candy kisses, unwrapped
- 1 (4.5 ounce) tube decorating gel

Directions

Step 1

Place a fudge stripe cookie with bottom side up onto a work surface. Smear a small dab (about 1/8 teaspoon) of honey onto the bottom of a chocolate kiss, and secure the candy piece to the center of the cookie, covering the hole. Use decorating gel to pipe a small bow onto the cookie at the base of the candy piece. Repeat with remaining ingredients.

Nutrition Facts

Per Serving:

203.7 calories; protein 2.4g 5% DV; carbohydrates 28.5g 9% DV; fat 8.7g 13% DV; cholesterol 1.7mg 1% DV; sodium 169.9mg 7% DV.

Sugar Cookie Icing

Prep: 15 mins **Total:** 15 mins **Servings:** 12 **Yield:** 1 dozen cookies' worth

Ingredients

- 1 cup confectioners' sugar
- 2 teaspoons milk
- 2 teaspoons light corn syrup
- ¼ teaspoon almond extract

- Recommended:
- assorted food coloring

Directions

Step 1

In a small bowl, stir together confectioners' sugar and milk until smooth. Beat in corn syrup and almond extract until icing is smooth and glossy. If icing is too thick, add more corn syrup.

Step 2

Divide into separate bowls, and add food colorings to each to desired intensity. Dip cookies, or paint them with a brush.

Nutrition Facts

Per Serving:

42.4 calories; proteing; carbohydrates 10.8g 4% DV; fatg; cholesterolmg; sodium 0.8mg.

Halloween Skeleton Cookies

Prep: 45 mins **Cook:** 8 mins **Additional:** 6 hrs 20 mins **Total:** 7 hrs 13 mins **Servings:** 40 **Yield:** 40 cookies

Ingredients

- 1 ½ cups white sugar
- 1 cup butter, softened
- 2 eaches eggs
- 1 ½ teaspoons vanilla extract
- 1 ½ teaspoons almond flavoring

- 3 ½ cups all-purpose flour
- 1 teaspoon baking powder
- ½ teaspoon salt
- 2 tablespoons confectioners' sugar

Icing:

- 1 cup confectioners' sugar
- 2 teaspoons milk, plus more as needed
- 2 teaspoons light corn syrup, or more as needed

- ¼ teaspoon vanilla extract
- 1 (1.5 ounce) tube black decorating gel

Directions

Step 1

Cream sugar and butter in a bowl with an electric mixer until creamy. Add eggs, 1 1/2 teaspoons vanilla extract, and almond flavoring and mix well.

Step 2

17

Stir flour, baking powder, and salt together in a second bowl. Add flour mixture to the creamed butter mixture and mix to combine. Wrap in plastic wrap and chill in the refrigerator for 3 to 4 hours or overnight.

Step 3

Preheat oven to 350 degrees F (175 degrees C). Line 2 baking sheets with parchment paper.

Step 4

Dust a work surface with 2 tablespoons confectioners' sugar and roll out dough into a 1/4-inch-thick circle. Cut out figure shapes with a gingerbread man cookie cutter and arrange cut-out cookies on prepared baking sheets.

Step 5

Bake in the preheated oven for 8 to 10 minutes. Remove from baking sheets carefully and transfer to wire racks. Cool completely, about 20 minutes.

Step 6

Stir 1 cup confectioners' sugar and milk together in a small bowl until smooth. Beat in corn syrup and 1/4 teaspoon vanilla extract until icing is smooth and glossy. Add more corn syrup if icing is too thick.

Step 7

Spoon icing into a piping bag with a small plain tip. Draw a filled-out circle inside the head for the skull and a skeleton on the body, including 3 horizontal lines for the ribs. Let cookies stand until icing dries completely, about 2 hour, best overnight.

Step 8

Use black decorating gel to draw eyes, a nose, and a mouth on the skull and let cookies dry again, about 1 hour.

Nutrition Facts

Per Serving:

131.2 calories; protein 1.5g 3% DV; carbohydrates 20.4g 7% DV; fat 4.9g 8% DV; cholesterol 20.4mg 7% DV; sodium 94.5mg 4% DV.

Apple Crisp Cookies

Prep: 30 mins **Cook:** 10 mins **Additional:** 50 mins **Total:** 1 hr 30 mins **Servings:** 24 **Yield:** 2 dozen cookies

Ingredients

- 2 cups whole wheat flour, plus
- 2 tablespoons whole wheat flour
- 1 ½ teaspoons ground cinnamon
- 1 teaspoon baking powder
- 1 teaspoon salt
- ½ cup butter, softened
- ½ cup demerara sugar

- ½ cup brown sugar
- 7 tablespoons apple butter
- 2 large eggs eggs
- 1 teaspoon vanilla extract
- 3 tablespoons apple juice
- 2 cups quick cooking oats
- 1 apple, finely chopped

Directions

Step 1

Preheat oven to 375 degrees F (190 degrees C). In a large bowl, mix all of the whole wheat flour together with the cinnamon, baking powder and salt.

Step 2

In a separate bowl, mash the butter, demerara sugar, and brown sugar together until thoroughly combined, then stir in the apple butter until smooth. Stir in eggs, vanilla extract, and apple juice until well mixed; pour the liquid mixture into the flour mixture about 1/3 cup at a time, stirring after each addition. Mix in the oats and chopped apple.

Step 3

With 2 teaspoons, form the dough into balls and place onto ungreased baking sheets about 2 inches apart.

Step 4

Bake in the preheated oven until the cookies are lightly browned and set in the centers, about 10 minutes; allow to cool for about 2 minutes on baking sheets until removing to finish cooling on wire racks.

Nutrition Facts

Per Serving:

147.6 calories; protein 3g 6% DV; carbohydrates 24.1g 8% DV; fat 4.9g 8% DV; cholesterol 25.7mg 9% DV; sodium 155mg 6% DV.

Pumpkin Cookies III

Prep: 15 mins **Cook:** 15 mins **Total:** 30 mins **Servings:** 36 **Yield:** 3 dozen

Ingredients

- 1 cup white sugar
- 1 egg
- 1 cup shortening
- 1 teaspoon vanilla extract
- 2 cups all-purpose flour
- 1 teaspoon baking soda
- 1 teaspoon baking powder
- 1 teaspoon salt
- 1 teaspoon ground cinnamon
- 1 cup canned pumpkin
- ½ cup raisins
- ½ cup chopped walnuts

Directions

Step 1

Preheat oven to 350 degrees F (175 degrees C). Grease cookie sheets.

Step 2

In a large bowl, cream together sugar, egg, shortening, and vanilla. Sift together flour, baking soda, baking powder, salt, and cinnamon; stir into the creamed mixture. Stir in the pumpkin, raisins, and walnuts. Drop dough by teaspoonfuls onto the prepared cookie sheets.

Step 3

Bake 10-15 minutes in the preheated oven.

Nutrition Facts

Per Serving:

119.5 calories; protein 1.3g 3% DV; carbohydrates 13.6g 4% DV; fat 7g 11% DV; cholesterol 5.2mg 2% DV; sodium 131.9mg 5% DV.

Iced Pumpkin Cookies

Prep: 20 mins **Cook:** 20 mins **Additional:** 40 mins **Total:** 1 hr 20 mins **Servings:** 36 **Yield:** 3 dozen

Ingredients

- 2 ½ cups all-purpose flour
- 1 teaspoon baking powder
- 1 teaspoon baking soda
- 2 teaspoons ground cinnamon

- ½ teaspoon ground nutmeg
- ½ teaspoon ground cloves
- ½ teaspoon salt
- ½ cup butter, softened
- 1 ½ cups white sugar
- 1 cup canned pumpkin puree

- 1 egg
- 1 teaspoon vanilla extract
- 2 cups confectioners' sugar
- 3 tablespoons milk
- 1 tablespoon melted butter
- 1 teaspoon vanilla extract

Directions

Step 1

Preheat oven to 350 degrees F (175 degrees C). Combine flour, baking powder, baking soda, cinnamon, nutmeg, ground cloves, and salt; set aside.

Step 2

In a medium bowl, cream together the 1/2 cup of butter and white sugar. Add pumpkin, egg, and 1 teaspoon vanilla to butter mixture, and beat until creamy. Mix in dry ingredients. Drop on cookie sheet by tablespoonfuls; flatten slightly.

Step 3

Bake for 15 to 20 minutes in the preheated oven. Cool cookies, then drizzle glaze with fork.

Step 4

To Make Glaze: Combine confectioners' sugar, milk, 1 tablespoon melted butter, and 1 teaspoon vanilla. Add milk as needed, to achieve drizzling consistency.

Nutrition Facts

Per Serving:

121.5 calories; protein 1.2g 3% DV; carbohydrates 22.4g 7% DV; fat 3.2g 5% DV; cholesterol 12.9mg 4% DV; sodium 120.5mg 5% DV.

Chocolate Mice

Prep: 20 mins **Additional:** 2 hrs **Total:** 2 hrs 20 mins **Servings:** 12 **Yield:** 1 dozen

Ingredients

- 4 (1 ounce) squares semisweet chocolate
- ⅓ cup sour cream
- 1 cup chocolate cookie crumbs
- ⅓ cup chocolate cookie crumbs

- ⅓ cup confectioners' sugar
- 24 eaches silver dragees decorating candy
- ¼ cup sliced almonds
- 12 (2 inch) pieces long red vine licorice

Directions

Step 1

Melt the chocolate, and combine with sour cream. Stir in 1 cup chocolate cookie crumbs. Cover and refrigerate until firm.

Step 2

Roll by level tablespoonfuls into balls. Mold to a slight point at one end (the nose).

Step 3

Roll dough in confectioners sugar (for white mice), and in chocolate cookie crumbs (for dark mice). On each mouse, place dragees in appropriate spot for eyes, almond slices for ears, and a licorice string for the tail.

Step 4

Refrigerate for at least two hours, until firm.

Nutrition Facts

Per Serving:

176.4 calories; protein 2.3g 5% DV; carbohydrates 27.4g 9% DV; fat 7.2g 11% DV; cholesterol 3.1mg 1% DV; sodium 89.8mg 4% DV.

The Best Rolled Sugar Cookies

Prep: 20 mins **Cook:** 8 mins **Additional:** 2 hrs 32 mins **Total:** 3 hrs **Servings:** 60 **Yield:** 5 dozen

Ingredients

- 1 ½ cups butter, softened
- 2 cups white sugar
- 4 large eggs eggs
- 1 teaspoon vanilla extract
- 5 cups all-purpose flour
- 2 teaspoons baking powder
- 1 teaspoon salt

Directions

Step 1

In a large bowl, cream together butter and sugar until smooth. Beat in eggs and vanilla. Stir in the flour, baking powder, and salt. Cover, and chill dough for at least one hour (or overnight).

Step 2

Preheat oven to 400 degrees F (200 degrees C). Roll out dough on floured surface 1/4 to 1/2 inch thick. Cut into shapes with any cookie cutter. Place cookies 1 inch apart on ungreased cookie sheets.

Step 3

Bake 6 to 8 minutes in preheated oven. Cool completely.

Nutrition Facts

Per Serving:

109.5 calories; protein 1.5g 3% DV; carbohydrates 14.7g 5% DV; fat 5g 8% DV; cholesterol 24.6mg 8% DV; sodium 92.6mg 4% DV.

Acorn Candy Cookies

Prep: 15 mins **Additional:** 30 mins **Total:** 45 mins **Servings:** 24 **Yield:** 2 dozen acorns

Ingredients

- 1 tablespoon prepared chocolate frosting
- 24 piece (blank)s milk chocolate candy kisses (such as Hershey's Kisses), unwrapped
- 24 wafers mini vanilla wafer cookies (such as Nilla)
- 24 eaches butterscotch chips

Directions

Step 1

Smear a small amount of frosting onto the flat bottom of a candy kiss. Press onto the flat bottom of the vanilla wafer. Smear a little more frosting onto the flat bottom of a butterscotch chip, and press onto the rounded top of the cookie. Repeat with remaining ingredients. Set aside to dry, about 30 minutes.

Nutrition Facts

Per Serving:

132 calories; protein 0.5g 1% DV; carbohydrates 15.6g 5% DV; fat 6.7g 10% DV; cholesterol 1mg; sodium 31.5mg 1% DV.

Haunted Oreos

Prep: 15 mins **Additional:** 1 hr 15 mins **Total:** 1 hr 30 mins **Servings:** 26 **Yield:** 26 servings

Ingredients

- 12 ounces white chocolate chips

- 26 cookies chocolate sandwich cookies (such as Oreo)
- 6 ounces milk chocolate chips

Directions

Step 1

Line a baking sheet with parchment paper.

Step 2

Melt white chocolate in the top of a double boiler over simmering water, stirring frequently and scraping down the sides with a rubber spatula to avoid scorching.

Step 3

Dip each sandwich cookie in melted white chocolate to coat completely; transfer cookies to the prepared baking sheet. Chill in the freezer until almost hardened, about 30 minutes.

Step 4

Press 2 chocolate chips into each cookie to resemble eyes and 1 chocolate chip below the "eyes" to resemble a mouth. Chill in the freezer until completely set, about 45 minutes.

Nutrition Facts

Per Serving:

154 calories; protein 1.9g 4% DV; carbohydrates 18.3g 6% DV; fat 8.6g 13% DV; cholesterol 4.9mg 2% DV; sodium 72.7mg 3% DV.

Cake Balls

Prep: 40 mins **Cook:** 30 mins **Additional:** 2 hrs **Total:** 3 hrs 10 mins **Servings:** 36 **Yield:** 3 dozen

Ingredients

- 1 (18.25 ounce) package chocolate cake mix
- 1 (16 ounce) container prepared chocolate frosting
- 1 (3 ounce) bar chocolate flavored confectioners coating

Directions

Step 1

Prepare the cake mix according to package directions using any of the recommended pan sizes. When cake is done, crumble while warm into a large bowl, and stir in the frosting until well blended.

Step 2

Melt chocolate coating in a glass bowl in the microwave, or in a metal bowl over a pan of simmering water, stirring occasionally until smooth.

Step 3

Use a melon baller or small scoop to form balls of the chocolate cake mixture. Dip the balls in chocolate using a toothpick or fork to hold them. Place on waxed paper to set.

Nutrition Facts

Per Serving:

123.6 calories; protein 1.1g 2% DV; carbohydrates 19.7g 6% DV; fat 5.2g 8% DV; cholesterol 0.5mg; sodium 143.4mg 6% DV.

Halloween Ghost Cookies

Prep: 45 mins **Cook:** 6 mins **Additional:** 2 hrs 15 mins **Total:** 3 hrs 6 mins **Servings:** 90 **Yield:** 90 cookies

Ingredients

- 1 cup butter
- 1 ½ cups confectioners' sugar
- 1 egg
- 1 teaspoon vanilla extract
- 2 ½ cups all-purpose flour
- 1 teaspoon baking soda
- 1 teaspoon cream of tartar
- ¼ teaspoon salt

- Icing:
- 1 cup confectioners' sugar
- 2 teaspoons milk, plus more if needed
- 2 teaspoons light corn syrup, or more as needed
- ¼ teaspoon vanilla extract
- 1 (12 ounce) package miniature semisweet chocolate chips

Directions

Step 1

Beat butter in a bowl with an electric mixer until creamy. Add 1 1/2 cups confectioners' sugar gradually, beating until light and fluffy. Beat in egg and 1 teaspoon vanilla extract.

Step 2

Combine flour, baking soda, cream of tartar, and salt in a second bowl. Add flour mixture to the creamed butter mixture and mix to combine. Wrap in plastic wrap and chill in the refrigerator for at least 1 hour.

Step 3

Preheat oven to 400 degrees F (200 degrees C).

Step 4

Dust a work surface with flour and roll out dough into a thin circle. Cut out tulip shapes; if your tulip cookie cutter has a stem, cut the stem off with a knife, so you have a stemless tulip shape. Arrange cut-out cookies on ungreased baking sheets.

Step 5

Bake in the preheated oven until lightly browned, 6 to 8 minutes. Remove from baking sheets carefully and transfer to wire racks. Cool completely, about 15 minutes.

Step 6

Stir 1 cup confectioners' sugar and milk together in a small bowl until smooth. Beat in corn syrup and 1/4 teaspoon vanilla extract until icing is smooth and glossy. Add more corn syrup if icing is too thick.

Step 7

Spoon icing into a piping bag with a small plain tip. Pipe icing around the edge of each cookie to create a border. Fill in the middle completely with icing. Stick 2 chocolate chip cookies into the wet icing for the eyes. Let cookies stand until icing dries, about 1 hour.

Nutrition Facts

Per Serving:

63.5 calories; protein 0.6g 1% DV; carbohydrates 8.6g 3% DV; fat 3.3g 5% DV; cholesterol 7.5mg 3% DV; sodium 36.4mg 2% DV.

Michelle's Soft Sugar Cookies

Servings: 60 **Yield:** 3 to 5 dozen

Ingredients

- 1 cup margarine
- 1 ½ cups white sugar
- 3 large eggs eggs
- 1 teaspoon vanilla extract

- 3 ½ cups all-purpose flour
- 2 teaspoons cream of tartar
- 1 teaspoon baking soda
- ½ teaspoon salt

Directions

Step 1

Cream the margarine and add the sugar gradually. Beat until light and fluffy. Add eggs one at time, mixing well after each addition.

Step 2

Stir in the vanilla. Add the flour, cream of tartar, baking soda and salt gradually to the creamed mixture, stirring in by hand. Cover and chill dough overnight.

Step 3

Preheat oven to 375 degrees F (190 degrees C). Line baking sheets with parchment paper.

Step 4

Roll dough out on a floured surface to 1/8 to 1/4 inch thick and cut into your favorite shapes. Place cookies onto the prepared baking sheets.

Step 5

Bake at 375 degrees F (190 degrees C) for 6 to 8 minutes or until cookie has a golden appearance.

Nutrition Facts

Per Serving:

76.7 calories; protein 1.1g 2% DV; carbohydrates 10.7g 3% DV; fat 3.3g 5% DV; cholesterol 9.3mg 3% DV; sodium 79.1mg 3% DV.

Meringue Bones

Prep: 30 mins **Cook:** 1 hr **Additional:** 1 hr **Total:** 2 hrs 30 mins **Servings:** 36 **Yield:** 3 dozen bones

Ingredients

- 6 large egg whites egg whites
- ½ teaspoon cream of tartar
- 1 pinch salt
- 1 ⅓ cups white sugar
- 2 teaspoons vanilla extract

Directions

Step 1

Preheat oven to 225 degrees F (110 degrees C). Line 2 baking sheets with aluminum foil and grease the foil.

Step 2

Beat egg whites with cream of tartar and salt in a bowl with an electric mixer until egg whites are foamy. Gradually beat in sugar, a few tablespoons at a time, beating until the sugar dissolves in the meringue before adding more. Continue beating until the meringue is glossy and forms a sharp peak when beaters are lifted straight up out of the bowl; beat in vanilla extract. Spoon the meringue into a pastry bag fitted with a small tip.

Step 3

Pipe meringue into small bone shapes on the prepared aluminum foil. You must pipe all the shapes at once or the meringue will deflate.

Step 4

Place cookie sheets into the preheated oven and bake for 1 hour. No not open oven door or peek during baking. Turn the oven off and let the meringue bones cool in the oven without opening door for 1 hour. Gently and carefully remove cookies from aluminum to prevent broken bones.

Nutrition Facts

Per Serving:

32.1 calories; protein 0.6g 1% DV; carbohydrates 7.5g 2% DV; fatg; cholesterolmg; sodium 9.3mg.

Chocolate Spiders

Prep: 5 mins **Cook:** 25 mins **Total:** 30 mins **Servings:** 20 **Yield:** 20 spiders

Ingredients

- 1 pound chocolate confectioners' coating
- 1 (8.5 ounce) package chow mein noodles

Directions

Step 1

Chop the chocolate confectioners' coating and place into a heatproof bowl over simmering water. Cook, stirring occasionally until melted and smooth. Remove from heat and stir in the chow mein noodles so they are evenly distributed. Spoon out to desired size onto waxed paper. Let cool completely before storing or serving.

Nutrition Facts

Per Serving:

172.1 calories; protein 2.8g 6% DV; carbohydrates 17.6g 6% DV; fat 12.7g 20% DV; cholesterolmg; sodium 53.7mg 2% DV.

Peanut Butter Spider Cookies

Prep: 45 mins **Cook:** 10 mins **Total:** 55 mins **Servings:** 48 **Yield:** 48 cookies

Ingredients

- ½ cup shortening
- ½ cup peanut butter
- ½ cup packed brown sugar
- ½ cup white sugar
- 1 egg, beaten
- 2 tablespoons milk
- 1 teaspoon vanilla extract
- 1 ¾ cups all-purpose flour
- 1 teaspoon baking soda
- ½ teaspoon salt
- ¼ cup white sugar for rolling
- 24 piece (blank)s chocolate candy spheres with smooth chocolate filling (such as Lindt Lindor Truffles), refrigerated until cold
- 48 eaches decorative candy eyeballs
- ½ cup prepared chocolate frosting

Directions

Step 1

Preheat oven to 375 degrees F (190 degrees C). Line baking sheets with baking parchment.

Step 2

Beat shortening, peanut butter, brown sugar, and 1/2 cup white sugar together with an electric mixer in a large bowl until smooth. Beat egg into the creamy mixture until fully incorporated. Stir milk and vanilla extract into the mixture until smooth.

Step 3

Mix flour, baking soda, and salt together in a small bowl; add to the wet mixture in the large bowl and stir until completely incorporated into a dough. Divide and shape dough into 48 balls.

Step 4

Spread 1/4 cup white sugar into a wide, shallow bowl. Roll dough balls in sugar to coat and arrange about 2 inches apart onto prepared baking sheets.

Step 5

Bake in preheated oven until golden brown, 10 to 12 minutes. Remove cookies from oven and quickly press a dimple into the middle of each cookie using the blunt end of a wooden spoon. Cool cookies on sheets for 10 minutes before transferring to a wire cooling rack to cool completely.

Step 6

Cut each chocolate sphere into two hemispheres. Put one piece atop each cookie with the rounded side facing upwards.

Step 7

Spoon frosting into a pastry bag with a small round tip or a plastic freezer bag with one end snipped off. Dab a small amount of frosting onto the back of each candy eyeball and stick two onto each chocolate candy to resemble eyes. Then pipe frosting in four thin lines, starting at the base of the candy, on each side atop the cookie to resemble spider legs.

Step 8

Let frosting harden at room temperature, about 30 minutes. Store cookies in an airtight container.

Nutrition Facts

Per Serving:

117.2 calories; protein 1.7g 3% DV; carbohydrates 14.4g 5% DV; fat 6.3g 10% DV; cholesterol 7mg 2% DV; sodium 78mg 3% DV.

Owl Cookies

Servings: 36 Yield: 72 cookies

Ingredients

- 1 ¼ cups candy-coated milk chocolate pieces
- 2 tablespoons milk

- 24 ounces dry sugar cookie mix
- 1 cup cashew halves

Directions

Step 1

In a small saucepan combine 3/4 cup of the candies and milk. Melt over low heat, stirring until smooth. Remove from heat.

Step 2

Prepare cookie mixes according to package directions. Stir melted chocolate into half the dough. Form chocolate dough into two 12-inch long rolls about 1 inch in diameter. Wrap in wax paper or foil. Chill until firm, about 2 hours.

Step 3

Divide plain dough in half. On a well-floured surface, roll each plain half out to a 12 x 6 inch rectangle. Place a chocolate roll on long edge. Roll up, pressing doughs lightly together so plain dough encases chocolate roll. Repeat with remaining dough.

Step 4

Wrap each roll in wax paper or foil. Chill about 2 hours until firm. Preheat oven to 375 F (190 C).

Step 5

Cut each roll into 1/4 inch slices. Place 2 slices so they are touching on greased baking sheet. In the center of each chocolate circle, place one of the remaining candies for eye. Where the slices touch, place a cashew to form nose.

Step 6

Bake until the plain cookie is lightly browned, 8 to 10 minutes. Cool cookies on baking sheets 2 to 3 minutes. Remove and cool on wire racks.

Nutrition Facts

Per Serving:

150.8 calories; protein 1.9g 4% DV; carbohydrates 19.9g 6% DV; fat 7.2g 11% DV; cholesterol 7.1mg 2% DV; sodium 103.8mg 4% DV.

Halloween Ghost Cookies

Prep: 45 mins **Cook:** 6 mins **Additional:** 2 hrs 15 mins **Total:** 3 hrs 6 mins **Servings:** 90 **Yield:** 90 cookies

Ingredients

- 1 cup butter
- 1 ½ cups confectioners' sugar
- 1 egg
- 1 teaspoon vanilla extract
- 2 ½ cups all-purpose flour
- 1 teaspoon baking soda
- 1 teaspoon cream of tartar

- ¼ teaspoon salt
- Icing:
- 1 cup confectioners' sugar
- 2 teaspoons milk, plus more if needed
- 2 teaspoons light corn syrup, or more as needed
- ¼ teaspoon vanilla extract

- 1 (12 ounce) package miniature semisweet   chocolate chips

Directions

Step 1

Beat butter in a bowl with an electric mixer until creamy. Add 1 1/2 cups confectioners' sugar gradually, beating until light and fluffy. Beat in egg and 1 teaspoon vanilla extract.

Step 2

Combine flour, baking soda, cream of tartar, and salt in a second bowl. Add flour mixture to the creamed butter mixture and mix to combine. Wrap in plastic wrap and chill in the refrigerator for at least 1 hour.

Step 3

Preheat oven to 400 degrees F (200 degrees C).

Step 4

Dust a work surface with flour and roll out dough into a thin circle. Cut out tulip shapes; if your tulip cookie cutter has a stem, cut the stem off with a knife, so you have a stemless tulip shape. Arrange cut-out cookies on ungreased baking sheets.

Step 5

Bake in the preheated oven until lightly browned, 6 to 8 minutes. Remove from baking sheets carefully and transfer to wire racks. Cool completely, about 15 minutes.

Step 6

Stir 1 cup confectioners' sugar and milk together in a small bowl until smooth. Beat in corn syrup and 1/4 teaspoon vanilla extract until icing is smooth and glossy. Add more corn syrup if icing is too thick.

Step 7

Spoon icing into a piping bag with a small plain tip. Pipe icing around the edge of each cookie to create a border. Fill in the middle completely with icing. Stick 2 chocolate chip cookies into the wet icing for the eyes. Let cookies stand until icing dries, about 1 hour.

Nutrition Facts

Per Serving:

63.5 calories; protein 0.6g 1% DV; carbohydrates 8.6g 3% DV; fat 3.3g 5% DV; cholesterol 7.5mg 3% DV; sodium 36.4mg 2% DV.

Meringue Bones and Ghosts

Prep: 15 mins **Cook:** 1 hr **Additional:** 1 hr **Total:** 2 hrs 15 mins **Servings:** 6 **Yield:** 24 bones and ghosts

Ingredients

- 2 large egg whites large egg whites
- 2 drops fresh lemon juice, or more to taste
- 7 tablespoons white sugar, or more to taste

- 2 eaches chocolate chips, melted, or as needed

Directions

Step 1

Preheat oven to 225 degrees F (110 degrees C). Line 2 baking sheets with silicone baking mats.

Step 2

Whisk eggs whites and lemon juice together in a bowl until thick, white, and foamy. Add sugar a spoonful at a time, whisking constantly, until meringue is shiny, thick, and holds its shape.

Step 3

Transfer meringue to a piping bag. Pipe 12 bone shapes onto a prepared baking sheet. Pipe 12 puffs to resemble ghosts onto the remaining baking sheet.

Step 4

Bake in the preheated oven until dried and firm, about 1 hour. Turn off the oven, close the door, and cool until completely dried, about 1 hour more.

Step 5

Dip the tip of a toothpick into melted chocolate and dot chocolate "eyes" on each of the ghosts.

Nutrition Facts

Per Serving:

87.4 calories; protein 1.4g 3% DV; carbohydrates 18.1g 6% DV; fat 1.6g 3% DV; cholesterolmg; sodium 19.1mg 1% DV.

Oreo Devils

Prep: 30 mins **Cook:** 5 mins **Additional:** 1 hr **Total:** 1 hr 35 mins **Servings:** 36 **Yield:** 36 servings

Ingredients

- 2 ounces red fondant
- 1 (12 ounce) package red confectioner's coating (such as Wilton Candy Melts)
- 1 (14 ounce) package chocolate sandwich cookies (such as Oreo)
- 72 eaches small candy eyeballs

Directions

Step 1

Shape red fondant into 72 little horns relative to the size of the cookies. Line 2 baking sheets with parchment paper.

Step 2

Place red confectioner's coating in the top of a double boiler over simmering water. Stir constantly, scraping down the sides with a rubber spatula to avoid scorching, until melted, about 5 minutes. Remove from heat.

Step 3

Use a spoon to cover the top and sides of each cookie with melted red coating. Place on the prepared baking sheet. Stick 2 small devil horns near the top and add 2 candy eyeballs. Let stand until dry, about 1 hour.

Nutrition Facts

Per Serving:

118.1 calories; protein 1.2g 2% DV; carbohydrates 16.3g 5% DV; fat 5.6g 9% DV; cholesterol 2mg 1% DV; sodium 62mg 3% DV.

Royal Icing I

Servings: 32 Yield: 2 cups

Ingredients

- 4 large egg whites egg whites
- 4 cups sifted confectioners' sugar
- 1 teaspoon lemon extract

Directions

Step 1

Pumpkin Whoopie Pies

Servings: 18 **Yield:** 3 dozen

Ingredients

- 2 cups packed brown sugar
- 1 cup vegetable oil
- 1 ½ cups solid pack pumpkin puree
- 2 large eggs eggs
- 3 cups all-purpose flour
- 1 teaspoon salt
- 1 teaspoon baking powder
- 1 teaspoon baking soda
- 1 teaspoon vanilla extract

- 1 ½ tablespoons ground cinnamon
- ½ tablespoon ground ginger
- ½ tablespoon ground cloves
- 1 egg white
- 2 tablespoons milk
- 1 teaspoon vanilla extract
- 2 cups confectioners' sugar
- ¾ cup shortening

Directions

Step 1

Preheat oven to 350 degrees F (175 degrees C). Lightly grease baking sheets.

Step 2

Combine the oil and brown sugar. Mix in the pumpkin and eggs, beating well. Add the flour, salt, baking powder, baking soda, 1 teaspoon vanilla, cinnamon, ginger and cloves. Mix well.

Step 3

Drop dough by heaping teaspoons onto the prepared baking sheets. Bake at 350 degrees F (175 degrees C) for 10 to 12 minutes. Let cookies cool then make sandwiches from two cookies filled with Whoopie Pie Filling.

Step 4

To Make Whoopie Pie Filling: Beat egg white and mix with the milk, 1 teaspoon vanilla and 1 cup of the confectioners' sugar. Mix well then beat in the shortening and the remaining cup of confectioners' sugar. Beat until light and fluffy.

Nutrition Facts

Per Serving:

424.8 calories; protein 3.4g 7% DV; carbohydrates 55.8g 18% DV; fat 21.7g 33% DV; cholesterol 20.8mg 7% DV; sodium 294.9mg 12% DV.

Chocolate Cut Out Cookies

Servings: 36 **Yield:** 6 dozen

Ingredients

- 1 cup butter
- 2 cups white sugar
- 3 large eggs eggs
- 3 teaspoons vanilla extract

- 3 cups all-purpose flour
- 1 teaspoon baking powder
- 10 tablespoons unsweetened cocoa powder

Directions

Step 1

Cream butter or margarine and sugar until light and fluffy; add eggs, one at a time, beating well. Mix in the vanilla. Combine flour, cocoa powder and baking powder; add and mix well. Wrap dough in waxed paper and chill for 2 hours.

Step 2

Preheat oven to 350 degrees F (175 degrees C).

Step 3

Divide dough in half. Roll out each half to 1/4 inch thick. Cut with desired shaped cookie cutters. Place on lightly greased cookie sheets and bake for 10-12 minutes.

Nutrition Facts

Per Serving:

136.5 calories; protein 1.9g 4% DV; carbohydrates 20g 7% DV; fat 5.8g 9% DV; cholesterol 29.1mg 10% DV; sodium 56.2mg 2% DV.

Pumpkin Cookies with Penuche Frosting

Prep: 15 mins **Cook:** 12 mins **Additional:** 18 mins **Total:** 45 mins **Servings:** 48 **Yield:** 4 dozen

Ingredients

36

- 1 cup shortening
- ½ cup packed brown sugar
- ½ cup white sugar
- 1 cup pumpkin puree
- 1 egg
- 1 teaspoon vanilla extract
- 2 cups all-purpose flour
- 1 teaspoon baking soda
- 1 teaspoon baking powder
- 1 teaspoon ground cinnamon
- ½ teaspoon salt
- 1 cup chopped walnuts
- 3 tablespoons butter
- ½ cup packed brown sugar
- ¼ cup milk
- 2 cups confectioners' sugar

Directions

Step 1

Preheat the oven to 350 degrees F (175 degrees C). Grease cookie sheets.

Step 2

In a large bowl, cream together shortening, 1/2 cup brown sugar, and white sugar. Mix in pumpkin, egg, and vanilla. Sift together flour, baking soda, baking powder, cinnamon, and salt; mix into the creamed mixture. Stir in walnuts. Drop dough by heaping spoonfuls onto the prepared baking sheets.

Step 3

Bake for 10 to 12 minutes in the preheated oven. Cool on wire racks.

Step 4

In a small saucepan over medium heat, combine the 3 tablespoons butter and 1/2 cup brown sugar. Bring to a boil; cook and stir for 1 minute, or until slightly thickened. Cool slightly, then stir in the milk, and beat until smooth. Gradually stir in 2 cups confectioners' sugar until frosting has reached desired consistency. Spread on cooled cookies.

Nutrition Facts

Per Serving:

128.2 calories; protein 1.2g 2% DV; carbohydrates 16.4g 5% DV; fat 6.8g 10% DV; cholesterol 5.9mg 2% DV; sodium 81.5mg 3% DV.

Pumpkin Shortbread Bars

Prep: 25 mins **Cook:** 35 mins **Additional:** 1 hr **Total:** 2 hrs **Servings:** 12 **Yield:** 12 bars

Ingredients

- ½ cup softened butter
- ⅓ cup white sugar

- ¼ teaspoon vanilla extract
- 1 cup all-purpose flour
- ⅓ cup all-purpose flour
- ½ teaspoon baking powder
- ¼ teaspoon salt
- 2 large eggs eggs
- 1 cup firmly packed brown sugar
- 1 cup canned solid pack pumpkin
- 1 teaspoon vanilla extract
- ½ cup chopped pecans
- 1 cup all-purpose flour
- ⅓ cup white sugar
- ¼ cup cold butter

Directions

Step 1

Preheat an oven to 400 degrees F (200 degrees C).

Step 2

Beat 1/2 cup butter, 1/3 cup sugar, and 1/4 teaspoon of vanilla extract together until blended. Mix in 1 cup flour until no longer dry. Press into a 9x13-inch baking dish.

Step 3

Bake in the preheated oven for 10 minutes. Remove and allow to cool for a few minutes. Reduce the oven to 350 degrees F (175 degrees C).

Step 4

Whisk together 1/3 cup flour, the baking powder, and salt together in a bowl; set aside. Beat the eggs, brown sugar, pumpkin, 1 teaspoon vanilla extract, and the pecans together in a bowl until the pumpkin is smooth. Stir in the flour mixture until just incorporated and spread the batter over the parbaked crust.

Step 5

Place 1 cup flour, 1/3 cup sugar, and 1/4 cup of cold butter into a bowl. Press the butter into the flour using a pastry blender or fork until no pieces of butter remain and the mixture resembles coarse crumbs. Sprinkle evenly over the pumpkin batter.

Step 6

Bake in the preheated oven until a toothpick inserted into the center comes out clean, 25 to 30 minutes. Cool completely in the pan. Cut into bars before serving.

Nutrition Facts

Per Serving:

357.5 calories; protein 4.5g 9% DV; carbohydrates 50.1g 16% DV; fat 16.2g 25% DV; cholesterol 61.5mg 21% DV; sodium 168.7mg 7% DV.

Pumpkin Protein Cookies

Prep: 15 mins **Cook:** 5 mins **Total:** 20 mins **Servings:** 14 **Yield:** 14 cookies

Ingredients

- ¾ cup SPLENDA Granular
- 1 cup rolled oats
- 1 cup whole wheat flour
- ½ cup soy flour
- 1 ¾ teaspoons baking soda
- ½ teaspoon baking powder
- ½ teaspoon salt
- 2 teaspoons ground cinnamon
- 1 teaspoon ground nutmeg
- ½ cup pumpkin puree
- 1 tablespoon canola oil
- 2 teaspoons water
- 2 large egg whites egg whites
- 1 teaspoon molasses
- 1 tablespoon flax seeds

Directions

Step 1

Preheat oven to 350 degrees F (175 degrees C).

Step 2

In a large bowl, whisk together Splenda, oats, wheat flour, soy flour, baking soda, baking powder, salt, cinnamon, and nutmeg. Stir in pumpkin, canola oil, water, egg whites, and molasses. Stir in flax seeds, if desired. Roll into 14 large balls, and flatten on a baking sheet.

Step 3

Bake for 5 minutes in preheated oven. DO NOT OVERBAKE: the cookies will come out really dry if overbaked.

Nutrition Facts

Per Serving:

84.8 calories; protein 4.2g 8% DV; carbohydrates 13.1g 4% DV; fat 2.2g 3% DV; cholesterolmg; sodium 284.1mg 11% DV.

White Chocolate Pumpkin Cookies

Servings: 18 **Yield:** 3 dozen

Ingredients

- 2 ¼ cups all-purpose flour
- 1 teaspoon pumpkin pie spice

- ½ teaspoon baking soda
- 1 cup unsalted butter
- 1 ½ cups packed brown sugar
- 1 cup solid pack pumpkin puree
- 2 large eggs eggs
- 1 tablespoon vanilla extract
- 2 cups white chocolate chips
- 1 cup chopped pecans

Directions

Step 1

In a small bowl, whisk together the flour, pumpkin pie spice and baking soda.

Step 2

In a medium bowl, with an electric mixer, cream butter and sugar. Beat in pumpkin pie puree. Beat in the eggs and vanilla. Beat in the flour mixture until just combined. Stir in the white chocolate and pecans.

Step 3

Drop dough by rounded tablespoon 2 inches apart on an ungreased cookie sheet. Bake at 300 degrees F (150 degrees C) for 20-22 minutes until just set.

Nutrition Facts

Per Serving:

386.5 calories; protein 4.6g 9% DV; carbohydrates 43.3g 14% DV; fat 22.4g 34% DV; cholesterol 52mg 17% DV; sodium 103.6mg 4% DV.

Almond Joy Cookies

Prep: 20 mins **Cook:** 8 mins **Additional:** 5 mins **Total:** 33 mins **Servings:** 36 **Yield:** 3 dozen cookies

Ingredients

- 4 ½ cups all-purpose flour
- 2 teaspoons baking soda
- 1 teaspoon salt
- 1 ½ cups white sugar
- 1 ½ cups brown sugar
- 1 ripe banana
- 4 large eggs eggs
- 1 tablespoon vanilla extract
- 5 cups chocolate chips
- 2 cups sweetened flaked coconut
- 2 cups chopped almonds

Directions

Step 1

Preheat oven to 375 degrees F (190 degrees C). Lightly grease baking sheets.

Step 2

Combine flour, baking soda, and salt in a bowl.

Step 3

Beat white sugar, brown sugar, and banana together in a separate bowl until smooth and creamy; beat in eggs, 1 at a time, until well mixed. Stir in vanilla extract.

Step 4

Stir banana mixture into flour mixture until batter is well mixed; fold in chocolate chips, coconut, and almonds. Drop batter by rounded spoonfuls onto the prepared baking sheets.

Step 5

Bake in the preheated oven until edges of cookies are beginning to crisp, 8 to 10 minutes. Cool cookies on baking sheet for 5 minutes before transferring to a wire rack to cool completely.

Nutrition Facts

Per Serving:

285 calories; protein 4.6g 9% DV; carbohydrates 44.9g 15% DV; fat 11.5g 18% DV; cholesterol 20.7mg 7% DV; sodium 158.7mg 6% DV.

Peanut Blossoms II

Prep: 30 mins **Cook:** 12 mins **Additional:** 48 mins **Total:** 1 hr 30 mins **Servings:** 84 **Yield:** 7 dozen

Ingredients

- 1 cup shortening
- 1 cup peanut butter
- 1 cup packed brown sugar
- 1 cup white sugar
- 2 large eggs eggs
- ¼ cup milk
- 2 teaspoons vanilla extract
- 3 ½ cups all-purpose flour
- 2 teaspoons baking soda
- 1 teaspoon salt
- ½ cup white sugar for decoration
- 2 (9 ounce) bags milk chocolate candy kisses, unwrapped

Directions

Step 1

Preheat oven to 375 degrees F (190 degrees C). Grease cookie sheets.

Step 2

In a large bowl, cream together the shortening, peanut butter, brown sugar, and 1 cup white sugar until smooth. Beat in the eggs one at a time, and stir in the milk and vanilla. Combine the flour, baking soda, and salt; stir into the peanut butter mixture until well blended. Shape tablespoonfuls of dough into balls, and roll in remaining white sugar. Place cookies 2 inches apart on the prepared cookie sheets.

Step 3

Bake for 10 to12 minutes in the preheated oven. Remove from oven, and immediately press a chocolate kiss into each cookie. Allow to cool completely; the kiss will harden as it cools.

Nutrition Facts

Per Serving:

115.5 calories; protein 1.9g 4% DV; carbohydrates 14.3g 5% DV; fat 6g 9% DV; cholesterol 5.8mg 2% DV; sodium 79.5mg 3% DV.

Royal Icing II

Prep: 15 mins **Total:** 15 mins **Servings:** 48 **Yield:** 3 cups

Ingredients

- 3 tablespoons meringue powder
- 4 cups sifted confectioners' sugar
- 6 tablespoons water

Directions

Step 1

Beat all ingredients at low speed for 7 to 10 minutes, or until icing forms peaks. Tip: Keep icing covered with a wet kitchen towel at all times. Icing can dry out quickly.

Nutrition Facts

Per Serving:

43.4 calories; protein 0.2g; carbohydrates 10.8g 4% DV; fatg; cholesterolmg; sodium 2.7mg.

Snickers Brownies

Prep: 15 mins **Cook:** 30 mins **Additional:** 30 mins **Total:** 1 hr 15 mins **Servings:** 12 **Yield:** 12 servings

Ingredients

- 1 ½ cups white sugar
- ¾ cup all-purpose flour
- ½ cup unsweetened cocoa powder
- ½ teaspoon salt
- ¼ teaspoon baking powder
- ¾ cup butter, melted
- 3 large eggs eggs
- 1 teaspoon vanilla extract
- 2 cups chocolate-coated caramel-peanut nougat candy (such as Snickers), chopped, divided

Directions

Step 1

Preheat the oven to 350 degrees F (175 degrees C). Grease a 9-inch square baking pan.

Step 2

Mix sugar, flour, cocoa powder, salt, and baking powder together in a mixing bowl.

Step 3

Mix butter, eggs, and vanilla extract together in a separate bowl; add butter mixture to the bowl with the flour mixture and stir batter until well mixed.

Step 4

Pour 1/2 the batter into the prepared baking pan. Top with 1/2 the candy bar pieces. Spread remaining batter on top, covering candy completely.

Step 5

Bake in the preheated oven until edges are brown and center is set, about 30 minutes.

Step 6

Remove brownies from the oven and spread remaining candy bar pieces on top, lightly pressing them in while the brownies are still hot. Let brownies cool completely before serving, about 30 minutes.

Nutrition Facts

Per Serving:

387.1 calories; protein 5.3g 11% DV; carbohydrates 50g 16% DV; fat 20g 31% DV; cholesterol 80.6mg 27% DV; sodium 276.1mg 11% DV.

Paul's Pumpkin Bars

Prep: 15 mins **Cook:** 30 mins **Total:** 45 mins **Servings:** 24 **Yield:** 2 dozen

Ingredients

- 4 large eggs eggs
- 1 ⅔ cups white sugar
- 1 cup vegetable oil
- 1 (15 ounce) can pumpkin puree
- 2 cups all-purpose flour
- 2 teaspoons baking powder
- 1 teaspoon baking soda
- 2 teaspoons ground cinnamon
- 1 teaspoon salt
- 1 (3 ounce) package cream cheese, softened
- ½ cup butter, softened
- 1 teaspoon vanilla extract
- 2 cups sifted confectioners' sugar

Directions

Step 1

Preheat oven to 350 degrees F (175 degrees C).

Step 2

In a medium bowl, mix the eggs, sugar, oil, and pumpkin with an electric mixer until light and fluffy. Sift together the flour, baking powder, baking soda, cinnamon and salt. Stir into the pumpkin mixture until thoroughly combined.

Step 3

Spread the batter evenly into an ungreased 10x15 inch jellyroll pan. Bake for 25 to 30 minutes in preheated oven. Cool before frosting.

Step 4

To make the frosting, cream together the cream cheese and butter. Stir in vanilla. Add confectioners' sugar a little at a time, beating until mixture is smooth. Spread evenly on top of the cooled bars. Cut into squares.

Nutrition Facts

Per Serving:

278.8 calories; protein 2.6g 5% DV; carbohydrates 34.1g 11% DV; fat 15.2g 23% DV; cholesterol 45.1mg 15% DV; sodium 282.5mg 11% DV.

Pumpkin Chocolate Chip Cookies III

Ingredients

- 1 cup canned pumpkin
- 1 cup white sugar
- ½ cup vegetable oil
- 1 egg
- 2 cups all-purpose flour
- 2 teaspoons baking powder
- 2 teaspoons ground cinnamon
- ½ teaspoon salt
- 1 teaspoon baking soda
- 1 teaspoon milk
- 1 tablespoon vanilla extract
- 2 cups semisweet chocolate chips
- ½ cup chopped walnuts

Directions

Step 1

Combine pumpkin, sugar, vegetable oil, and egg. In a separate bowl, stir together flour, baking powder, ground cinnamon, and salt. Dissolve the baking soda with the milk and stir in. Add flour mixture to pumpkin mixture and mix well.

Step 2

Add vanilla, chocolate chips and nuts.

Step 3

Drop by spoonful on greased cookie sheet and bake at 350 degrees F (175 degrees C) for approximately 10 minutes or until lightly brown and firm.

Nutrition Facts

Per Serving:

202.4 calories; protein 2.4g 5% DV; carbohydrates 26.6g 9% DV; fat 10.7g 17% DV; cholesterol 7.8mg 3% DV; sodium 170.9mg 7% DV.

Pumpkin Oatmeal Chocolate Chip Cookies

Prep: 15 mins **Cook:** 10 mins **Total:** 25 mins **Servings:** 72 **Yield:** 6 dozen cookies

Ingredients

- 1 ½ cups butter, softened
- 2 cups packed brown sugar
- 1 cup white sugar
- 1 (15 ounce) can pumpkin puree
- 1 egg
- 1 teaspoon vanilla extract
- 4 cups all-purpose flour
- 2 cups quick-cooking oats

- 2 teaspoons ground cinnamon
- 2 teaspoons baking soda
- 1 teaspoon baking powder
- 1 teaspoon salt
- 2 cups miniature chocolate chips

Directions

Step 1

Preheat oven to 375 degrees F (190 degrees C).

Step 2

Beat butter, brown sugar, and white sugar together in a bowl until creamy. Add pumpkin, egg, and vanilla extract; beat until smooth.

Step 3

Mix flour, oats, cinnamon, baking soda, baking powder, and salt in a separate bowl; stir into creamed butter until combined. Fold chocolate chips into batter. Drop 1 to 2 tablespoons batter for each cookie onto a baking sheet.

Step 4

Bake in the preheated oven until the edges of each cookie are lightly browned, 10 to 12 minutes.

Nutrition Facts

Per Serving:

128.1 calories; protein 1.4g 3% DV; carbohydrates 19.2g 6% DV; fat 5.6g 9% DV; cholesterol 12.8mg 4% DV; sodium 119mg 5% DV.

Pumpkin Spice Cookie

Prep: 15 mins **Cook:** 20 mins **Total:** 35 mins **Servings:** 24 **Yield:** 2 dozen cookies

Ingredients

- 1 (18.25 ounce) package spice cake mix
- 1 (15 ounce) can solid pack pumpkin

Directions

Step 1

Preheat oven to 350 degrees F (175 degrees C). Grease cookie sheets.

Step 2

In a large bowl, stir together the cake mix and pumpkin until well blended. Drop by rounded spoonfuls onto the prepared cookie sheet.

Step 3

Bake for 18 to 20 minutes in the preheated oven. Allow cookies to cool on baking sheet for 5 minutes before removing to a wire rack to cool completely.

Nutrition Facts

Per Serving:

98 calories; protein 1.5g 3% DV; carbohydrates 17.2g 6% DV; fat 2.7g 4% DV; cholesterolmg; sodium 187.8mg 8% DV.

Pumpkin Pie Bars

Prep: 15 mins **Cook:** 45 mins **Additional:** 1 hr **Total:** 2 hrs **Servings:** 24 **Yield:** 1 9x13-inch pan

Ingredients

- 1 (18.25 ounce) package yellow cake mix
- ½ cup melted butter
- 3 large eggs eggs
- 3 cups pumpkin pie filling
- ⅔ cup milk
- ¼ cup white sugar
- 1 teaspoon ground cinnamon
- ¼ cup butter

Directions

Step 1

Preheat oven to 350 degrees F (190 degrees C). Grease the bottom of a 9x13 inch pan.

Step 2

Pour one cup of yellow cake mix into a medium size mixing bowl; set aside.

Step 3

Combine remaining cake mix, 1/2 cup melted butter and 1 egg; mix well. Press into the baking pan.

Step 4

Combine pumpkin pie filling, 2 eggs and milk in a medium size mixing bowl; mix until smooth. Pour evenly over the crust in the 9x13 inch pan.

Step 5

Pour the sugar and cinnamon into the mixing bowl containing the 1 cup of yellow cake mix. Cut in the butter until the mixture looks crumbly. Sprinkle this mixture over the pumpkin filling.

Step 6

Bake for 45 to 50 minutes or until a knife inserted into the bars come out clean. Let cool before slicing.

Nutrition Facts

Per Serving:

188.3 calories; protein 2.4g 5% DV; carbohydrates 28.3g 9% DV; fat 7.8g 12% DV; cholesterol 36.2mg 12% DV; sodium 262.9mg 11% DV.

Pumpkin Cookies with Cream Cheese Frosting (The World's Best!)

Prep: 30 mins **Cook:** 10 mins **Additional:** 30 mins **Total:** 1 hr 10 mins **Servings:** 36 **Yield:** 3 dozen cookies

Ingredients

- 2 cups all-purpose flour
- 1 teaspoon baking powder
- 1 teaspoon ground cinnamon
- ½ teaspoon baking soda
- ½ teaspoon ground nutmeg
- ½ teaspoon ground ginger
- 1 cup butter
- ¾ cup white sugar

- ¾ cup brown sugar
- 2 teaspoons vanilla extract
- 1 egg
- 1 (15 ounce) can pumpkin puree
- 1 (3 ounce) package cream cheese, softened
- ¼ cup butter, softened
- 1 teaspoon vanilla extract
- 2 cups confectioners' sugar

Directions

Step 1

Preheat oven to 350 degrees F (175 degrees C). Lightly grease baking sheets.

Step 2

Whisk flour, baking powder, cinnamon, baking soda, nutmeg, and ginger together in a bowl. Beat 1 cup butter, white sugar, brown sugar, 2 teaspoons vanilla extract, and egg with an electric mixer in a separate large bowl, beating until mixture is smooth. Beat in pumpkin puree. Gradually stir dry ingredients into pumpkin mixture. Batter will be moist.

Step 3

Spoon batter by teaspoonfuls about 2 inches apart onto prepared baking sheets.

Step 4

Bake in the preheated oven until cookies are lightly browned, 10 to 12 minutes. Let cookies cool for about 5 minutes on sheets before removing to finish cooling on waxed paper.

Step 5

Beat cream cheese, 1/4 cup butter, and 1 teaspoon vanilla extract in a bowl with an electric mixer until soft and creamy. Beat in confectioners' sugar, about 1/2 cup at a time, until frosting is smooth and spreadable. Frost cooled cookies with cream cheese frosting.

Nutrition Facts

Per Serving:

152.3 calories; protein 1.3g 3% DV; carbohydrates 20.6g 7% DV; fat 7.5g 12% DV; cholesterol 24.7mg 8% DV; sodium 115mg 5% DV.

Pumpkin Chocolate Chip Cookies I

Prep: 15 mins **Cook:** 15 mins **Additional:** 15 mins **Total:** 45 mins **Servings:** 48 **Yield:** 4 dozen

Ingredients

- ½ cup shortening
- 1 ½ cups white sugar
- 1 egg
- 1 cup canned pumpkin
- 1 teaspoon vanilla extract
- 2 ½ cups all-purpose flour
- 1 teaspoon baking powder
- 1 teaspoon baking soda
- 1 teaspoon salt
- 1 teaspoon ground nutmeg
- 1 teaspoon ground cinnamon
- ½ cup chopped walnuts
- 1 cup semisweet chocolate chips

Directions

Step 1

Preheat oven to 350 degrees F (175 degrees C). Grease cookie sheets.

Step 2

In a large bowl, cream together the shortening and sugar until light and fluffy. Beat in the egg, then stir in the pumpkin and vanilla. Combine the flour, baking powder, baking soda, salt, nutmeg, and cinnamon; gradually mix into the creamed mixture. Stir in the walnuts and chocolate chips. Drop dough by teaspoonfuls onto the prepared cookie sheets.

Step 3

Bake for 15 minutes in the preheated oven, or until light brown. Cool on wire racks.

Nutrition Facts

Per Serving:

95.5 calories; protein 1.2g 2% DV; carbohydrates 14.1g 5% DV; fat 4.2g 6% DV; cholesterol 3.9mg 1% DV; sodium 99.1mg 4% DV.

Extra Easy Pumpkin Cookies

Prep: 15 mins **Cook:** 8 mins **Total:** 23 mins **Servings:** 24 **Yield:** 2 dozen cookies

Ingredients

- 1 (14 ounce) can 100% pure pumpkin
- 2 large eggs eggs
- ½ cup applesauce
- ½ teaspoon vanilla extract
- 1 (18.25 ounce) package spice cake mix
- 1 teaspoon cinnamon
- ½ teaspoon ground nutmeg
- ¼ teaspoon ground cloves

Directions

Step 1

Preheat oven to 350 degrees F (175 degrees C). Lightly grease two baking sheets.

Step 2

Beat the pumpkin, eggs, applesauce, and vanilla together in a large mixing bowl. Stir in the cake mix, cinnamon, nutmeg, and cloves until well blended and creamy. Drop by spoonfuls on prepared baking sheets.

Step 3

Bake in preheated oven until tops are firm when lightly touched, 8 to 10 minutes. Cool on racks.

Nutrition Facts

Per Serving:

106.6 calories; protein 2g 4% DV; carbohydrates 17.8g 6% DV; fat 3.2g 5% DV; cholesterol 15.5mg 5% DV; sodium 190.9mg 8%

> And let us not be weary in well doing: for in due season we shall reap, if we faint not. GALATIANS 6:9

Choc... Cookies

Prep: 10 mins **Cook:** 15 mins **Additional:** 10 mins **Total:** 35 mins **Servings:** 84 **Yield:** 7 dozen

Ingredients

- 1 cup shortening
- 2 cups white sugar
- 2 large eggs eggs
- 2 teaspoons vanilla extract
- 1 (15 ounce) can pumpkin puree
- 4 cups all-purpose flour
- 1 ½ teaspoons baking soda
- 1 ½ teaspoons baking powder
- 1 teaspoon salt
- 1 teaspoon ground cinnamon
- 1 pinch ground nutmeg
- 1 cup semisweet chocolate chips
- 1 cup chopped walnuts

Directions

Step 1

Preheat the oven to 375 degrees F (190 degrees C). Grease cookie sheets.

Step 2

In a large bowl, cream together the shortening and white sugar until smooth. Beat in the eggs one at a time. Stir in the vanilla and pumpkin until well blended. Combine the flour, baking soda, baking powder, salt, cinnamon and nutmeg; stir into the pumpkin mixture. Mix in the chocolate chips. Stir in the walnuts if desired. Drop by teaspoonfuls onto the prepared cookie sheets.

Step 3

Bake for 12 to 15 minutes in the preheated oven, until edges begin to brown. Allow to cool for a few minutes on the baking sheets before removing to wire racks to cool completely.

Nutrition Facts

Per Serving:

84.2 calories; protein 1.1g 2% DV; carbohydrates 11.2g 4% DV; fat 4.1g 6% DV; cholesterol 4.4mg 2% DV; sodium 70.9mg 3% DV.

Root Beer Float Cookies

Prep: 15 mins **Cook:** 8 mins **Total:** 23 mins **Servings:** 24 **Yield:** 24 cookies

Ingredients

- ¾ cup butter
- ¾ cup brown sugar
- ¼ cup white sugar
- 1 (3.5 ounce) package instant vanilla pudding mix
- 2 large eggs eggs
- 1 teaspoon root beer concentrate
- 2 ¼ cups all-purpose flour
- 1 teaspoon baking soda
- 1 cup white chocolate chips, or more to taste

Directions

Step 1

Preheat oven to 350 degrees F (175 degrees C). Grease 2 baking sheets.

Step 2

Beat butter, brown sugar, and white sugar together in a bowl with an electric mixer until creamy; beat in pudding mix. Add eggs and root beer concentrate; stir in flour and baking soda. Fold chocolate chips into the dough.

Step 3

Drop spoonfuls of dough 2 inches apart on the baking sheets.

Step 4

Bake in the preheated oven until golden, 8 to 10 minutes.

Nutrition Facts

Per Serving:

182.1 calories; protein 2.3g 5% DV; carbohydrates 23.5g 8% DV; fat 8.9g 14% DV; cholesterol 32.3mg 11% DV; sodium 167.4mg 7% DV.

Soft Pumpkin Cookies

Servings: 12 Yield: 1 dozen

Ingredients

- 1 cup white sugar
- 1 tablespoon butter
- 1 egg, beaten
- 1 teaspoon vanilla extract
- 1 cup pumpkin puree
- ½ cup chopped walnuts
- 2 cups all-purpose flour
- 1 teaspoon baking powder
- ½ teaspoon salt

Directions

Step 1

Preheat oven to 375 degrees F (190 degrees C).

Step 2

Cream together sugar and butter. Add egg, vanilla, pumpkin and walnuts.

Step 3

Stir in flour, baking powder and salt; mix well.

Step 4

Drop by the tablespoon on cookie sheet and bake for 15 minutes.

Nutrition Facts

Per Serving:

192 calories; protein 3.6g 7% DV; carbohydrates 34.4g 11% DV; fat 4.8g 7% DV; cholesterol 18mg 6% DV; sodium 150.9mg 6% DV.

Broiler S'mores

Prep: 5 mins **Cook:** 3 mins **Total:** 8 mins **Servings:** 4 **Yield:** 4 servings

Ingredients

- 4 cracker (2-1/2" square)s graham crackers
- 2 eaches milk chocolate candy bars
- 12 regulars marshmallows

Directions

Step 1

Preheat the oven broiler. Line a small pan with aluminum foil and lightly coat with cooking spray.

Step 2

Break the graham crackers in half and lay 4 of the squares out on a serving plate. Break the candy bars in half and lay one piece on each of the graham crackers on the plate.

Step 3

Arrange the marshmallows in a single layer in the prepared pan.

Step 4

Broil the marshmallows until the tops brown, turn the marshmallows to brown the undersides. Keep a close eye on the marshmallows so they do not burn. They will brown very quickly.

Step 5

Remove the marshmallows from the pan and place three on each of the chocolate squares. Top with the remaining graham cracker halves.

Nutrition Facts

Per Serving:

208.3 calories; protein 1.9g 4% DV; carbohydrates 35.9g 12% DV; fat 7.3g 11% DV; cholesterol 5mg 2% DV; sodium 72.1mg 3% DV.

Pumpkin Cookies V

Servings: 18 **Yield:** 3 dozen

Ingredients

- 2 cups shortening
- 2 cups white sugar
- 2 cups canned pumpkin
- 2 large eggs eggs
- 2 teaspoons baking soda
- 1 ½ teaspoons ground cinnamon
- 1 teaspoon salt
- 4 cups all-purpose flour
- 6 tablespoons butter
- 8 tablespoons milk
- 2 cups confectioners' sugar
- 1 ½ teaspoons vanilla extract
- 1 cup packed brown sugar

Directions

Step 1

Cream shortening, white sugar and pumpkin. Add eggs and mix well. Sift together the baking soda, ground cinnamon, salt and flour. Add to pumpkin mixture and mix well.

Step 2

Drop from spoon to cookie sheet. Bake 10 minutes at 350 degrees F (175 degrees C).

Step 3

To Make Frosting: Cook butter, milk, and brown sugar until dissolved. Cool and add confectioners' sugar and vanilla. Spread over warm cookies.

Nutrition Facts

Per Serving:

542.8 calories; protein 4.2g 8% DV; carbohydrates 71.4g 23% DV; fat 27.7g 43% DV; cholesterol 31.4mg 11% DV; sodium 376.6mg 15% DV.

Peanut Candy Bar Cake

Servings: 24 **Yield:** 1 -9x13 inch cake

Ingredients

- 1 (18.25 ounce) package yellow cake mix
- ⅓ cup butter
- 3 cups miniature marshmallows
- ⅔ cup light corn syrup
- 1 egg

- 2 teaspoons vanilla extract
- 2 cups peanut butter chips
- 2 cups salted peanuts
- 1 ½ cups crisp rice cereal
- ¼ cup butter

Directions

Step 1

Preheat oven to 350 degrees F (175 degrees C).

Step 2

Mix together the cake mix, 1/3 cup butter or margarine and, the egg. Press into the bottom of one 9x13 inch pan and bake at 350 degrees F (175 degrees C) for 12 to 18 minutes. Remove from oven and sprinkle with miniature marshmallows. Return to oven for 1 to 2 minutes or until the marshmallows begin to puff.

Step 3

In a saucepan over medium heat cook corn syrup, 1/4 cup butter of margarine, vanilla, and peanut butter chips until melted. Remove from heat and stir in the puffed rice cereal and salted peanuts. Spoon mixture over top of marshmallow topped cake and spread to cover. Allow to cool before serving.

Nutrition Facts

Per Serving:

373.2 calories; protein 8.6g 17% DV; carbohydrates 43g 14% DV; fat 18.9g 29% DV; cholesterol 20mg 7% DV; sodium 348.8mg 14% DV.

Peanutty Candy Corn Cereal Bars

Prep: 15 mins **Cook:** 5 mins **Additional:** 30 mins **Total:** 50 mins **Servings:** 12 **Yield:** 1 9x13-inch pan

Ingredients

- ¼ cup margarine
- 1 tablespoon peanut butter
- 5 cups miniature marshmallows, divided
- 6 cups honey nut-flavored cereal squares (such as Honey Nut Chex)
- 2 cups candy corn
- ½ cup peanuts

Directions

Step 1

Grease a 9x13-inch baking pan.

Step 2

Cook and stir margarine and peanut butter together in a saucepan over medium heat until smooth, 2 to 3 minutes. Add 4 cups marshmallows to margarine mixture; cook and stir until marshmallows are melted, 2 to 3 minutes. Remove saucepan from heat.

Step 3

Stir cereal squares into marshmallow mixture until fully coated and slightly cooled; fold in candy corn, peanuts, and remaining 1 cup marshmallows. Pour mixture into the prepared baking pan, pressing down in an even layer with buttered hands or a buttered wooden spoon. Cool completely before cutting into squares.

Nutrition Facts

Per Serving:

343.3 calories; protein 3.2g 6% DV; carbohydrates 63.9g 21% DV; fat 7.8g 12% DV; cholesterolmg; sodium 226.3mg 9% DV.

Halloween Finger Cookies

Prep: 30 mins **Cook:** 20 mins **Total:** 50 mins **Servings:** 50 **Yield:** 50 cookies

Ingredients

- 1 cup unsalted butter
- ¾ cup confectioners' sugar
- 1 teaspoon vanilla extract
- ½ teaspoon salt
- 1 ¾ cups all-purpose flour
- 1 cup ground pecans
- 50 almonds almonds

Directions

Step 1

Preheat the oven to 300 degrees F (150 degrees C). Line a baking sheet with parchment paper.

Step 2

Beat butter and sugar together using an electric mixer until fluffy. Blend in vanilla extract and salt. Mix in flour and ground pecans. Shape about 1 tablespoon of dough into a finger, about 3 inches long and 3/4 inch wide. Repeat with remaining dough to form about 50 fingers total.

Step 3

Place fingers 2 inches apart on the prepared baking sheet; they will expand a little while baking. Stick an almond 'nail' onto the end of each finger. Lightly score some 'knuckles' into the centers using a knife.

Step 4

Bake in the preheated oven until set and very lightly browned, about 20 minutes. Let cool.

Nutrition Facts

Per Serving:

74.2 calories; protein 0.9g 2% DV; carbohydrates 5.6g 2% DV; fat 5.5g 9% DV; cholesterol 9.8mg 3% DV; sodium 23.9mg 1% DV.

Spiderweb Brownies

Prep: 15 mins **Cook:** 40 mins **Additional:** 30 mins **Total:** 1 hr 25 mins **Servings:** 16 **Yield:** 16 servings

Ingredients

- 1 (18.25 ounce) package chocolate brownie mix
- 2 (2.1 ounce) bars NESTLE BUTTERFINGER Original, chopped
- 1 (3 ounce) package cream cheese, at room temperature
- ¼ cup granulated sugar
- 2 tablespoons milk

Directions

Step 1

Preheat oven to 350 degrees F. Grease 9- or 10-inch-round baking pan.

Step 2

Prepare brownie batter according to package directions; stir in chopped Butterfinger. Spoon into prepared pan.

Step 3

Beat cream cheese, sugar and milk in small mixer bowl until smooth. Pipe cream cheese mixture into concentric circles over brownie batter. Using wooden pick or tip of knife, pull tip through cream cheese from center to last circle to create a spiderweb effect.

Step 4

Bake for 40 minutes or until wooden pick inserted near center comes out almost clean. Cool completely in pan on wire rack. Cut into wedges using wet knife.

Nutrition Facts

Per Serving:

205.7 calories; protein 2.3g 5% DV; carbohydrates 33.5g 11% DV; fat 8.1g 12% DV; cholesterol 6mg 2% DV; sodium 131.4mg 5% DV.

Halloween Candy Blondies

Prep: 20 mins **Cook:** 30 mins **Additional:** 30 mins **Total:** 1 hr 20 mins **Servings:** 12 **Yield:** 12 blondies

Ingredients

- 1 cup all-purpose flour
- ½ teaspoon baking powder
- ½ cup salted butter, softened
- ½ cup white sugar
- ¼ cup dark brown sugar
- ¼ cup sugar and sucralose blend for baking (such as Natur Bakers Blend)
- 1 large egg
- 1 teaspoon vanilla extract
- ½ cup white chocolate chips
- ¼ cup candy-coated milk chocolate pieces
- ¼ cup candy corn
- 3 tablespoons sliced almonds

Directions

Step 1

Preheat the oven to 350 degrees F (175 degrees C). Lightly butter an 8-inch square baking pan.

Step 2

Whisk flour and baking powder in a small bowl to remove any lumps.

Step 3

Beat butter with white sugar, brown sugar, and sugar blend in a large bowl until well combined. Stir in egg and vanilla extract, beating until smooth. Add flour mixture and blend until just combined, taking care not to overbeat the batter.

Step 4

Gently fold white chocolate chips, milk chocolate pieces, candy corn, and almonds into the batter. Spread batter into the prepared pan.

Step 5

Bake in the preheated oven until a toothpick inserted in the center comes out clean, 30 to 35 minutes. Let cool for at least 30 minutes before cutting into bars.

Nutrition Facts

Per Serving:

269 calories; protein 2.7g 5% DV; carbohydrates 36g 12% DV; fat 12.5g 19% DV; cholesterol 38mg 13% DV; sodium 93.1mg 4% DV.

Pumpkin Cookies with Maple Icing

Prep: 15 mins **Cook:** 15 mins **Additional:** 25 mins **Total:** 55 mins **Servings:** 24 **Yield:** 24 cookies

Ingredients

Cookies:

- 2 cups all-purpose flour
- 1 teaspoon baking powder
- 1 teaspoon baking soda
- ½ teaspoon salt
- 1 teaspoon pumpkin pie spice
- ½ cup shortening
- 1 cup brown sugar
- 1 cup pumpkin puree
- 1 large egg
- 1 teaspoon vanilla extract

Icing:

- ½ cup unsalted butter, at room temperature
- ¼ cup maple syrup
- 2 tablespoons pumpkin puree
- 1 teaspoon pumpkin pie spice
- 1 teaspoon vanilla extract
- 1 (16 ounce) package powdered sugar
- 1 drop orange gel food coloring, or as desired

- 1 tablespoon black sprinkles, or as desired

Directions

Step 1

Preheat the oven to 350 degrees F (175 degrees C). Line 2 baking sheets with parchment paper.

Step 2

Sift flour, baking powder, baking soda, salt, and pumpkin pie spice for cookies together in a large bowl. Set aside.

Step 3

Combine shortening and brown sugar in a second large bowl. Beat using an electric mixer until light and fluffy, about 1 minute. Add pumpkin, egg, and vanilla extract; mix well until combined. Add 1/2 of the flour mixture and mix well. Add remaining flour mixture and mix again.

Step 4

Scoop tablespoonfuls of dough onto the prepared baking sheets, arranging 2 inches apart.

Step 5

Bake in the preheated oven until lightly browned at the edges, about 14 minutes, rotating baking sheets from top to bottom and front to back halfway through baking time.

Step 6

While the cookies bake, combine butter and maple syrup for icing in a medium bowl. Beat using an electric mixer until smooth. Add pumpkin, pumpkin pie spice, and vanilla extract. Mix well. Add powdered sugar and beat until fluffy. Add food coloring and beat until uniform. Set aside.

Step 7

Remove cookies from the oven and let cool on baking sheets for 5 minutes. Transfer cookies to a wire rack to cool completely, 20 to 30 minutes more. Pipe or spread icing onto cooled cookies and decorate with sprinkles as desired.

Nutrition Facts

Per Serving:

224.7 calories; protein 1.5g 3% DV; carbohydrates 36.2g 12% DV; fat 8.6g 13% DV; cholesterol 17.9mg 6% DV; sodium 154.9mg 6% DV.

Crispy Rice Candy Corn Treats

Prep: 5 mins **Cook:** 10 mins **Additional:** 5 mins **Total:** 20 mins **Servings:** 24 **Yield:** 1 15x10-inch pan

Ingredients

- 9 cups miniature marshmallows
- ½ cup butter
- 10 cups crispy rice cereal
- 2 cups candy corn
- ¾ cup mini chocolate chips

Directions

Step 1

Butter a 10x15 baking pan.

Step 2

Melt marshmallows and butter together in a large saucepan over medium heat, stirring until mixture is smooth, about 10 minutes.

Step 3

Combine cereal, candy corn, and chocolate chips together in a large bowl. Add marshmallow mixture to cereal mixture and stir together until cereal is well coated. Spread in prepared pan. Cool to room temperature and cut into squares.

Nutrition Facts

Per Serving:

225.2 calories; protein 1g 2% DV; carbohydrates 42.9g 14% DV; fat 5.6g 9% DV; cholesterol 10.2mg 3% DV; sodium 141.9mg 6% DV.

Halloween Mummy Cookies

Prep: 1 hr **Cook:** 10 mins **Additional:** 45 mins **Total:** 1 hr 55 mins **Servings:** 30 **Yield:** 30 cookies

Ingredients

- ⅔ cup butter, softened
- 1 cup white sugar
- 2 large eggs eggs
- 2 teaspoons vanilla extract
- 2 ½ cups all-purpose flour
- ½ cup unsweetened cocoa powder
- ¼ teaspoon baking soda
- ½ teaspoon salt
- 2 (11 ounce) packages white chocolate chips, or as needed
- 1 ½ tablespoons solid vegetable shortening, or as needed
- miniature chocolate chips

Directions

Step 1

Beat butter and sugar with electric mixer in a large bowl until smooth. Mix in eggs one at a time, beating the first egg in until fully incorporated before adding the second. Stir in vanilla extract.

Step 2

Sift together flour, cocoa powder, baking soda, and salt in a bowl; stir into butter mixture. Shape dough into a log and wrap with waxed paper, parchment, or plastic wrap. Refrigerate until firm, about 30 minutes.

Step 3

Preheat oven to 350 degrees F (175 degrees C).

Step 4

Slice pieces off the log and shape them into narrow wedges about 3 inches long. Set cookies on baking tray. Cut more slices and pull off teaspoon-sized pieces and roll into balls; flatten and press balls onto wide ends of wedges for the mummies' "heads."

Step 5

Bake in preheated until cookies are set and edges are dry, about 8 minutes. Let cool in pan for 1 minute; remove to wire rack to cool completely.

Step 6

Combine white chocolate chips with vegetable shortening in a microwave-safe bowl. Heat in microwave on low until melted, 1 to 2 minutes, stirring every 20 seconds, until coating is warm and smooth. Coat the tops of each cookie with melted white chocolate using a small spatula or butter knife. Reheat white chocolate mixture in microwave for a few seconds and stir again if it becomes too thick to work with. Repeat coating remaining cookies with white chocolate.

Step 7

Use a toothpick to score lines for "bandages" on each cookie, and place mini chocolate chips on the mummy heads for eyes.

Nutrition Facts

Per Serving:

237.2 calories; protein 3.3g 7% DV; carbohydrates 28g 9% DV; fat 13g 20% DV; cholesterol 27.6mg 9% DV; sodium 105.4mg 4% DV.

Huge Scary Spiders

Ingredients

- 2 (1 ounce) squares unsweetened chocolate
- 1 ¼ cups all-purpose flour
- 1 ½ teaspoons baking powder
- ¼ teaspoon salt
- ¼ cup butter

- 1 cup white sugar
- 1 egg
- 1 teaspoon vanilla extract
- 40 eaches cinnamon red hot candies

Directions

Step 1

Preheat oven to 375 degrees F (190 degrees C). Lightly grease baking sheet.

Step 2

In a saucepan melt chocolate over low heat. Let cool.

Step 3

In a small bowl mix flour, baking powder and salt.

Step 4

In a medium bowl beat margarine on low speed until smooth. Add sugar and beat until creamy. Stir in egg, vanilla and chocolate. Add flour mixture and mix well, forming a stiff dough.

Step 5

To make spider, shape a 2 inch flat oval for the body. Make the spider's head by flattening a circle about 1/2 inch wide. Shape dough for legs each about 2 inches long and less than 1/4 inch wide.

Step 6

Attach the head and legs to body. Put two red candies into head for eyes. Bake for 5-8 minutes. Let spiders cool on baking sheet to avoid breaking when moving.

Nutrition Facts

Per Serving:

216.5 calories; protein 3g 6% DV; carbohydrates 35.1g 11% DV; fat 8.2g 13% DV; cholesterol 30.8mg 10% DV; sodium 173.1mg 7% DV.

Pumpkin-Pine Cookies

Prep: 10 mins **Cook:** 8 mins **Additional:** 8 mins **Total:** 26 mins **Servings:** 60 **Yield:** 5 dozen

Ingredients

- 2 cups all-purpose flour
- ½ teaspoon baking soda
- ½ teaspoon baking powder
- 1 teaspoon ground cinnamon
- ¼ teaspoon ground cloves
- ½ cup butter, softened
- 1 ⅓ cups white sugar
- 1 egg
- 1 ½ cups canned pumpkin puree
- ¼ cup heavy cream
- 1 cup rolled oats
- ½ cup crushed pineapple, drained
- 1 cup chopped pecans

Directions

Step 1

Preheat the oven to 400 degrees F (200 degrees C). Grease cookie sheets. Stir together the flour, baking soda, baking powder, cinnamon and cloves; set aside.

Step 2

In a large bowl, cream together the butter, sugar and egg until smooth. Stir in the pumpkin and cream. Gradually mix in the dry ingredients until well blended and then stir in the oats, pineapple and pecans. Drop dough by tablespoonfuls onto the prepared cookie sheets.

Step 3

Bake for 8 to 10 minutes in the preheated oven, until bottoms begin to brown. Allow cookies to cool on baking sheets for a few minutes before removing to wire racks to cool completely.

Nutrition Facts

Per Serving:

71.8 calories; protein 1g 2% DV; carbohydrates 9.7g 3% DV; fat 3.5g 5% DV; cholesterol 8.5mg 3% DV; sodium 26.4mg 1% DV.

Candy Bar Squares

Servings: 12 **Yield:** 2 dozen

Ingredients

- 1 cup butter, softened
- 1 cup white sugar
- ½ cup packed brown sugar
- 2 large eggs eggs
- 3 cups all-purpose flour
- 1 teaspoon baking soda
- 1 teaspoon salt

- 6 (2.1 ounce) bars chocolate-coated peanut

and nougat candy (such as Baby Ruth(R))

Directions

Step 1

Preheat oven to 350 degrees F (175 degrees C).

Step 2

Beat the butter or margarine with the white and brown sugars until light and fluffy. Blend in the eggs, mixing well.

Step 3

Mix in the flour, baking soda and salt to the egg mixture. Reserve 1/2 cup of the chopped candy bars for the topping. Stir the remaining candy into the flour mixture. Spread the batter into one 13x9 inch baking pan. Sprinkle the reserved candy on top.

Step 4

Bake at 350 degrees F (175 degrees C) for 25 to 30 minutes or until lightly browned. Cool in pan on a wire rack then cut into squares.

Nutrition Facts

Per Serving:

504.9 calories; protein 6.7g 13% DV; carbohydrates 69.1g 22% DV; fat 22.8g 35% DV; cholesterol 72.9mg 24% DV; sodium 490.3mg 20% DV.

Oats and Pumpkin Pinwheels

Servings: 24 Yield: 4 dozen

Ingredients

- 1 ½ cups all-purpose flour
- 1 cup rolled oats
- ¼ teaspoon baking soda
- 1 ½ cups white sugar
- ½ cup butter, softened

- 2 large egg whites egg whites
- 1 cup canned pumpkin
- ½ teaspoon pumpkin pie spice
- ⅓ cup sesame seeds

Directions

Step 1

In small bowl, combine flour, oats and baking soda; set aside. In large mixing bowl, beat 1 cup sugar and butter or margarine until fluffy; mix in egg whites. Stir in dry ingredients. On waxed paper, press dough into 16 x 12 inch rectangle.

Step 2

In small bowl, combine pumpkin, remaining 1/2 cup sugar and pumpkin pie spice; mix well. Spread mixture over dough to 1/2 inch of edge. Roll dough, beginning at the narrow end. Sprinkle sesame seeds over roll, pressing gently into dough. Wrap in waxed paper; freeze until firm or overnight.

Step 3

Preheat oven to 400 degrees F (200 degrees C).

Step 4

Spray cookie sheet with non-stick cooking spray. Cut frozen dough into 1/4 inch slices; place on cookie sheet. Bake 9 - 11 minutes or until golden brown. Remove to wire rack; cool completely.

Nutrition Facts

Per Serving:

139.9 calories; protein 2.1g 4% DV; carbohydrates 22.1g 7% DV; fat 5.2g 8% DV; cholesterol 10.2mg 3% DV; sodium 70.2mg 3% DV.

Pumpkin Bars IV

Prep: 10 mins **Cook:** 25 mins **Total:** 35 mins **Servings:** 48 **Yield:** 48 bars

Ingredients

- 4 large eggs eggs
- 1 cup vegetable oil
- 2 cups white sugar
- 1 (15 ounce) can pumpkin puree
- 2 cups all-purpose flour
- 2 teaspoons baking powder

- 1 teaspoon baking soda
- ½ teaspoon salt
- 2 teaspoons ground cinnamon
- ½ teaspoon ground ginger
- ½ teaspoon ground cloves
- ½ teaspoon ground nutmeg

Directions

Step 1

Preheat oven to 350 degrees F (175 degrees C). Grease a 12x18 inch half sheet pan.

Step 2

In a large bowl, using a wooden spoon, mix together the eggs, oil, sugar and pumpkin until well blended. Combine the flour, baking powder, baking soda, salt, cinnamon, ginger, cloves and nutmeg; stir into the pumpkin mixture until just blended. Spread evenly into the prepared pan.

Step 3

Bake for 25 to 30 minutes in the preheated oven, until bars spring back when lightly touched. Cool before cutting into bars.

Nutrition Facts

Per Serving:

100.9 calories; protein 1.2g 2% DV; carbohydrates 13.2g 4% DV; fat 5g 8% DV; cholesterol 15.5mg 5% DV; sodium 92.8mg 4% DV.

Jack-O'-Crispies

Prep: 30 mins **Cook:** 5 mins **Additional:** 20 mins **Total:** 55 mins **Servings:** 24 **Yield:** 24 small jack-o-crispies

Ingredients

- 3 tablespoons butter
- 6 cups miniature marshmallows
- 1 teaspoon vanilla extract
- 6 drops orange food coloring, or as needed
- 4 cups crispy rice cereal (such as Rice Krispies), or more to taste
- 6 pieces green licorice string, or as needed
- 1 (.75 ounce) package green fruit roll-up (such as General Mills Fruit Roll-Ups)
- 1 (.75 ounce) tube black decorating gel

Directions

Step 1

Melt butter in a saucepan over low heat. Add marshmallows and vanilla extract. Stir in food coloring. Add rice cereal, 1 cup at a time, stirring after each addition, until blended. Scoop out mixture and shape into small pumpkins using buttered hands.

Step 2

Cut string candy into stems and cut fruit roll-up into leaves. Decorate pumpkins while still soft. Let cool completely, at least 20 minutes. Draw faces onto pumpkins using decorating gel.

Nutrition Facts

Per Serving:

89.3 calories; protein 0.4g 1% DV; carbohydrates 17.8g 6% DV; fat 1.5g 2% DV; cholesterol 3.8mg 1% DV; sodium 79.8mg 3% DV.

Pattern Cookies

Servings: 12 **Yield:** 2 dozen

Ingredients

- ⅔ cup shortening
- 1 cup white sugar
- 2 large eggs eggs
- 1 teaspoon vanilla extract
- ⅓ cup milk
- 3 cups all-purpose flour
- 1 tablespoon baking powder
- ½ teaspoon salt

Directions

Step 1

In a medium bowl, cream together the shortening and sugar. Beat in the eggs, one at a time, then stir in the vanilla and milk. Combine the flour , baking powder and salt, stir into the wet mixture. Cover and chill for about 1 hour.

Step 2

Preheat oven to 350 degrees F (175 degrees C). Line baking sheets with parchment paper. On a lightly floured surface, roll dough out to 1/4 to 1/8 inch thickness. Cut into desired shapes with cookie cutters.

Step 3

Bake for 8 to 10 minutes in the preheated oven, until middle of cookie springs back when touched. Cool on wire racks. Frost with frosting if desired.

Nutrition Facts

Per Serving:

295.7 calories; protein 4.5g 9% DV; carbohydrates 41.3g 13% DV; fat 12.6g 20% DV; cholesterol 31.5mg 11% DV; sodium 233.9mg 9% DV.

Halloween Vegan Yacon Syrup Cookies

Prep: 25 mins **Cook:** 10 mins **Total:** 35 mins **Servings:** 30 **Yield:** 30 cookies

Ingredients

Cookies:

- 2 ½ cups gluten-free flour
- 1 teaspoon baking soda
- ½ teaspoon ground ginger
- ½ teaspoon ground cinnamon
- ¼ teaspoon ground nutmeg
- 1 dash salt
- ½ cup coconut oil, or more as needed
- ½ cup yacon syrup

Icing:

- ¼ cup yacon syrup
- 2 ½ tablespoons melted dark chocolate (85% cacao)

Directions

Step 1

Preheat the oven to 340 degrees F (170 degrees C). Line a baking sheet with parchment paper.

Step 2

Combine flour, baking soda, ginger, cinnamon, nutmeg, and salt in a large bowl. Combine coconut oil and yacon syrup in a separate bowl. Add oil mixture to dry ingredients and mix until dough forms.

Step 3

Roll dough out to about 1/2-inch thickness. Use Halloween-themed cookie cutters to cut out cookies; place them on the prepared baking sheet.

Step 4

Bake in the preheated oven for 10 minutes.

Step 5

While cookies bake, combine yacon syrup and melted chocolate.

Step 6

Remove cookies from oven and apply icing while still hot.

Nutrition Facts

Per Serving:

91.8 calories; protein 1.2g 2% DV; carbohydrates 13.1g 4% DV; fat 4.4g 7% DV; cholesterol 0.1mg; sodium 55mg 2% DV.

Pumpkin Spice Pudding Cookies

Prep: 15 mins **Cook:** 20 mins **Additional:** 5 mins **Total:** 40 mins **Servings:** 36 **Yield:** 3 dozen cookies

Ingredients

- 2 ¼ cups all-purpose flour
- 1 (3.4 ounce) package instant pumpkin-spice pudding mix (such as Jello)
- 1 teaspoon baking soda
- ½ teaspoon pumpkin pie spice
- ½ teaspoon salt
- ¾ cup softened butter
- ½ cup canned pumpkin
- ½ cup white sugar
- ½ cup brown sugar
- 2 eaches eggs
- 1 tablespoon honey
- 1 teaspoon vanilla extract
- 1 cup white chocolate chips
- 1 (14 ounce) package pumpkin-spice flavored candy-coated milk chocolate pieces (such as M&Ms)

Directions

Step 1

Preheat the oven to 350 degrees F (175 degrees C).

Step 2

Combine flour, pudding mix, baking soda, pumpkin pie spice, and salt in a bowl.

Step 3

Combine butter, pumpkin, white sugar, and brown sugar in a large bowl; beat with an electric mixer until fluffy. Beat in eggs, honey, and vanilla extract until incorporated. Mix in the dry ingredients slowly, being careful not to overmix. Stir in the white chocolate chips and pumpkin spice-flavored candies by hand. Drop tablespoonfuls of dough 2 inches apart onto ungreased baking sheets.

Step 4

Bake in the preheated oven until edges are browned and set, about 10 minutes. Cool on the baking sheets for 3 to 4 minutes before removing to a wire rack to cool completely.

Nutrition Facts

Per Serving:

183.9 calories; protein 2.1g 4% DV; carbohydrates 25.7g 8% DV; fat 8.3g 13% DV; cholesterol 21.9mg 7% DV; sodium 149.3mg 6% DV.

Owl Cupcakes

Prep: 30 mins **Cook:** 12 mins **Additional:** 20 mins **Total:** 1 hr 2 mins **Servings:** 24 **Yield:**

24 cupcakes

Ingredients

Cupcakes:

- 2 cups white sugar
- 2 cups all-purpose flour, sifted
- 1 cup unsweetened cocoa powder
- 2 teaspoons baking powder
- 1 teaspoon salt
- ½ teaspoon baking soda

- 1 cup buttermilk
- ½ cup vegetable oil
- 2 large eggs eggs
- 1 teaspoon vanilla extract
- 1 cup hot water

Frosting:

- ¾ cup heavy whipping cream
- 1 ½ tablespoons heavy whipping cream
- 1 ½ cups mascarpone cheese
- 2 tablespoons mascarpone cheese
- 7 tablespoons unsweetened cocoa powder
- ¼ cup white sugar
- Decoration:

- 48 cookies chocolate sandwich cookies (such as Oreo)
- 48 piece (blank)s brown candy-coated milk chocolate pieces (such as M&M's)
- 24 piece (blank)s orange or yellow candy-coated milk chocolate pieces (such as M&M's)

Directions

Step 1

Preheat oven to 350 degrees F (175 degrees C). Line 2 muffin tins with paper liners.

Step 2

Combine 2 cups sugar, flour, 1 cup cocoa powder, baking powder, salt, and baking soda in a bowl.

Step 3

Whisk buttermilk, vegetable oil, eggs, and vanilla extract in a large bowl. Add flour mixture; mix until well-combined. Pour in hot water; stir until batter is smooth. Divide batter evenly among muffin tins.

Step 4

Bake in the preheated oven until a toothpick inserted into the center comes out clean, about 12 minutes. Transfer cupcakes to a wire rack and let cool completely, about 20 minutes.

Step 5

Whip 3/4 cup plus 1 1/2 tablespoon heavy cream in a bowl with an electric mixer until soft peaks form. Fold in 1 1/2 cup plus 2 tablespoons mascarpone cheese, 7 tablespoons cocoa powder, and 1/4 cup sugar gently to make frosting.

Step 6

Spread 1 tablespoon frosting over each cooled cupcake.

Step 7

Twist chocolate sandwich cookies open, leaving all cream filling on 1 side. Place 2 cookies, cream filling-side up, on each cupcake to make owl eyes. Place a brown milk chocolate piece on each cookie to create pupils. Insert an orange or yellow milk chocolate piece in the center to make a beak.

Nutrition Facts

Per Serving:

372.1 calories; protein 5.4g 11% DV; carbohydrates 46.4g 15% DV; fat 20.3g 31% DV; cholesterol 46.7mg 16% DV; sodium 291.3mg 12% DV.

Halloween Fondant Ghost Cupcakes

Prep: 40 mins **Cook:** 16 mins **Additional:** 2 hrs 15 mins **Total:** 3 hrs 11 mins **Servings:**

12 **Yield:** 12 cupcakes

Ingredients

- 1 cup all-purpose flour
- 2 tablespoons all-purpose flour
- ½ cup unsweetened cocoa powder
- 1 teaspoon baking soda
- 1 teaspoon salt

- 1 cup white sugar
- ½ cup butter
- 1 egg
- 1 teaspoon vanilla extract
- 1 cup milk

Decorating:

- 1 (16 ounce) package vanilla frosting
- 6 eaches large marshmallows, cut in half crosswise

- 2 tablespoons confectioners' sugar, or as needed
- 8 ounces ready-to-use white fondant
- 12 eaches raisins, halved

Directions

Step 1

Preheat oven to 350 degrees F (175 degrees C). Grease a 12-cup muffin tin or line cups with paper liners.

Step 2

Sift 1 cup plus 2 tablespoons flour, cocoa powder, baking soda, and salt together in a bowl.

Step 3

Combine sugar and butter in a large bowl; beat with an electric mixer until light and fluffy. Beat in egg and vanilla extract. Mix in flour mixture alternately with milk. Beat until batter is just blended.

Step 4

Bake in the preheated oven until tops spring back when lightly pressed and a toothpick inserted into the center comes out clean, 16 to 20 minutes. Remove from oven and cool on a wire rack for 15 minutes. Remove cupcakes from tin and cool completely, about 2 hours.

Step 5

Frost each cupcake with a thin layer of white vanilla frosting. Place 1 marshmallow half, cut-side up, in the center of each cupcake.

Step 6

Dust a work surface with confectioners' sugar. Pinch off walnut-sized pieces of white fondant; roll into thin circles that are slightly bigger than the cupcakes. Drape over the marshmallows so they look like ghosts. Poke 2 holes near the top for the eyes. Stuff 1 raisin half into each hole.

Nutrition Facts

Per Serving:

454.3 calories; protein 3.2g 6% DV; carbohydrates 75.6g 24% DV; fat 16.4g 25% DV; cholesterol 35.6mg 12% DV; sodium 441.4mg 18% DV.

Chocolate Cupcakes with Pumpkin Cheesecake Filling

Prep: 15 mins **Cook:** 25 mins **Total:** 40 mins **Servings:** 12 **Yield:** 12 cupcakes

Ingredients

Filling:

- 1 (8 ounce) package cream cheese, at room temperature
- ⅓ cup white sugar
- 1 egg
- 2 tablespoons 100% pure pumpkin

- 6 drops yellow food coloring
- 3 drops red food coloring
- ⅛ teaspoon salt
- ½ cup semisweet chocolate chips, or more to taste

Cake:

- 1 ½ cups all-purpose flour
- 1 cup white sugar
- ¼ cup unsweetened cocoa powder
- 1 teaspoon baking soda
- ½ teaspoon salt

- ⅓ cup vegetable oil
- 1 cup water
- 1 teaspoon white vinegar
- 1 teaspoon vanilla extract

Directions

Step 1

Preheat oven to 350 degrees F (175 degrees C). Line a muffin tin with paper liners.

Step 2

Place cream cheese, 1/3 cup sugar, egg, pumpkin, yellow food coloring, red food coloring, and salt in a bowl. Beat using an electric mixer until thoroughly combined and no lumps remain. Stir in chocolate chips.

Step 3

Whisk flour, 1 cup sugar, cocoa powder, baking soda, and 1/2 teaspoon salt together in a large bowl. Mix in water, oil, vinegar, and vanilla extract until batter is well blended.

Step 4

Fill muffin cups 1/2-full with batter; top with 1 tablespoon of the cream cheese mixture. Sprinkle a few chocolate chips on top.

Step 5

Bake in the preheated oven until a toothpick inserted into the center comes out clean, about 25 minutes.

Nutrition Facts

Per Serving:

306.2 calories; protein 4.2g 8% DV; carbohydrates 40.1g 13% DV; fat 15.5g 24% DV; cholesterol 36mg 12% DV; sodium 289.2mg 12% DV.

Pumpkin Ginger Cupcakes

Prep: 20 mins **Cook:** 20 mins **Additional:** 50 mins **Total:** 1 hr 30 mins **Servings:** 24 **Yield:** 24 cupcakes

Ingredients

- 2 cups all-purpose flour
- 1 (3.4 ounce) package instant butterscotch pudding mix
- 2 teaspoons baking soda
- ¼ teaspoon salt
- 1 tablespoon ground cinnamon
- ½ teaspoon ground ginger
- ½ teaspoon ground allspice
- ¼ teaspoon ground cloves
- ⅓ cup finely chopped crystallized ginger
- 1 cup butter, room temperature
- 1 cup white sugar
- 1 cup packed brown sugar
- 4 large eggs eggs, room temperature
- 1 teaspoon vanilla extract
- 1 (15 ounce) can pumpkin puree

Directions

Step 1

Preheat an oven to 350 degrees F (175 degrees C). Grease 24 muffin cups, or line with paper muffin liners. Whisk together the flour, pudding mix, baking soda, salt, cinnamon, ground ginger, allspice, cloves, and crystallized ginger in a bowl; set aside.

Step 2

Beat the butter, white sugar, and brown sugar with an electric mixer in a large bowl until light and fluffy. The mixture should be noticeably lighter in color. Add the eggs one at a time, allowing each egg to blend into the butter mixture before adding the next. Beat in the vanilla and pumpkin puree with the last egg. Stir in the flour mixture, mixing until just incorporated. Pour the batter into the prepared muffin cups.

Step 3

Bake in the preheated oven until golden and the tops spring back when lightly pressed, about 20 minutes. Cool in the pans for 10 minutes before removing to cool completely on a wire rack.

Nutrition Facts

Per Serving:

210.6 calories; protein 2.4g 5% DV; carbohydrates 31.8g 10% DV; fat 8.7g 13% DV; cholesterol 51.3mg 17% DV; sodium 303.2mg 12% DV.

Bat Cupcakes

Prep: 10 mins **Cook:** 20 mins **Total:** 30 mins **Servings:** 24 **Yield:** 2 dozen

Ingredients

- 1 (18.25 ounce) package chocolate cake mix
- 1 (16 ounce) container prepared chocolate frosting
- 1 (11.5 ounce) package fudge stripe cookies
- 1 (6 ounce) bag milk chocolate candy kisses, unwrapped
- 1 tablespoon red gel icing

Directions

Step 1

Prepare the cake mix according to package directions for cupcakes. Cool. Frost cupcakes with chocolate frosting.

Step 2

Break the cookies in half, and press two halves into the top of each cupcake for wings, stripes facing the frosting. Place a chocolate kiss in front of the cookies with the point facing forward for the body. Make two beady little eyes with the red gel icing towards the point of the kiss. Let the fun begin!

Nutrition Facts

Per Serving:

272.6 calories; protein 2.8g 6% DV; carbohydrates 41g 13% DV; fat 11.8g 18% DV; cholesterol 1.5mg 1% DV; sodium 271.9mg 11% DV.

Cupcake Graveyard

Prep: 30 mins **Cook:** 25 mins **Total:** 55 mins **Servings:** 24 **Yield:** 2 dozen

Ingredients

- 1 (18.25 ounce) package chocolate cake mix
- 2 (16 ounce) packages vanilla frosting
- ¾ cup chocolate sandwich cookie crumbs
- 24 eaches chocolate covered graham cracker cookies

Directions

Step 1

Prepare and bake cake mix according to package directions for cupcakes.

Step 2

In a medium bowl stir 1 package of frosting with the cookie crumbs. Frost cooled cupcakes.

Step 3

Fill a pastry bag, fitted with a plain tip, with remaining white frosting. Write R.I.P. on each chocolate covered graham cracker cookie. Stand a decorated cookie on top of each cupcake so that it looks like a tombstone. Place the cupcakes on a large cookie sheet that has been covered with green paper. Place paper ghosts and bats randomly through the graveyard. Serve!

Nutrition Facts

Per Serving:

311.5 calories; protein 1.7g 4% DV; carbohydrates 49.3g 16% DV; fat 12.4g 19% DV; cholesterolmg; sodium 284mg 11% DV.

Creepy Halloween Skull Cupcakes

Prep: 30 mins **Cook:** 18 mins **Additional:** 1 hr 45 mins **Total:** 2 hrs 33 mins **Servings:** 24 **Yield:** 24 cupcakes

Ingredients

- 1 (18.25 ounce) package devil's food cake mix (such as Duncan Hines)
- 1 cup water
- 3 eaches eggs
- ⅓ cup vegetable oil

- 1 ½ (16 ounce) packages prepared vanilla frosting
- 1 (7 ounce) pouch prepared chocolate frosting

Directions

Step 1

Preheat oven to 350 degrees F (175 degrees C). Line two 12-cup muffin tins with paper liners, preferable dark-colored or Halloween-themed ones.

Step 2

Combine cake mix, water, eggs, and oil in a large bowl; beat with an electric mixer on low speed until moistened, about 30 seconds. Beat at medium speed until batter is smooth and creamy, about 2 minutes. Spoon batter into the prepared muffin cups, filling each 3/4 full.

Step 3

Bake in the preheated oven until a toothpick inserted in the center comes out clean, 18 to 21 minutes. Remove from oven and cool tins on a wire rack for 15 minutes. Remove cupcakes from the tins and cool completely on a wire rack before decorating, about 1 hour.

Step 4

Frost each cupcake with a thin layer of white vanilla frosting and refrigerate for 30 minutes to make decorating easier.

Step 5

Remove cupcakes from fridge and apply a second layer of white frosting. Fill a piping bag outfitted with a small round tip with chocolate frosting and draw a skull face on the cupcakes: pipe large ovals for the eyes, two dots for the nostrils, and a large "stitched" smile for the mouth.

Nutrition Facts

Per Serving:

275.8 calories; protein 2.8g 6% DV; carbohydrates 38.6g 13% DV; fat 13.1g 20% DV; cholesterol 24.7mg 8% DV; sodium 234.4mg 9% DV.

Pumpkin Spice Cupcakes With Cream Cheese Frosting

Prep: 20 mins **Cook:** 20 mins **Additional:** 10 mins **Total:** 50 mins **Servings:** 24 **Yield:** 2 dozen cupcakes

Ingredients

Cupcakes:

- 2 ½ cups white sugar
- ¾ cup butter, softened
- 3 large eggs eggs
- 1 (15 ounce) can solid-pack pumpkin puree
- 2 ⅓ cups all-purpose flour

- 1 tablespoon pumpkin pie spice
- 1 tablespoon ground cinnamon
- ¾ teaspoon baking powder
- ½ teaspoon ground ginger
- 1 cup buttermilk

Frosting:

- 1 (8 ounce) package cream cheese, softened
- ½ cup butter, softened
- 4 cups confectioners' sugar

- 2 teaspoons ground cinnamon
- 1 teaspoon vanilla extract

Directions

Step 1

Preheat oven to 350 degrees F (175 degrees C). Line 24 muffin cups with paper liners.

Step 2

Beat white sugar and 3/4 cup butter together in a bowl using an electric mixer until smooth and creamy; add eggs, 1 at a time, beating well after each addition. Beat pumpkin into creamed butter mixture.

Step 3

Mix flour, pumpkin pie spice, 1 tablespoon cinnamon, baking powder, and ginger together in a bowl; stir into creamed butter mixture, alternating with buttermilk, until batter is smooth. Fill each muffin cup 3/4-full with batter.

Step 4

Bake in the preheated oven until a toothpick inserted in the center of a cupcake comes out clean, 20 to 25 minutes. Cool in muffin tin for 10 minutes before transferring to wire rack.

Step 5

Beat cream cheese and 1/2 cup butter together in a bowl using an electric mixer until fluffy. Beat confectioners' sugar, 2 teaspoons cinnamon, and vanilla extract into creamed butter until frosting is smooth. Spread frosting on each cupcake.

Nutrition Facts

Per Serving:

345.3 calories; protein 3.4g 7% DV; carbohydrates 53.8g 17% DV; fat 13.8g 21% DV; cholesterol 59.3mg 20% DV; sodium 173.9mg 7% DV.

Pumpkin Spice Cupcakes

Prep: 25 mins **Cook:** 25 mins **Additional:** 50 mins **Total:** 1 hr 40 mins **Servings:** 24 **Yield:** 24 cupcakes

Ingredients

- 2 ¼ cups all-purpose flour
- 1 teaspoon ground cinnamon
- ½ teaspoon ground nutmeg
- ½ teaspoon ground ginger
- ½ teaspoon ground cloves
- ½ teaspoon ground allspice
- ½ teaspoon salt
- 1 tablespoon baking powder
- ½ teaspoon baking soda
- ½ cup butter, softened
- 1 cup white sugar

- ⅓ cup brown sugar
- 2 large eggs eggs, room temperature
- ¾ cup milk
- 1 cup pumpkin puree
- Cinnamon Cream Cheese Frosting
- 1 (8 ounce) package cream cheese, softened
- ¼ cup butter, softened
- 3 cups confectioners' sugar
- 1 teaspoon vanilla extract
- 1 teaspoon ground cinnamon

Directions

Step 1

Preheat an oven to 375 degrees F (190 degrees C). Grease 24 muffin cups, or line with paper muffin liners. Sift together the flour, 1 teaspoon cinnamon, nutmeg, ginger, clove, allspice, salt, baking powder, and baking soda; set aside.

Step 2

Beat 1/2 cup of butter, the white sugar, and brown sugar with an electric mixer in a large bowl until light and fluffy. The mixture should be noticeably lighter in color. Add the room-temperature eggs one at a time, allowing each egg to blend into the butter mixture before adding the next. Stir in the milk and pumpkin puree after the last egg. Stir in the flour mixture, mixing until just incorporated. Pour the batter into the prepared muffin cups.

Step 3

Bake in the preheated oven until golden and the tops spring back when lightly pressed, about 25 minutes. Cool in the pans for 5 minutes before removing to cool completely on a wire rack.

Step 4

While the cupcakes are cooling, make the frosting by beating the cream cheese and 1/4 butter with an electric mixer in a bowl until smooth. Beat in the confectioners' sugar a little at a time until incorporated. Add the vanilla extract and 1 teaspoon ground cinnamon; beat until fluffy. Once the cupcakes are cool, frost with the cream cheese icing.

Nutrition Facts

Per Serving:

243.9 calories; protein 2.9g 6% DV; carbohydrates 37.2g 12% DV; fat 9.8g 15% DV; cholesterol 41.6mg 14% DV; sodium 220.1mg 9% DV.

Carrot Cupcakes with White Chocolate Cream Cheese Icing

Prep: 30 mins **Cook:** 25 mins **Additional:** 1 hr **Total:** 1 hr 55 mins **Servings:** 12 **Yield:** 12 muffins

Ingredients

Cream Cheese Icing:

- 2 ounces white chocolate
- 1 (8 ounce) package cream cheese, softened
- ½ cup unsalted butter, softened
- 1 teaspoon vanilla extract

- ½ teaspoon orange extract
- 4 cups confectioners' sugar
- 2 tablespoons heavy cream

Carrot Cake:

- 2 large eggs eggs, lightly beaten
- 1 ⅛ cups white sugar
- ⅓ cup brown sugar
- ½ cup vegetable oil
- 1 teaspoon vanilla extract
- 2 cups shredded carrots
- ½ cup crushed pineapple

- 1 ½ cups all-purpose flour
- 1 ¼ teaspoons baking soda
- ½ teaspoon salt
- 1 ½ teaspoons ground cinnamon
- ½ teaspoon ground nutmeg
- ¼ teaspoon ground ginger
- 1 cup chopped walnuts

Directions

Step 1

Preheat oven to 350 degrees F (175 degrees C). Lightly grease 12 muffin cups.

Step 2

In small saucepan, melt white chocolate over low heat. Stir until smooth, and allow to cool to room temperature.

Step 3

In a bowl, beat together the cream cheese and butter until smooth. Mix in white chocolate, 1 teaspoon vanilla, and orange extract. Gradually beat in the confectioners' sugar until the mixture is fluffy. Mix in heavy cream.

Step 4

Beat together the eggs, white sugar, and brown sugar in a bowl, and mix in the oil and vanilla. Fold in carrots and pineapple. In a separate bowl, mix the flour, baking soda, salt, cinnamon, nutmeg, and ginger. Mix flour mixture into the carrot mixture until evenly moist. Fold in 1/2 cup walnuts. Transfer to the prepared muffin cups.

Step 5

Bake 25 minutes in the preheated oven, or until a toothpick inserted in the center of a muffin comes out clean. Cool completely on wire racks before topping with the icing and sprinkling with remaining walnuts.

Nutrition Facts

Per Serving:

639.1 calories; protein 6g 12% DV; carbohydrates 84.7g 27% DV; fat 32.2g 50% DV; cholesterol 76.2mg 25% DV; sodium 317.4mg 13% DV.

Harvest Pumpkin Cupcakes

Prep: 20 mins **Cook:** 30 mins **Additional:** 30 mins **Total:** 1 hr 20 mins **Servings:** 32 **Yield:**

32 servings

Ingredients

Cupcakes:

- 4 large eggs eggs, slightly beaten
- ¾ cup Mazola Vegetable Plus! Oil
- 2 cups sugar
- 1 (15 ounce) can pumpkin
- 1 ¾ cups all-purpose flour
- ¼ cup Argo OR Kingsford's Corn Starch

- 4 teaspoons Spice Islands Pumpkin Pie Spice
- 2 teaspoons Argo Baking Powder
- 1 teaspoon baking soda
- ¾ teaspoon salt

Frosting:

- 1 (8 ounce) package cream cheese, softened
- 3 tablespoons butter OR margarine, softened
- 1 tablespoon orange juice

- 2 teaspoons Spice Islands 100% Pure Bourbon Vanilla Extract
- 1 ½ teaspoons freshly grated orange peel
- 4 cups powdered sugar

Directions

Step 1

To make cupcakes: Blend the eggs, oil, sugar, and pumpkin in a large mixing bowl; set aside. Stir together dry ingredients in a separate bowl. Add dry ingredients to pumpkin mixture and beat until well blended. POUR into lined muffin tins. Fill about 2/3 full. Bake in preheated 350 degrees oven for 30 minutes or until center springs back when touched. Cool 30 minutes. Spread with frosting.

Step 2

To make frosting: Beat cream cheese and butter until fluffy. Add remaining ingredients and beat until smooth. Spread over cooled cupcakes.

Nutrition Facts

Per Serving:

233.4 calories; protein 2.2g 4% DV; carbohydrates 35.9g 12% DV; fat 9.6g 15% DV; cholesterol 33.8mg 11% DV; sodium 193.9mg 8% DV.

Bloody Broken Glass Cupcakes

Prep: 30 mins **Cook:** 30 mins **Additional:** 20 mins **Total:** 1 hr 20 mins **Servings:** 24 **Yield:**

24 cupcakes

Ingredients

- 1 (18.25 ounce) package white cake mix
- 1 cup water
- ⅓ cup vegetable oil

- 3 large eggs eggs
- 1 (16 ounce) can white frosting

Sugar Glass:

- 2 cups water
- 1 cup light corn syrup
- 3 ½ cups white sugar
- ¼ teaspoon cream of tartar
- Edible Blood:

- ½ cup light corn syrup
- 1 tablespoon cornstarch
- ¼ cup water, or more as needed
- 15 drops red food coloring
- 3 drops blue food coloring

Directions

Step 1

Preheat an oven to 350 degrees F (175 degrees C). Line 2, 12-cupcake tins with paper cupcake liners.

Step 2

Blend cake mix, 1 cup water, vegetable oil, and eggs in a large bowl. Beat with a mixer on low speed for 2 minutes. Divide cake batter between lined cupcake tins.

Step 3

Bake cupcakes in preheated oven until a toothpick inserted in the center comes out clean, 18 to 22 minutes. Cool completely. Frost cupcakes with white frosting.

Step 4

Make the sugar glass. Mix 2 cups water, 1 cup corn syrup, white sugar, and cream of tartar in a large saucepan; bring to a boil. Use a candy thermometer and boil sugar syrup until temperature reaches 300 degrees (hard ball), stirring constantly. The mixture will thicken as water evaporates. When sugar reaches 300 degrees, quickly pour onto a metal baking pan. Cool until completely hardened. Break into "shards" using a meat mallet.

Step 5

Make the edible blood. Mix together 1/2 cup corn syrup and cornstarch in a large bowl. Slowly stir in the 1/4 cup of water, adding more if necessary, until the corn syrup mixture has thickened to the consistency of blood. Stir in the red and blue food coloring.

Step 6

Stab each frosted cupcake with a few shards of broken sugar glass. Drizzle on drops of "blood" to complete the effect.

Nutrition Facts

Per Serving:

376.7 calories; protein 1.7g 4% DV; carbohydrates 74.6g 24% DV; fat 9g 14% DV; cholesterol 23.3mg 8% DV; sodium 198.2mg 8% DV.

Spider Cupcakes

Prep: 1 hr **Cook:** 30 mins **Total:** 1 hr 30 mins **Servings:** 24 **Yield:** 24 cupcakes

Ingredients

- 1 (18.25 ounce) package chocolate cake mix
- 1 pound black shoestring licorice
- 1 (16 ounce) can white frosting
- 48 eaches pieces candy corn
- 48 eaches cinnamon red hot candies
- ¼ cup orange decorator sugar

Directions

Step 1

Prepare cupcakes according to package directions. Let cool completely.

Step 2

Cut licorice into 3 inch sections. Working with one or two cupcakes at a time, so the frosting doesn't set before decorating, frost the cupcakes with the white frosting. Insert licorice pieces into the outer edges of the cupcakes to make the legs of the spider, 3 legs on each side (4 takes up too much space). Place two pieces of candy corn on the front of the cupcake for fangs and use two red hots as eyes. Sprinkle with decorator sugar. Repeat with remaining cupcakes.

Nutrition Facts

Per Serving:

259.5 calories; protein 1.7g 4% DV; carbohydrates 49.8g 16% DV; fat 6.4g 10% DV; cholesterol1mg; sodium 241.1mg 10% DV.

Candy Corn Cupcakes

Prep: 15 mins **Cook:** 20 mins **Additional:** 20 mins **Total:** 55 mins **Servings:** 24 **Yield:** 2 dozen cupcakes

Ingredients

- 1 (18.25 ounce) package white cake mix
- 1 cup water
- ⅓ cup vegetable oil
- 3 large eggs eggs
- 14 drops red food coloring, or as needed - divided
- 22 drops yellow food coloring, or as needed - divided
- 6 drops green food coloring, or as needed
- 2 cups prepared white frosting
- 12 eaches pieces of yellow, orange, and white candy corn
- 12 eaches pieces of brown, orange, and white candy corn

Directions

Step 1

Preheat oven to 350 degrees F (175 degrees C). Line 24 cupcake cups with paper liners.

Step 2

Place cake mix in a bowl, and pour in water and vegetable oil; add 3 eggs. With electric mixer on low speed, beat the cake mix with water, oil, and eggs until thoroughly combined, about 2 minutes. Pour half the cake mix into a second bowl; divide the remaining cake mix in half, and place into 2 separate small bowls.

Step 3

Color the largest portion of the cake mix orange by mixing in 4 drops of red food coloring and 6 drops of yellow food coloring. Into a second, smaller bowl of cake mix, mix in 10 drops of red food coloring, 12 drops of yellow food coloring, and 6 drops of green food coloring, to color that bowl brown. Into the last remaining small bowl of cake mix, stir in 5 drops of yellow food coloring to color that bowl yellow.

Step 4

Spoon yellow cake batter into the bottoms of 12 prepared cupcake cups, filling them about 1/3 full. Spoon the brown batter into the bottoms of the remaining 12 prepared cupcake cups, filling them about 1/3 full. Spoon orange cupcake mix over the yellow and brown layers, filling the cupcakes about 2/3 full. Try not to jar or shake the filled cupcakes, to avoid mixing layers.

Step 5

Carefully place cupcakes into the preheated oven, and bake until a toothpick inserted into the center of a cupcake comes out clean, 18 to 22 minutes. Allow to cool.

Step 6

Frost each cooled cupcake with the white frosting; place a piece of yellow, orange, and white candy corn on top of each yellow and orange cupcake. Place a brown, orange, and white piece of candy corn on top of each brown and orange cupcake.

Nutrition Facts

Per Serving:

238.3 calories; protein 2g 4% DV; carbohydrates 35g 11% DV; fat 10.6g 16% DV; cholesterol 23.3mg 8% DV; sodium 199.3mg 8% DV.

Rick's Special Buttercream Frosting

Prep: 30 mins **Total:** 30 mins **Servings:** 12 **Yield:** 7 cups

Ingredients

- 2 cups shortening
- 8 cups confectioners' sugar
- ½ teaspoon salt
- 2 teaspoons vanilla extract
- 1 cup heavy whipping cream

Directions

Step 1

In a mixing bowl, cream shortening until fluffy. Add sugar, and continue creaming until well blended.

Step 2

Add salt, vanilla, and 6 ounces whipping cream. Blend on low speed until moistened. Add additional 2 ounces whipping cream if necessary. Beat at high speed until frosting is fluffy.

Nutrition Facts

Per Serving:

683.7 calories; protein 0.4g 1% DV; carbohydrates 80.3g 26% DV; fat 41.6g 64% DV; cholesterol 27.2mg 9% DV; sodium 105.3mg 4% DV.

Ann's Chocolate Chip Carrot Cake Pumpkins

Prep: 20 mins **Cook:** 20 mins **Additional:** 30 mins **Total:** 1 hr 10 mins **Servings:** 12 **Yield:** 12 servings

Ingredients

Cupcakes:

- 2 cups cake flour
- 2 teaspoons ground cinnamon
- 1 ½ teaspoons baking soda
- 1 teaspoon baking powder
- 1 teaspoon salt
- 2 cups white sugar
- 1 ½ cups vegetable oil
- 4 large eggs eggs
- 2 cups grated carrots
- 1 (8 ounce) can crushed pineapple, drained
- 1 tablespoon cake flour
- ½ cup chopped walnuts
- ½ cup semisweet chocolate chips

Frosting:

- ½ cup butter
- 1 (8 ounce) package cream cheese, softened
- 1 tablespoon vanilla extract
- 2 cups confectioners' sugar, or more as needed
- 1 tablespoon lemon juice
- 3 drops orange food coloring
- 1 (1.5 ounce) tube black decorating gel

Directions

Step 1

Preheat oven to 325 degrees F (165 degrees C). (If using a countertop induction oven, preheat to 325 degrees F.) Grease 12 pumpkin-shaped cupcake molds (silicon molds work well).

Step 2

Sift 2 cups cake flour, cinnamon, baking soda, baking powder, and salt together in a bowl. Mix in sugar, oil, and eggs until combined. Stir carrots and pineapple into the batter.

Step 3

Place 1 tablespoon cake flour in a bowl. Toss walnuts and chocolate chips in flour until coated; fold into batter.

Step 4

Pour batter into cupcake molds to about two-thirds full; gently tap molds onto work surface to remove air bubbles.

Step 5

Bake in preheated oven (or countertop induction oven) until a toothpick inserted into the center of a cupcake comes out clean, 20 to 25 minutes (or 15 to 20 minutes in the countertop induction oven). Cool to room temperature, 15 to 20 minutes; remove from molds.

Step 6

Combine butter, cream cheese, and vanilla extract in a bowl; beat with an electric mixer until well blended, 4 to 6 minutes. Mix in confectioners' sugar on low speed, 1/2 cup at a time, until frosting is smooth and spreadable. Add lemon juice and orange food coloring; stir until combined. Refrigerate until set, 15 to 20 minutes.

Step 7

Frost cupcakes with the cream cheese frosting; decorate with black decorating gel.

Nutrition Facts

Per Serving:

818.3 calories; protein 7.3g 15% DV; carbohydrates 89.4g 29% DV; fat 49.4g 76% DV; cholesterol 102.9mg 34% DV; sodium 595.3mg 24% DV.

Halloween Cyclops Cupcakes

Prep: 30 mins **Cook:** 10 mins **Additional:** 1 hr 30 mins **Total:** 2 hrs 10 mins **Servings:** 12

Yield: 12 cupcakes

Ingredients

Cupcakes:

- 9 tablespoons unsweetened cocoa powder
- 5 tablespoons boiling water, or more if needed
- ¾ cup unsalted butter
- ¾ cup white sugar

- 2 tablespoons white sugar
- 3 eaches eggs
- 1 cup all-purpose flour
- 2 teaspoons baking powder

Frosting:

- 1 (8 ounce) package cream cheese, softened and cubed
- ¼ cup unsalted butter, softened

- ½ teaspoon vanilla extract
- 1 cup confectioners' sugar
- 3 drops green food coloring

Cyclops:

- 1 (.68 oz. tube) black decorating gel

- 12 piece (blank)s blue candy-coated milk chocolate pieces
- 4 eaches marshmallows
- 3 eaches dark colored fruit leather
- 2 tablespoons confectioners' sugar

- ½ teaspoon lemon juice, or more as needed
- 3 tablespoons silver dragees decorating candy
- 24 eaches sunflower seeds

Directions

Step 1

Preheat the oven to 400 degrees F (200 degrees C). Grease a 12-cup muffin tin or line cups with paper liners.

Step 2

Sift cocoa powder into a large bowl and add 5 tablespoons boiling water. Stir into a thick paste, adding more water, 1 tablespoon at a time, if needed. Add 3/4 cup butter and 3/4 cup plus 2 tablespoons sugar and beat with an electric mixer until smooth and creamy. Beat in eggs one at a time, beating well after each addition, until batter is smooth.

Step 3

Mix flour and baking powder in a bowl and stir into the batter until well combined. Spoon batter into the prepared muffin cups, filling each 2/3 to the top using an ice cream scoop.

Step 4

Bake in the preheated oven until tops spring back when lightly pressed and a toothpick comes out clean, 10 to 15 minutes. Allow to cool in muffin tin for a few minutes; transfer to wire rack and cool completely, about 1 hour.

Step 5

Beat cream cheese and 1/4 cup butter together in a bowl until creamy. Mix in vanilla extract. Stir in 1 cup confectioners' sugar gradually until frosting is smooth. Mix in green food coloring.

Step 6

Frost each cupcake with a thin layer of green frosting and refrigerate for 30 minutes to make decorating easier. Frost with a second thin layer of green frosting.

Step 7

Draw a small dot with the black decorating gel on each candy-coated milk chocolate piece for the pupil. Cut marshmallows into 4 slices with a sharp knife and stick 1 blue pupil in the center of each marshmallow piece.

Step 8

Cut fruit leather into crescent shapes or semi-circles for the mouths using small sharp scissors.

Step 9

Mix 2 tablespoons confectioners' sugar with lemon juice in a bowl to make icing. Glue silver dragees onto the fruit leather mouths using a toothpick dipped in icing.

Step 10

Assemble cyclops by placing a mouth and one marshmallow eye onto each cupcake. Stick 2 sunflower seeds on top of the cupcake for the horns.

Nutrition Facts

Per Serving:

424.6 calories; protein 5.3g 11% DV; carbohydrates 48.2g 16% DV; fat 25.2g 39% DV; cholesterol 102.2mg 34% DV; sodium 275.9mg 11% DV.

Halloween Chocolate Cupcakes with Monster Peanut Butter Eyes

Prep: 50 mins **Cook:** 15 mins **Additional:** 2 hrs **Total:** 3 hrs 5 mins **Servings:** 12 **Yield:**

12 cupcakes

Ingredients

Chocolate Cupcakes:

- 9 tablespoons unsweetened cocoa powder
- 5 tablespoons boiling water, or more if needed
- ¾ cup unsalted butter
- ¾ cup white sugar

- 2 tablespoons white sugar
- 1 cup all-purpose flour
- 2 teaspoons baking powder
- 3 eaches eggs
- 1 teaspoon vanilla extract

Peanut Butter Eyes:

- 4 cups confectioners' sugar
- 1 ¾ cups peanut butter
- 1 cup white chocolate chips
- ¼ cup butter

- 1 (1.5 ounce) tube red decorating gel
- 1 (16 ounce) package prepared chocolate frosting
- 1 (1.5 ounce) tube white decorating gel

Directions

Step 1

Preheat oven to 200 degrees F (95 degrees C). Grease a 12-cup muffin tin or line cups with paper liners.

Step 2

Sift cocoa powder into a large bowl and add 5 tablespoons boiling water. Stir into a thick paste, adding more water, 1 tablespoon at a time, if needed. Add 3/4 cup butter and 3/4 cup plus 2 tablespoons sugar and beat with an electric mixer until smooth and creamy. Beat in eggs one at a time, beating well after each addition, until batter is smooth.

Step 3

Mix flour and baking powder in a bowl and stir into the batter until well combined. Spoon batter into the prepared muffin cups, filling each 2/3 to the top using an ice cream scoop.

Step 4

Bake in the preheated oven until tops spring back when lightly pressed and a toothpick comes out clean, 10 to 15 minutes. Allow to cool in muffin tin for a few minutes; transfer to wire rack and cool completely, about 1 hour.

Step 5

Beat confectioners' sugar, peanut butter, 1/4 cup butter, and vanilla extract in a bowl until a thick dough forms. Refrigerate for 30 minutes.

Step 6

Line a baking sheet with baking parchment.

Step 7

Remove the peanut butter mixture from the fridge and roll into small balls to make monster eyes. Chill mixture or moisten hands if it starts to stick. Arrange balls on the prepared baking sheet and freeze for 30 minutes.

Step 8

Place white chocolate in top of a double boiler over simmering water. Stir continuously, scraping down the sides with a rubber spatula to avoid scorching, until chocolate is melted, about 5 minutes.

Step 9

Remove the eyes from the freezer and individually pick them up with a toothpick. Dip balls into melted chocolate leaving a small circle on one side blank. Twirl the toothpick to remove excess chocolate and put back on the parchment lined baking sheet.

Step 10

Dig out a bit of the peanut butter mixture from each ball where it isn't covered with chocolate to make room for the red decorating gel. Fill the holes with red decorating gel.

Step 11

Frost cupcakes with chocolate frosting. Place 2 peanut butter eyes on top. Draw on a mouth with the white decorating gel.

Nutrition Facts

Per Serving:

889.7 calories; protein 14.3g 29% DV; carbohydrates 109.8g 35% DV; fat 48.2g 74% DV; cholesterol 84.8mg 28% DV; sodium 499.6mg 20% DV.

Monster Mini Cupcakes

Prep: 45 mins **Cook:** 14 mins **Additional:** 1 hr 5 mins **Total:** 2 hrs 4 mins **Servings:** 24

Yield: 24 mini cupcakes

Ingredients

Mini Chocolate Cupcakes:

- ½ cup milk
- 1 tablespoon white vinegar
- ½ cup unsalted butter, at room temperature
- 10 tablespoons white sugar
- 2 teaspoons vanilla sugar
- 2 large eggs
- ¾ cup all-purpose flour
- 1 tablespoon all-purpose flour
- ½ cup unsweetened cocoa powder
- ½ teaspoon baking powder
- ¼ teaspoon baking soda
- 1 pinch salt

Cream Cheese Frosting:

- 1 (8 ounce) package cream cheese, softened
- ¼ cup unsalted butter, at room temperature
- 1 teaspoon vanilla extract
- 1 cup confectioners' sugar, sifted
- 2 drops orange food coloring
- 48 eaches small candy eyeballs
- 2 pieces dried mango

Directions

Step 1

Combine milk and vinegar in a bowl. Let stand until milk curdles, about 5 minutes.

Step 2

Preheat oven to 350 degrees F (175 degrees C). Grease a 24-cup mini muffin tin or line cups with paper liners.

Step 3

Combine 1/2 cup butter, white sugar, and vanilla sugar in a large bowl; beat with an electric mixer until smooth and creamy. Add eggs one at a time, beating well after each addition.

Step 4

Mix 3/4 cup plus 1 tablespoon flour, cocoa powder, baking powder, baking soda, and salt in a bowl. Alternate adding flour mixture and curdled milk to the creamed butter mixture, mixing until batter is well blended. Spoon batter into the prepared muffin cups, filling each 3/4 full.

Step 5

Bake in the preheated oven until tops spring back when lightly pressed and a toothpick inserted in the center of 1 cupcake comes back clean, about 14 minutes. Cool in the muffin tin for a few minutes, then transfer to a wire rack to cool completely, about 1 hour.

Step 6

Combine cream cheese and 1/4 cup butter in a bowl; beat with an electric mixer until well combined. Mix in vanilla extract. Stir in confectioners' sugar gradually. Color frosting orange with a few drops of food coloring.

Step 7

Place orange frosting in a pastry bag fitted with a grass tip. Hold the pastry bag at a 90-degree angle 1/8 inch above the surface of a cupcake. Squeeze bag to form orange 'fur' by pulling tip up and away when the icing strand is about 1/2 inch high. Repeat to cover cupcake evenly with fur.

Step 8

Add 2 eyes to each cupcake. Cut dried mango into small strips and arrange into the frosting as 'horns'.

Nutrition Facts

Per Serving:

163.4 calories; protein 2.3g 5% DV; carbohydrates 17g 6% DV; fat 10.2g 16% DV; cholesterol 41.4mg 14% DV; sodium 67.1mg 3% DV.

Vegan Halloween Chocolate Cupcakes with Vegan Matcha Icing

Prep: 30 mins **Cook:** 20 mins **Additional:** 1 hr **Total:** 1 hr 50 mins **Servings:** 12 **Yield:**

12 cupcakes

Ingredients

- 2 ⅓ cups all-purpose flour
- 2 cups white sugar
- ¾ cup dark cocoa powder
- 2 teaspoons baking powder
- 1 teaspoon instant espresso powder
- ½ teaspoon baking soda
- ¼ teaspoon salt
- 1 cup almond milk
- ½ cup canola oil

- 2 teaspoons apple cider vinegar
- 2 teaspoons vanilla extract
- Matcha Vegan Icing:
- 1 cup confectioners' sugar
- 1 teaspoon green tea powder (matcha)
- ½ teaspoon almond extract
- ½ teaspoon vanilla extract
- 1 tablespoon almond milk, or as needed

Directions

Step 1

Preheat the oven to 350 degrees F (175 degrees C). Place liners into a 12-cup muffin tin.

Step 2

Combine flour, sugar, cocoa powder, baking powder, espresso powder, baking soda, and salt in a large bowl. Sift flour mixture into another bowl and sift again back to the first bowl. Add almond milk, oil, vinegar, and vanilla extract and beat using an electric mixer on medium speed until well combined. Fill each lined muffin cup 1/3 full of batter.

Step 3

Bake in the preheated oven until a toothpick inserted in the center of a cupcake comes out clean, 20 to 25 minutes.

Step 4

While cupcakes are baking, sift confectioners' sugar into a bowl and add matcha powder. Whisk together to blend. Add almond extract and vanilla extract and stir to combine. Mix in almond milk 1 teaspoon at a time using a whisk or spoon until icing reaches a good spreading consistency.

Step 5

Allow cupcakes to cool completely before icing, about 1 hour.

Cook's Note:

I use unbleached flour and raw sugar.

Nutrition Facts

Per Serving:

362.7 calories; protein 3.7g 7% DV; carbohydrates 66.4g 21% DV; fat 10.6g 16% DV; cholesterolmg; sodium 198.2mg 8% DV.

Easy Halloween Mummy Cupcakes

Prep: 30 mins **Cook:** 18 mins **Additional:** 1 hr 15 mins **Total:** 2 hrs 3 mins **Servings:** 24 **Yield:** 24 cupcakes

Ingredients

- 1 (18.25 ounce) package devil's food cake mix (such as Duncan Hines)
- 1 cup water
- 3 large eggs eggs
- ⅓ cup vegetable oil
- 1 (16 ounce) can vanilla frosting
- 48 eaches chocolate chips

Directions

Step 1

Preheat oven to 350 degrees F (175 degrees C). Line two 12-cup muffin tins with paper liners, preferable dark-colored or Halloween-themed ones.

Step 2

Combine cake mix, water, eggs, and oil in a large bowl; beat with an electric mixer on low speed until moistened, about 30 seconds. Beat at medium speed until batter is smooth and creamy, about 2 minutes. Spoon batter into the prepared muffin cups, filling each 3/4 full.

Step 3

Bake in the preheated oven until a toothpick inserted in the center comes out clean, 18 to 21 minutes. Remove from oven and cool tins on a wire rack for 15 minutes. Remove cupcakes from the tins and cool completely on a wire rack before decorating, about 1 hour.

Step 4

Spoon frosting in an pastry bag or a plastic bag with the corner cut off. Pipe strands of frosting onto the top and bottom of the cupcakes, leaving an oval eye shape exposed in the middle. Pipe 2 dots in the exposed middle for the mummy's eyes. Place 2 chocolate chips flat-side up in the middle of each dot for the pupils.

Nutrition Facts

Per Serving:

360.7 calories; protein 3.8g 8% DV; carbohydrates 48g 16% DV; fat 19.3g 30% DV; cholesterol 27.5mg 9% DV; sodium 205.2mg 8% DV.

Frankenstein Cupcakes

Prep: 30 mins **Cook:** 20 mins **Additional:** 30 mins **Total:** 1 hr 20 mins **Servings:** 24 **Yield:** 24 cupcakes

Ingredients

Cupcakes:

- 1 (15.25 ounce) package yellow cake mix
- 1 cup water
- 3 large eggs eggs
- ⅓ cup vegetable oil

Frosting:

- 1 cup shortening
- 1 cup butter, softened
- 2 teaspoons vanilla extract
- 8 cups confectioners' sugar
- ⅓ cup milk
- 3 drops green food coloring, or as desired

Decorations:

- 3 (1.75 ounce) packages chocolate sprinkles (jimmies)
- 48 piece (blank)s dark brown candy-coated milk chocolate pieces
- 48 piece (blank)s blue candy-coated milk chocolate pieces
- ⅔ ounce black gel food coloring
- ⅔ ounce red gel food coloring

Directions

Step 1

Preheat oven to 350 degrees F (175 degrees C). Grease or line 12 muffin cups with paper liners.

Step 2

Mix cake mix, water, eggs, and vegetable oil together in a bowl; beat with an electric mixer until batter is smooth, about 2 minutes. Fill muffin cups with batter.

Step 3

Bake in the preheated oven until a toothpick inserted in the center comes out clean, 19 to 23 minutes. Cool cupcakes in the pan for 10 minutes before transferring to a wire rack to cool.

Step 4

Beat shortening and butter together in a bowl using an electric mixer until smooth; add vanilla extract and mix well. Beat confectioners' sugar, alternating with milk, into butter-shortening mixture until frosting is stiff and holds its shape; mix in green food coloring until desired color is reached.

Step 5

Fill a piping bag, or large resealable freezer bag with a corner snipped, with frosting. Pipe frosting around the top half perimeter and top of each cupcake creating the "head" and "face"; smooth out the frosting using a small spatula, flattening the top into a square-shape for the top of his "head."

Step 6

Pour chocolate sprinkles into a shallow bowl and dip the top of each cupcake into the sprinkles, slightly angling the cupcake to get sprinkles around the uppermost top side of the "head" for the "hair."

Step 7

Press 2 dark brown chocolate pieces on the sides of each cupcake creating the "bolts." Press 2 blue chocolate pieces into the top front of each cupcake creating the "eyes." Put a dot of black food gel in the center of each blue candy for the "pupil." Make a "stitch" onto the "face" using the red food gel.

Nutrition Facts

Per Serving:

460.1 calories; protein 2g 4% DV; carbohydrates 60.9g 20% DV; fat 24g 37% DV; cholesterol 44.7mg 15% DV; sodium 186.4mg 8% DV.

Pumpkin Cheesecake Cupcakes

Prep: 25 mins **Cook:** 15 mins **Additional:** 30 mins **Total:** 1 hr 10 mins **Servings:** 24 **Yield:** 24 cupcakes

Ingredients

Crust:

- 1 (4.8 ounce) package graham crackers
- 2 tablespoons ground ginger
- 6 tablespoons butter, melted

Filling:

- 3 (8 ounce) packages cream cheese, softened
- ½ cup white sugar
- ½ cup packed brown sugar
- 1 (15 ounce) can pumpkin puree
- 1 tablespoon ground cinnamon

- 1 tablespoon ground ginger
- 2 teaspoons ground nutmeg
- 1 teaspoon ground cloves
- ¼ teaspoon salt
- 3 large eggs eggs

Topping:

- 1 cup sour cream
- 3 tablespoons confectioners' sugar, or to taste

- 1 tablespoon vanilla extract
- 1 pinch ground cinnamon, for garnish

Directions

Step 1

Preheat oven to 350 degrees F (175 degrees C). Line 24 muffin cups with foil liners.

Step 2

Crush graham crackers and 2 tablespoons ground ginger together in a resealable plastic bag; pour into a bowl. Add butter to graham cracker mixture and mix with a fork or pastry blender until blended.

Step 3

Beat cream cheese, white sugar, and brown sugar together in a large bowl until creamy; beat in pumpkin puree. Add cinnamon, 1 tablespoon ginger, nutmeg, cloves, and salt; add eggs 1 at a time, beating well after each addition.

Step 4

Press 1 tablespoon graham cracker mixture into the base of each prepared muffin cup, pressing mixture slightly up the sides of the liners. Fill each cup with cream cheese mixture.

Step 5

Bake in the preheated oven until tops are smooth and cupcakes jiggle slightly when moved, about 15 minutes. Cool in the pans for 10 minutes before transferring to a wire rack to cool.

Step 6

Stir sour cream, confectioners' sugar, and vanilla extract together in a bowl until frosting is smooth. Top each cheesecake with the topping and sprinkle with cinnamon.

Nutrition Facts

Per Serving:

226.1 calories; protein 3.9g 8% DV; carbohydrates 17.6g 6% DV; fat 16g 25% DV; cholesterol 65.9mg 22% DV; sodium 220.3mg 9% DV.

Simple 'N' Delicious Chocolate Cake

Prep: 15 mins **Cook:** 35 mins **Additional:** 30 mins **Total:** 1 hr 20 mins **Servings:** 8 **Yield:** 1 8-inch pan

Ingredients

- 1 cup white sugar
- 1.063 cups all-purpose flour
- ½ cup unsweetened cocoa powder
- 1 teaspoon baking soda
- 1 teaspoon salt

- ½ cup butter
- 1 egg
- 1 teaspoon vanilla extract
- 1 cup cold, strong, brewed coffee

Directions

Step 1

Preheat oven to 350 degrees F (175 degrees C). Grease and flour an 8-inch pan (see Editor's Note). Sift together flour, cocoa, baking soda and salt. Set aside.

Step 2

In a medium bowl, cream butter and sugar until light and fluffy. Add egg and vanilla and beat well. Add flour mixture, alternating with coffee. Beat until just incorporated.

Step 3

Bake at 350 degrees F (175 degrees C) for 35 to 45 minutes, or until a toothpick inserted into the cake comes out clean. Allow to cool before frosting.

Nutrition Facts

Per Serving:

282 calories; protein 3.7g 7% DV; carbohydrates 40.7g 13% DV; fat 13g 20% DV; cholesterol 53.8mg 18% DV; sodium 540.6mg 22% DV.

Chocolate Cupcakes with Caramel Frosting

Prep: 20 mins **Cook:** 20 mins **Additional:** 1 hr **Total:** 1 hr 40 mins **Servings:** 15 **Yield:** 15 cupcakes

Ingredients

- 1 cup white sugar
- 2 cups all-purpose flour
- ¼ cup unsweetened cocoa powder
- 2 teaspoons baking soda
- 1 cup water
- 2 tablespoons grape jelly
- 1 cup mayonnaise
- 1 teaspoon vanilla extract
- ¼ cup butter, melted
- ⅓ cup half-and-half cream
- ¾ cup packed brown sugar
- ½ teaspoon vanilla extract
- 1 ¾ cups confectioners' sugar

Directions

Step 1

Preheat oven to 350 degrees F (175 degrees C). Grease 15 muffin cups or line with paper baking cups.

Step 2

In a large bowl, stir together the white sugar, flour, cocoa, and baking soda. Make a well in the center, and pour in the water, grape jelly, mayonnaise, and 1 teaspoon of vanilla. Mix just until blended. Spoon the batter into the prepared cups, dividing evenly.

Step 3

Bake in the preheated oven until the tops spring back when lightly pressed, 20 to 25 minutes. Cool in the pan set over a wire rack. When cool, arrange the cupcakes on a serving platter.

Step 4

Make the frosting while the cupcakes cool. Combine the butter, half-and-half and brown sugar in a medium saucepan. Bring to a boil, stirring frequently. Remove from the heat and stir in the confectioners' sugar and vanilla. Set the pan over a bowl of ice water and whisk or beat with an electric mixer until fluffy. Frost cupcakes when they are completely cool.

Nutrition Facts

Per Serving:

361.6 calories; protein 2.3g 5% DV; carbohydrates 54.7g 18% DV; fat 15.7g 24% DV; cholesterol 15.7mg 5% DV; sodium 279.5mg 11% DV.

Caramel Apple Cupcakes

Prep: 20 mins **Cook:** 25 mins **Additional:** 30 mins **Total:** 1 hr 15 mins **Servings:** 24 **Yield:** 2 dozen cupcakes

Ingredients

- 1 (18.25 ounce) package spice cake mix
- 1 ⅓ cups water
- ⅓ cup vegetable oil
- 3 large eggs eggs
- 1 large Granny Smith apple, cored and chopped
- 35 caramels caramels
- ¼ cup evaporated milk
- ½ cup chopped peanuts
- 24 eaches wooden craft sticks

Directions

Step 1

Preheat oven to 350 degrees F (175 degrees C). Line 24 cupcake cups with paper liners.

Step 2

Place cake mix into a large bowl, and pour in water, vegetable oil, and eggs. With an electric mixer on low speed, beat until moistened and combined, about 30 seconds. Increase mixer speed to medium, and beat for 2 minutes. Stir in the chopped apple, and fill the prepared cupcake cups about 2/3 full.

Step 3

Bake in the preheated oven until lightly browned and a wooden toothpick inserted into the center of a cupcake comes out clean, about 20 minutes. Remove cupcake pans to a wire rack to cool.

Step 4

When cupcakes have cooled, melt the caramels with evaporated milk in a saucepan over low heat, stirring constantly until smooth and combined, about 4 minutes. Spread the caramel icing over the cupcakes, and sprinkle with chopped peanuts. Insert a wooden stick into the center of each cupcake.

Nutrition Facts

Per Serving:

209.1 calories; protein 3.7g 7% DV; carbohydrates 29.2g 9% DV; fat 9.2g 14% DV; cholesterol 25mg 8% DV; sodium 193.3mg 8% DV.

Chocolate-Orange Cupcakes with Pistachio Buttercream

Prep: 20 mins **Cook:** 20 mins **Additional:** 30 mins **Total:** 1 hr 10 mins **Servings:** 12 **Yield:** 1 dozen cupcakes

Ingredients

- 1 teaspoon shortening, or as needed

- 1 teaspoon all-purpose flour, or as needed

Cake:

- 1 ½ cups all-purpose flour, sifted
- 1 cup white sugar
- 3 tablespoons cocoa powder
- 1 teaspoon baking soda
- ¼ teaspoon salt

- 1 cup cold water
- ⅓ cup olive oil
- 2 tablespoons orange juice
- ½ teaspoon vanilla extract
- 1 tablespoon grated orange zest

Icing:

- ½ cup unsalted butter
- ⅔ cup confectioners' sugar, sifted
- 2 tablespoons instant pistachio pudding mix

- 2 tablespoons cold water
- 1 ounce dark chocolate, grated

Directions

Step 1

Preheat oven to 350 degrees F (175 degrees C). Grease 12 muffin cups with shortening using a paper towel and dust with about 1 teaspoon flour or line with paper liners.

Step 2

Combine 1 1/2 cups flour, white sugar, cocoa powder, baking soda, and salt in the bowl of a stand mixer. Beat 1 cup cold water, olive oil, orange juice, and vanilla extract into flour mixture on medium-low speed until batter is just combined, about 2 minutes. Fold orange zest into batter. Pour batter into prepared muffin cups, 2/3-full.

Step 3

Bake in the preheated oven until a toothpick inserted into a cupcake comes out clean, about 20 minutes. Transfer cupcakes to a wire rack to cool completely, about 30 minutes.

Step 4

Beat butter in a bowl using an electric mixer in medium speed until fluffy, about 1 minute. Slowly pour confectioners' sugar into creamed butter and beat until incorporated, about 2 minutes. Beat pudding mix into butter mixture until just combined. Add water, 1 tablespoon at a time, until desired consistency of icing is reached. Ice the cooled cupcakes; garnish with grated chocolate.

Nutrition Facts

Per Serving:

300.6 calories; protein 2.1g 4% DV; carbohydrates 40.4g 13% DV; fat 15.2g 23% DV; cholesterol 20.5mg 7% DV; sodium 189.6mg 8% DV.

Worm Cake

Servings: 24 **Yield:** 24 cupcakes

Ingredients

- 1 (18.25 ounce) package chocolate cake mix
- 3 cups chocolate cookie crumbs
- 1 (16 ounce) package prepared chocolate frosting
- 1 (16 ounce) package gummi worms

Directions

Step 1

Prepare cake mix according to package directions. Pour batter into cupcake pans and bake as directed on cake mix box. Let cupcakes cool thoroughly before frosting.

Step 2

Spread cupcakes lightly with chocolate icing. Sprinkle cookie crumbs on top.

Step 3

Cut gummi worms in half (as many as you like). Put icing onto cut end of the worms and stick to the top of cupcakes. You can use as few or as many as will fit on each cupcake. Let icing set for 10 minutes and then enjoy.

Nutrition Facts

Per Serving:

299.6 calories; protein 4.2g 8% DV; carbohydrates 54.3g 18% DV; fat 8.7g 13% DV; cholesterol 0.3mg; sodium 296.3mg 12% DV.

Candied Yam Cupcakes

Prep: 20 mins **Cook:** 35 mins **Additional:** 30 mins **Total:** 1 hr 25 mins **Servings:** 24 **Yield:** 24 cupcakes

Ingredients

- 1 pound yams, peeled and cubed
- 4 large eggs eggs

103

- 1 cup canola oil
- 1 cup white sugar
- 1 teaspoon vanilla extract
- 2 cups all-purpose flour
- 2 teaspoons baking powder
- 1 teaspoon baking soda
- 2 teaspoons ground cinnamon
- 1 teaspoon salt
- 3 ounces cream cheese
- ½ cup butter, softened
- 1 teaspoon vanilla extract
- 2 cups confectioners' sugar

Directions

Step 1

Place a steamer insert into a large saucepan, and fill with water to just below the bottom of the steamer. Cover, and bring the water to a boil over high heat. Add the yams, recover, and steam until very tender, about 15 minutes. Remove yams from steamer and allow to cool slightly.

Step 2

Preheat oven to 350 degrees F (175 degrees C). Line 2-12 cup cupcake tins with paper liners.

Step 3

Place eggs, oil, sugar, vanilla extract, and cooked yams in a large bowl; beat with an electric mixer until light and fluffy. Sift together flour, baking powder, baking soda, cinnamon, and salt. Stir dry ingredients into yam mixture, mixing just until combined. Pour batter into paper liners, filling 2/3 full.

Step 4

Bake in preheated oven until a toothpick inserted in the center of a cupcake comes out clean, 17 to 20 minutes. Cool in pans for 5 minutes, transfer to wire rack to cool completely.

Step 5

Beat together cream cheese and butter until fluffy. Beat in the vanilla extract and confectioners sugar; mix until smooth. Frost cool cupcakes with cream cheese frosting.

Nutrition Facts

Per Serving:

275.6 calories; protein 2.7g 6% DV; carbohydrates 32.4g 11% DV; fat 15.4g 24% DV; cholesterol 45.1mg 15% DV; sodium 241.4mg 10% DV.

Fluffy Pumpkin Spiced Cupcakes

Prep: 15 mins **Cook:** 30 mins **Additional:** 1 hr **Total:** 1 hr 45 mins **Servings:** 24 **Yield:** 2 dozen

Ingredients

104

- 1 (15 ounce) can pumpkin puree
- 1 ½ cups white sugar
- 1 cup packed brown sugar
- ½ cup butter-flavored shortening
- ½ cup butter, softened
- ¼ cup whole milk
- ¼ cup vegetable oil
- 4 large eggs eggs
- 2 cups cake flour
- ¼ cup dry buttermilk powder
- ¼ cup cornstarch
- 2 teaspoons pumpkin pie spice
- 2 teaspoons baking powder
- 1 teaspoon baking soda
- ¾ teaspoon salt

Directions

Step 1

Preheat oven to 350 degrees F (175 degrees C). Line 24 muffin cups with paper muffin liners.

Step 2

Beat the pumpkin puree, white sugar, brown sugar, shortening, butter, milk, vegetable oil, and eggs together in a large bowl until smooth. Whisk the cake flour, dry buttermilk powder, cornstarch, pumpkin pie spice, baking powder, baking soda, and salt together in another bowl. Add the dry ingredients to the pumpkin mixture, stirring until mixed. Pour batter into the prepared muffin cups, filling each cup about 2/3 full.

Step 3

Bake in the preheated until the center of the cupcakes spring back when touched, about 30 minutes. Cool in the pans for 10 minutes before removing to cool completely on a wire rack.

Nutrition Facts

Per Serving:

249.9 calories; protein 2.8g 6% DV; carbohydrates 34.5g 11% DV; fat 11.7g 18% DV; cholesterol 42.3mg 14% DV; sodium 257.9mg 10% DV.

Pumpkin Cupcakes with Cream Cheese Frosting

Prep: 20 mins **Cook:** 20 mins **Additional:** 1 hr **Total:** 1 hr 40 mins **Servings:** 36 **Yield:** 36 servings

Ingredients

Cupcakes:

- 3 cups baking mix (such as Bisquick)
- 1 (15 ounce) can pumpkin puree
- 1 cup white sugar
- 1 cup brown sugar
- 4 large eggs eggs
- ¼ cup butter, softened

- ¼ cup milk

Cream Cheese Frosting:

- ½ (8 ounce) package cream cheese, softened
- ½ cup butter, softened

- 2 teaspoons pumpkin pie spice

- 4 ½ cups confectioners' sugar, divided
- 2 teaspoons vanilla extract

Directions

Step 1

Preheat oven to 350 degrees F (175 degrees C). Grease or line 36 muffin cups with paper liners.

Step 2

Beat baking mix, pumpkin puree, white sugar, brown sugar, eggs, 1/4 cup butter, milk, and pumpkin pie spice together in a bowl using an electric mixer on low speed until well mixed; spoon into the prepared muffin cups.

Step 3

Bake in the preheated oven until a toothpick inserted in the center comes out clean, 20 to 30 minutes. Cool cupcakes in pan for 5 minutes before transferring to a wire rack to cool completely.

Step 4

Beat cream cheese and 1/2 cup butter together in a bowl using an electric mixer on low speed until smooth and creamy. Beat 2 cups confectioners' sugar and vanilla extract into creamed butter mixture on low speed until well mixed; increase to high speed and beat until fluffy. Gradually pour 2 1/2 cups confectioners' sugar into frosting and beat on medium speed until frosting is thickened.

Step 5

Spoon frosting into a resealable plastic bag and snip 1 corner. Pipe frosting onto the cooled cupcakes.

Nutrition Facts

Per Serving:

197.2 calories; protein 1.9g 4% DV; carbohydrates 32.5g 11% DV; fat 7.1g 11% DV; cholesterol 34.4mg 12% DV; sodium 200.8mg 8% DV.

Monster Chocolate Cupcakes for Halloween

Prep: 45 mins **Cook:** 14 mins **Additional:** 1 hr 5 mins **Total:** 2 hrs 4 mins **Servings:** 12 **Yield:** 12 chocolate cupcakes

Ingredients

Chocolate Cupcakes:

- ½ cup milk
- 1 tablespoon white vinegar
- ½ cup unsalted butter, at room temperature
- 10 tablespoons white sugar
- 2 teaspoons vanilla sugar
- 2 large eggs
- ¾ cup all-purpose flour
- 1 tablespoon all-purpose flour
- ½ cup unsweetened cocoa powder
- ½ teaspoon baking powder
- ¼ teaspoon baking soda
- 1 pinch salt

Cream Cheese Frosting:

- 1 (8 ounce) package cream cheese, softened
- ¼ cup unsalted butter, at room temperature
- 1 teaspoon vanilla extract
- 1 cup confectioners' sugar, sifted
- 2 drops green food coloring
- 24 eaches candy eyeballs

Directions

Step 1

Combine milk and vinegar in a bowl. Let stand until milk curdles, about 5 minutes.

Step 2

Preheat oven to 350 degrees F (175 degrees C). Grease a 12-cup muffin tin or line cups with paper liners.

Step 3

Combine 1/2 cup butter, white sugar, and vanilla sugar in a large bowl; beat with an electric mixer until smooth and creamy. Add eggs one at a time, beating well after each addition.

Step 4

Mix 3/4 cup plus 1 tablespoon flour, cocoa powder, baking powder, baking soda, and salt in a bowl. Alternate adding flour mixture and curdled milk to the creamed butter mixture, mixing until batter is well blended. Spoon batter into the prepared muffin cups, filling each 3/4 full.

Step 5

Bake in the preheated oven until tops spring back when lightly pressed and a toothpick inserted in the center of 1 cupcake comes back clean, about 14 minutes. Cool in the muffin tin for a few minutes, then transfer to a wire rack to cool completely, about 1 hour.

Step 6

Combine cream cheese and 1/4 cup butter in a bowl; beat with an electric mixer until well combined. Mix in vanilla extract. Stir in confectioners' sugar gradually. Color frosting green with a few drops of food coloring.

Step 7

Place green frosting in a pastry bag fitted with a grass tip. Hold the pastry bag at a 90-degree angle 1/8 inch above the surface of a cupcake. Squeeze bag to form green 'fur' by pulling tip up and away when the icing strand is about 1/2 inch high. Repeat to cover cupcake evenly with fur. Add 2 eyes to each cupcake.

Nutrition Facts

Per Serving:

315.5 calories; protein 4.5g 9% DV; carbohydrates 32.1g 10% DV; fat 20g 31% DV; cholesterol 82.9mg 28% DV; sodium 133.4mg 5% DV.

Spiced Spider Cupcakes

Prep: 1 hr **Cook:** 25 mins **Additional:** 2 hrs **Total:** 3 hrs 25 mins **Servings:** 24 **Yield:** 2 dozen cupcakes

Ingredients

Spice Cake:

- 3 cups all-purpose flour
- 2 cups white sugar
- 2 teaspoons baking soda
- 1 teaspoon salt
- 1 teaspoon ground cinnamon
- ½ teaspoon ground cloves

- ½ teaspoon ground nutmeg
- 2 cups water
- ⅔ cup canola oil
- 2 tablespoons distilled white vinegar
- 2 teaspoons vanilla extract

Cream Cheese Frosting:

- 2 (3 ounce) packages cream cheese, softened
- ½ cup butter, softened
- 2 teaspoons vanilla extract
- ¼ teaspoon salt

- ⅛ teaspoon ground cinnamon
- 5 cups sifted confectioners' sugar, or more as needed

Decorations:

- 1 (.68 oz. tube) black decorating gel
- 24 large gumdrop (1" dia)s large spiced gumdrops
- black shoestring licorice

Directions

Step 1

Preheat oven to 350 degrees F (175 degrees C). Line cupcake pans with paper liners.

Step 2

Combine flour, white sugar, baking soda, 1 teaspoon salt, 1 teaspoon cinnamon, cloves, and nutmeg in bowl; whisk to mix. In separate bowl, mix water, canola oil, vinegar, and 2 teaspoons vanilla extract. Pour liquids into dry mixture and stir until smooth. The batter will be very thin.

Step 3

Transfer batter into a measuring cup or pitcher; pour batter into prepared cupcake pans.

Step 4

Bake in preheated oven until tops spring back when gently pressed with a fingertip and a toothpick inserted in the center comes out clean, about 25 minutes. Allow cupcakes to cool completely on a wire rack.

Step 5

Beat cream cheese, butter, 2 teaspoons vanilla extract, 1/4 teaspoon salt, and 1/8 teaspoon cinnamon with an electric mixer until smooth. Gradually mix in confectioners' sugar until frosting is creamy and spreadable. Frost the cooled cupcakes.

Step 6

To decorate cupcakes, use black decorating gel to draw a small circle in the center of each cupcake. Draw a larger circle around the first, and continue making larger circles until the last circle is about 1/4 inch from the edge. There should be about 5 rings on each cupcake. Use a toothpick to draw about 8 lines radiating from the center of the cupcake to the edge, like spokes on a wheel, to make webs.

Step 7

Cut the licorice strings into pieces about 1 1/4 inch long for legs. Poke four licorice legs into both sides of each gumdrop. Use decorating gel to make eyes and a smiley mouth on each gumdrop. Place a gumdrop spider onto each cupcake in the center of the webs.

Nutrition Facts

Per Serving:

402.5 calories; protein 2.3g 5% DV; carbohydrates 70.7g 23% DV; fat 12.7g 20% DV; cholesterol 18mg 6% DV; sodium 302.3mg 12% DV.

Halloween Gingerbread Cupcakes

Prep: 40 mins **Cook:** 20 mins **Additional:** 5 mins **Total:** 1 hr 5 mins **Servings:** 12 **Yield:** 12 cupcakes

Ingredients

Reynolds StayBrite Baking Cups

- 6 tablespoons butter, softened
- ½ cup granulated sugar
- 1 ½ teaspoons baking powder
- 1 teaspoon ground cinnamon
- ¼ teaspoon ground ginger
- ¼ teaspoon baking soda

- ¼ teaspoon salt
- 2 large eggs eggs
- 1 cup milk
- ½ cup molasses
- 1 ¾ cups all-purpose flour
- Orange and black decorating sugar

Cinnamon Vanilla Frosting:

- ⅓ cup butter, softened
- ⅓ cup sour cream
- 1 teaspoon vanilla

- 4 cups powdered sugar
- 1 teaspoon ground cinnamon

Directions

Step 1

Preheat oven to 350 degrees F. Line muffin pans with 12 to 18 Reynolds StayBrite Baking Cups with a black swirl design.

Step 2

Beat butter and sugar together in a large bowl with an electric mixer on medium speed for 30 seconds. Add baking powder, cinnamon, ginger, baking soda, and salt. Beat until combined, scraping down sides of the bowl as necessary. Beat in eggs, one at a time.

Step 3

Whisk together the milk and molasses in a medium bowl. Alternately add flour and milk mixture to the butter mixture, beating on low speed after each addition just until combined. Spoon batter evenly into prepared muffin cups, filling each about three-fourths full.

Step 4

Bake 18 to 20 minutes or until a wooden toothpick inserted near centers comes out clean. Cool in pans on a wire rack for 5 minutes. Carefully remove cupcakes from pans; cool completely on a wire rack.

Step 5

Frost with Cinnamon Vanilla Frosting. Sprinkle colored decorating sugars.

Step 6

Cinnamon Vanilla Frosting: Combine butter, sour cream, and vanilla in a large mixing bowl. Beat with an electric mixer on medium speed for 30 seconds. Gradually beat in powdered sugar and ground cinnamon. Thin with 1 to 2 tablespoons milk, if needed to reach desired consistency.

Nutrition Facts

Per Serving:

436.8 calories; protein 3.9g 8% DV; carbohydrates 76.2g 25% DV; fat 13.8g 21% DV; cholesterol 64.3mg 21% DV; sodium 242.2mg 10% DV.

Pull-Apart Spider Web Cupcakes

Prep: 20 mins **Cook:** 20 mins **Additional:** 40 mins **Total:** 1 hr 20 mins **Servings:** 24 **Yield:** 24 cupcakes

Ingredients

- 1 (18.25 ounce) package white cake mix
- 1 cup water
- ⅓ cup vegetable oil
- 3 large eggs eggs

- 2 (16 ounce) containers prepared fluffy white frosting
- 3 drops orange gel food coloring, or as needed
- 1 (.68 oz. tube) black decorating gel

Directions

Step 1

Preheat oven to 350 degrees F (175 degrees C). Line 24 muffin cups with paper muffin liners.

Step 2

Beat cake mix, water, oil, and eggs in a large bowl with an electric mixer on medium speed until batter is completely smooth, about 2 minutes. Divide batter between prepared muffin cups, filling each about 2/3-full.

Step 3

Bake in the preheated oven until tops spring back when pressed, 19 to 23 minutes. Cool for 10 minutes in the pans before removing to a wire rack to cool completely.

Step 4

Beat frosting and orange food coloring together in a bowl until desired shade and consistency are reached.

Step 5

Arrange cooled cupcakes close together in a solid circle shape on a large platter. Spread frosting over cupcakes to create one large, round frosted surface. Squeeze 1 large dot of black decorating gel in the center of the frosting. Draw concentric circles around the dot about 2 inches apart. Drag a toothpick from the center dot to the outermost circle; repeat 12 times to make the surface appear to be a spider's web.

Nutrition Facts

Per Serving:

284.6 calories; protein 1.7g 4% DV; carbohydrates 42.5g 14% DV; fat 12g 19% DV; cholesterol 23.3mg 8% DV; sodium 232mg 9% DV.

Halloween-Inspired Cupcakes

Prep: 1 hr **Total:** 1 hr **Servings:** 12 **Yield:** 12 cupcakes

Ingredients

- 12 eaches unfrosted cupcakes

Spider Cupcake Decoration:

- ½ cup prepared chocolate frosting
- 8 strips red licorice
- 12 piece (blank)s candy-coated milk chocolate pieces (such as M&M's)

Worm Cupcake Decoration:

- ½ cup prepared chocolate frosting
- ¼ cup chocolate cookie crumbs
- 4 piece (blank)s gummy worm candies

Graveyard Cupcake Decoration:

- 1 cup prepared chocolate frosting
- 4 eaches rectangular or oval sandwich cookies (such as Milano)
- ¼ cup chocolate cookie crumbs

Directions

Step 1

For spider cupcakes: Frost 4 cupcakes with a thin layer of chocolate frosting. Cut each licorice strip into 3 pieces. Poke 6 holes around the sides of each cupcake with a skewer. Insert 1 licorice piece into each hole for the spider legs. Place 2 candy-coated milk chocolate pieces as eyes and one for the nose. Add drops of icing to the eyes to make pupils.

Step 2

For worm cupcakes: Frost 4 cupcakes with a thin layer of chocolate frosting. Sprinkle cookie crumbs on top to resemble dirt. Cut gummy worms in half and brush the cut side with some frosting. Stick onto the cupcakes on either side.

Step 3

For graveyard cupcakes: Frost 4 cupcakes with a thin layer of chocolate frosting. Fill a pastry bag fitted with a small plain tip with remaining chocolate frosting. Write "RIP" or draw a cross on each sandwich cookie. Insert decorated cookies into the cupcake so that they look like tombstones. Sprinkle chocolate cookie crumbs around the cookie tombstones to resemble dirt.

Nutrition Facts

Per Serving:

410.5 calories; protein 3.1g 6% DV; carbohydrates 65.9g 21% DV; fat 16.3g 25% DV; cholesterol 19.7mg 7% DV; sodium 254.7mg 10% DV.

Chocolate-Pumpkin Cupcakes

Prep: 15 mins **Cook:** 20 mins **Additional:** 10 mins **Total:** 45 mins **Servings:** 24 **Yield:** 24 cupcakes

Ingredients

- 2 cups white sugar
- 1 ¾ cups all-purpose flour
- ⅓ cup cocoa powder
- 1 ½ teaspoons baking powder
- 1 ½ teaspoons baking soda
- 1 teaspoon salt

- 2 large eggs eggs
- 1 cup pumpkin puree
- 1 cup milk
- ½ cup canola oil
- 2 teaspoons vanilla extract
- ⅓ cup boiling water

Directions

Step 1

Preheat the oven to 350 degrees F (175 degrees C). Line two 12-cup muffin tins with paper liners.

Step 2

Combine sugar, flour, cocoa powder, baking powder, baking soda, and salt in the bowl of an electric mixer. Mix briefly until combined. Add pumpkin, milk, canola oil, and vanilla extract; mix on medium speed for 2 minutes. Add water and mix until just blended.

Step 3

Spoon batter into the prepared muffin cups, filling each almost all the way to the top.

Step 4

Bake in the preheated oven until a toothpick inserted into the center of a cupcake comes out clean, about 20 minutes. Let cool in trays for about 10 minutes before transferring to wire racks to cool completely.

Nutrition Facts

Per Serving:

157.3 calories; protein 2.1g 4% DV; carbohydrates 25.7g 8% DV; fat 5.6g 9% DV; cholesterol 16.3mg 5% DV; sodium 241.2mg 10% DV.

Halloween Buttermilk Bundt Cake

Prep: 15 mins **Cook:** 50 mins **Additional:** 15 mins **Total:** 1 hr 20 mins **Servings:** 8
Yield:

8 servings

Ingredients

- 2 tablespoons butter, or as needed
- 2 ¼ cups cake flour
- 1 cup white sugar
- 2 teaspoons baking powder
- 1 cup buttermilk, at room temperature
- ¾ cup butter, at room temperature

- 3 eaches eggs, at room temperature
- 1 teaspoon vanilla extract
- 2 teaspoons orange food coloring powder
- ½ cup cocoa powder
- 1 teaspoon black food coloring powder

Directions

Step 1

Preheat the oven to 350 degrees F (175 degrees C). Grease a fluted tube pan (such as Bundt) with 2 tablespoons butter.

Step 2

Mix flour, sugar, and baking powder in a large bowl. Beat in buttermilk using an electric mixer. Add 3/4 cup butter and beat until fully incorporated. Mix in eggs and vanilla extract until smooth.

Step 3

Pour 1/3 of the batter into a small bowl; mix in orange food coloring. Add cocoa powder and black food coloring to the large bowl. Mix well, scraping down the sides.

Step 4

Pour black batter into the cake pan. Pour orange batter on top. Rap pan against the counter to release any air bubbles.

Step 5

Bake in the preheated oven until a toothpick inserted into the center comes out clean, about 50 minutes. Cool for 15 minutes before removing from the pan.

Nutrition Facts

Per Serving:

470.9 calories; protein 7.7g 15% DV; carbohydrates 61.3g 20% DV; fat 23.1g 36% DV; cholesterol 116mg 39% DV; sodium 322.2mg 13% DV.

Rolled Fondant

Prep: 30 mins **Cook:** 5 mins **Total:** 35 mins **Servings:** 16 **Yield:** 1 - 10 x 4 inch high cake (enough to cover)

Ingredients

- 1 (.25 ounce) package unflavored gelatin
- ¼ cup cold water
- ½ cup glucose syrup
- 1 tablespoon glycerin
- 2 tablespoons shortening
- 1 teaspoon vanilla extract
- 8 cups sifted confectioners' sugar

Directions

Step 1

Combine gelatin and cold water; let stand until thick. Place gelatin mixture in top of double boiler and heat until dissolved.

Step 2

Add glucose and glycerin, mix well. Stir in shortening and just before completely melted, remove from heat and stir in vanilla. Mixture should cool until lukewarm.

Step 3

Place 4 cups confectioners' sugar in a large bowl. Make a well in the center and using a wooden spoon, stir in the lukewarm gelatin mixture. Mix in sugar and add more a little at a time, until stickiness disappears. Knead in remaining sugar. Knead until the fondant is smooth, pliable and does not stick to your hands. If fondant is too soft, add more sugar; if too stiff, add water (a drop at a time). Use fondant immediately or store in airtight container in fridge. When ready to use, bring to room temperature and knead again until soft.

Nutrition Facts

Per Serving:

292.9 calories; protein 0.4g 1% DV; carbohydrates 69.8g 23% DV; fat 1.7g 3% DV; cholesterolmg; sodium 1.7mg.

Chocolate Web Cake

Servings: 12 **Yield:** 1 -4 layer 9 inch round cake

Ingredients

- 1 ⅓ cups all-purpose flour
- 2 teaspoons baking powder
- 1 teaspoon salt
- ¼ teaspoon baking soda
- 1 ½ cups white sugar
- ½ cup shortening
- 1 ¼ cups evaporated milk
- 2 large eggs eggs

- 2 (1 ounce) squares unsweetened chocolate, melted
- 1 ⅓ cups shortening
- 1 ⅓ cups white sugar
- ¾ cup evaporated milk
- 2 teaspoons vanilla extract
- 2 (1 ounce) squares unsweetened chocolate, melted

Directions

Step 1

Preheat oven to 350 degrees F(175 degrees C). Grease two 9 inch round cake pans.

Step 2

Sift flour, baking powder, salt, baking soda and 1 1/2 cups of the white sugar together in a large mixing bowl. Add 1/2 cup of the shortening and 1-1/4 cup of the evaporated milk. Beat at medium speed with an electric mixer for 2 minutes. Beat in the eggs and beat for 2 minutes longer. Spread the batter evenly into the prepared pans. Drizzle 1 square of the melted chocolate in a spiral on top of each cake. Feather lines with a knife to form a web pattern.

Step 3

Bake at 350 degrees F (175 degrees C) for 30 to 40 minutes or until a toothpick inserted in the center comes out clean. Let cakes cool in pans for 10 minutes then remove from pans and let cakes cool completely.

Step 4

To Make Filling: Combine the 2 squares unsweetened melted chocolate, 1 1/3 cups shortening, 1 cup white sugar, 3/4 cup evaporated milk and the vanilla together and beat with an electric mixer until smooth.

Step 5

To Assemble Cake: Cut each cooled cake layer in half horizontally. Spread 1/4 of the filling between each layer making a 4 layer cake with a web design on top. Frost sides with the remaining filling.

Nutrition Facts

Per Serving:

627.6 calories; protein 6.5g 13% DV; carbohydrates 65.2g 21% DV; fat 40.3g 62% DV; cholesterol 43.2mg 14% DV; sodium 360mg 14% DV.

Rick's Special Buttercream Frosting

Prep: 30 mins **Total:** 30 mins **Servings:** 12 **Yield:** 7 cups

Ingredients

- 2 cups shortening
- 8 cups confectioners' sugar
- ½ teaspoon salt
- 2 teaspoons vanilla extract
- 1 cup heavy whipping cream

Directions

Step 1

In a mixing bowl, cream shortening until fluffy. Add sugar, and continue creaming until well blended.

Step 2

Add salt, vanilla, and 6 ounces whipping cream. Blend on low speed until moistened. Add additional 2 ounces whipping cream if necessary. Beat at high speed until frosting is fluffy.

Nutrition Facts

Per Serving:

683.7 calories; protein 0.4g 1% DV; carbohydrates 80.3g 26% DV; fat 41.6g 64% DV; cholesterol 27.2mg 9% DV; sodium 105.3mg 4% DV.

Popcorn Cake II

Prep: 20 mins **Cook:** 5 mins **Additional:** 5 mins **Total:** 30 mins **Servings:** 14 **Yield:** 1 - 10 inch bundt cake

Ingredients

- 18 cups popped popcorn
- 1 ½ cups gumdrops
- 1 cup whole peanuts
- 1 (10.5 ounce) package miniature marshmallows
- ½ cup butter

Directions

Step 1

Butter one 10 inch tube or bundt pan.

Step 2

Toss the popcorn with the gumdrops and cashews.

Step 3

Melt the marshmallows with the butter or margarine. Pour over the popcorn mixture and mix well. Press the mixture into the prepared pan. Butter hands before pressing firmly into pan. Chill and remove from pan.

Nutrition Facts

Per Serving:

343.6 calories; protein 3.9g 8% DV; carbohydrates 45g 15% DV; fat 18g 28% DV; cholesterol 17.4mg 6% DV; sodium 222.3mg 9% DV.

Marshmallow Fondant

Prep: 29 mins **Cook:** 1 min **Additional:** 8 hrs **Total:** 8 hrs 30 mins **Servings:** 10 **Yield:** 2 1/4 pounds of fondant

Ingredients

- ¼ cup butter
- 1 (16 ounce) package miniature marshmallows
- ¼ cup water
- 1 teaspoon vanilla extract
- 2 pounds confectioners' sugar, divided

Directions

Step 1

Place the butter in a shallow bowl, and set aside.

Step 2

Place the marshmallows in a large microwave-safe bowl, and microwave on High for 30 seconds to 1 minute to start melting the marshmallows. Carefully stir the water and vanilla extract into the hot marshmallows, and stir until the mixture is smooth. Slowly beat in the confectioners' sugar, a cup at a time, until you have a sticky dough. Reserve 1 cup of powdered sugar for kneading. The dough will be very stiff.

Step 3

Rub your hands thoroughly with butter, and begin kneading the sticky dough. As you knead, the dough will become workable and pliable. Turn the dough out onto a working surface dusted with confectioners' sugar and continue kneading until the fondant is smooth and no longer sticky to the touch, 5 to 10 minutes.

Step 4

Form the fondant into a ball, wrap it tightly in plastic wrap, and refrigerate overnight. To use, allow the fondant to come to room temperature, and roll it out onto a flat surface dusted with confectioners' sugar.

Nutrition Facts

Per Serving:

555.1 calories; proteing; carbohydrates 127.3g 41% DV; fat 4.7g 7% DV; cholesterol 12.2mg 4% DV; sodium 89.8mg 4% DV.

Black Magic Cake

Prep: 15 mins **Cook:** 35 mins **Additional:** 10 mins **Total:** 1 hr **Servings:** 24 **Yield:** 1 - 9x13 inch or 2 - 9 inch round pans

Ingredients

- 1 ¾ cups all-purpose flour
- 2 cups white sugar
- ¾ cup unsweetened cocoa powder
- 2 teaspoons baking soda
- 1 teaspoon baking powder
- 1 teaspoon salt

- 2 large eggs eggs
- 1 cup strong brewed coffee
- 1 cup buttermilk
- ½ cup vegetable oil
- 1 teaspoon vanilla extract

Directions

Step 1

Preheat oven to 350 degrees F (175 degrees C). Grease and flour two 9 inch round cake pans or one 9x13 inch pan.

Step 2

In large bowl combine flour, sugar, cocoa, baking soda, baking powder and salt. Make a well in the center.

Step 3

Add eggs, coffee, buttermilk, oil and vanilla. Beat for 2 minutes on medium speed. Batter will be thin. Pour into prepared pans.

Step 4

Bake at 350 degrees F (175 degrees C) for 30 to 40 minutes, or until toothpick inserted into center of cake comes out clean. Cool for 10 minutes, then remove from pans and finish cooling on a wire rack. Fill and frost as desired.

Nutrition Facts

Per Serving:

155.1 calories; protein 2.3g 5% DV; carbohydrates 25.7g 8% DV; fat 5.5g 9% DV; cholesterol 15.9mg 5% DV; sodium 239.6mg 10% DV.

Pumpkin Cake

Servings: 16 Yield: 1 10-inch bundt cake

Ingredients

- 1 cup vegetable oil
- 3 large eggs eggs
- 1 (15 ounce) can pumpkin puree
- 1 teaspoon vanilla extract
- 2 ½ cups white sugar
- 2 ½ cups all-purpose flour
- 1 teaspoon baking soda
- 1 teaspoon ground nutmeg
- 1 teaspoon ground allspice
- 1 teaspoon ground cinnamon
- 1 teaspoon ground cloves
- ¼ teaspoon salt
- ¼ cup chopped nuts

Directions

Step 1

Preheat oven to 350 degrees F (175 degrees C). Grease one 10 inch bundt or tube pan.

Step 2

Cream oil, beaten eggs, pumpkin, and vanilla together.

Step 3

Sift the flour, sugar, baking soda, ground nutmeg, ground allspice, ground cinnamon, ground cloves and salt together. Add the flour mixture to the pumpkin mixture and mix until just combined. If desired, stir in some chopped nuts. Pour batter into the prepared pan.

Step 4

Bake at 350 degrees F (175 degrees C) for 1 hour or until a toothpick inserted in the middle comes out clean. Let cake cool in pan for 5 minutes then turn out onto a plate and sprinkle with confectioners' sugar.

Nutrition Facts

Per Serving:

352.6 calories; protein 3.9g 8% DV; carbohydrates 49.3g 16% DV; fat 16.3g 25% DV; cholesterol 34.9mg 12% DV; sodium 193.4mg 8% DV.

Dirt Cake I

Servings: 10 **Yield:** 1 medium size flower pot

Ingredients

- ½ cup butter, softened
- 1 (8 ounce) package cream cheese, softened
- ½ cup confectioners' sugar
- 2 (3.5 ounce) packages instant vanilla pudding mix
- 3 ½ cups milk
- 1 (12 ounce) container frozen whipped topping, thawed
- 32 ounces chocolate sandwich cookies with creme filling

Directions

Step 1

Chop cookies very fine in food processor. The white cream will disappear.

Step 2

Mix butter, cream cheese, and sugar in bowl.

122

Step 3

In a large bowl mix milk, pudding and whipped topping together.

Step 4

Combine pudding mixture and cream mixture together.

Step 5

Layer in flower pot, starting with cookies then cream mixture. Repeat layers.

Step 6

Chill until ready to serve.

Step 7

Add artificial flower and trowel. Enjoy!

Nutrition Facts

Per Serving:

827.3 calories; protein 9.9g 20% DV; carbohydrates 101.5g 33% DV; fat 44.6g 69% DV; cholesterol 55.9mg 19% DV; sodium 895.8mg 36% DV.

Pumpkin Cake III

Prep: 30 mins **Cook:** 30 mins **Total:** 1 hr **Servings:** 14 **Yield:** 1 - 12x18 inch pan

Ingredients

- 2 cups white sugar
- 1 ¼ cups vegetable oil
- 1 teaspoon vanilla extract
- 2 cups canned pumpkin
- 4 large eggs eggs
- 2 cups all-purpose flour
- 3 teaspoons baking powder
- 2 teaspoons baking soda
- ¼ teaspoon salt
- 2 teaspoons ground cinnamon
- 1 cup chopped walnuts

Directions

Step 1

Preheat oven to 350 degrees F (175 degrees C). Grease and flour a 12x18 inch pan. Sift together the flour, baking powder, baking soda, salt and cinnamon. Set aside.

Step 2

In a large bowl combine sugar and oil. Blend in vanilla and pumpkin, then beat in eggs one at a time. Gradually beat in flour mixture. Stir in nuts. Spread batter into prepared 12x18 inch pan.

Step 3

Bake in the preheated oven for 30 minutes, or until a toothpick inserted into the center of the cake comes out clean. Allow to cool.

Nutrition Facts

Per Serving:

438.4 calories; protein 5.3g 11% DV; carbohydrates 46.8g 15% DV; fat 26.8g 41% DV; cholesterol 53.1mg 18% DV; sodium 404.1mg 16% DV.

Great Pumpkin Dessert

Servings: 24 **Yield:** 1 - 9x13 inch pan

Ingredients

- 1 (15 ounce) can pumpkin puree
- 1 (12 fluid ounce) can evaporated milk
- 3 large eggs eggs
- 1 cup white sugar
- 4 teaspoons pumpkin pie spice
- 1 (18.25 ounce) package yellow cake mix
- ¾ cup butter, melted
- 1 ½ cups chopped walnuts

Directions

Step 1

Preheat oven to 350 degrees F (175 degrees C). Grease a 9x13 inch baking pan.

Step 2

In a large bowl, combine pumpkin, milk, eggs, sugar and spice. Mix well, and pour into a 9x13 inch pan.

Step 3

Sprinkle dry cake mix over the top, then drizzle with melted butter. Top with walnuts.

Step 4

Bake at 350 degrees F (175 degrees C) for 1 hour or until a knife inserted near the center comes out clean.

Nutrition Facts

Per Serving:

261 calories; protein 4.2g 8% DV; carbohydrates 29.4g 10% DV; fat 14.9g 23% DV; cholesterol 43.5mg 15% DV; sodium 250.9mg 10% DV.

Pumpkin Squares

Servings: 24 **Yield:** 1 9x13 inch pan.

Ingredients

- 4 large eggs eggs
- 1 cup vegetable oil
- 2 cups white sugar
- 1 (15 ounce) can solid pack pumpkin puree
- 2 cups all-purpose flour
- 2 teaspoons ground cinnamon

- ½ teaspoon ground cloves
- ½ teaspoon ground ginger
- ½ teaspoon ground nutmeg
- 1 teaspoon baking soda
- 2 teaspoons baking powder
- ½ teaspoon salt

Directions

Step 1

Preheat oven to 350 degrees F (175 degrees C). Grease a 9x13 inch baking pan.

Step 2

In a medium bowl, mix together the eggs, oil, sugar and pumpkin until smooth. Sift together the flour, cinnamon, cloves, ginger, nutmeg, baking soda, baking powder and salt. Stir into the pumpkin mixture.

Step 3

Spread evenly into the prepared pan and bake for 25 to 30 minutes. The bars should spring back to the touch when done. Allow to cool before frosting.

Nutrition Facts

Per Serving:

202.7 calories; protein 2.3g 5% DV; carbohydrates 26.5g 9% DV; fat 10.2g 16% DV; cholesterol 31mg 10% DV; sodium 196.3mg 8% DV.

Graveyard Cake for Halloween

Prep: 30 mins **Cook:** 26 mins **Additional:** 2 hrs 15 mins **Total:** 3 hrs 11 mins **Servings:** 16

Yield: 16 servings

Ingredients

- cooking spray
- 1 (15.25 ounce) package chocolate cake mix (such as Duncan Hines)
- 1 cup water
- 3 eaches eggs
- ⅓ cup vegetable oil
- 1 (16 ounce) package prepared chocolate frosting
- 15 eaches rectangular or oval sandwich cookies (such as Milano)
- 10 eaches chocolate wafer cookies, crushed

Directions

Step 1

Preheat oven to 350 degrees F (175 degrees C). Grease sides and bottom of a 9x13-inch cake pan with cooking spray.

Step 2

Combine cake mix, water, eggs, and oil in a large bowl; beat with an electric mixer on low speed until moistened, about 30 seconds. Beat at medium speed until batter is smooth and creamy, about 2 minutes. Pour batter into the prepared pan.

Step 3

Bake in the preheated oven until a toothpick inserted in the center comes out clean, 26 to 31 minutes. Remove from oven and cool pan on wire rack for 15 minutes. Remove cake from pan and cool completely on wire rack before decorating, about 2 hours.

Step 4

Spread a layer of chocolate frosting over top of the cake.

Step 5

Fill a pastry bag, fitted with a small plain tip, with a few tablespoons of chocolate frosting. Write "RIP" or draw a cross on sandwich cookies. Insert decorated cookies into the cake so that they look like tombstones in a graveyard. Sprinkle chocolate cookie crumbs in between the cookie tombstones to resemble dirt.

Nutrition Facts

Per Serving:

338.6 calories; protein 3.6g 7% DV; carbohydrates 44.6g 14% DV; fat 17.8g 27% DV; cholesterol 33.8mg 11% DV; sodium 312.8mg 13% DV.

Grandma Carol's Pumpkin Roll

Prep: 30 mins **Cook:** 10 mins **Additional:** 1 hr 10 mins **Total:** 1 hr 50 mins **Servings:** 24

Yield: 1 cake

Ingredients

- 3 large eggs eggs, beaten
- 1 cup white sugar
- ⅔ cup pumpkin puree
- ¾ cup all-purpose flour

- 1 teaspoon baking soda
- 1 teaspoon ground cinnamon
- ½ teaspoon ground cloves
- ½ teaspoon ground nutmeg
- 1 (8 ounce) package cream cheese, softened
- 2 tablespoons butter
- 1 (16 ounce) package confectioners' sugar
- 1 teaspoon vanilla extract
- 1 cup chopped pecans
- 2 teaspoons confectioners' sugar for dusting, or as needed

Directions

Step 1

Preheat oven to 400 degrees F (200 degrees C). Butter a 12x17-inch jelly roll pan and line with parchment paper; butter the parchment paper. Generously dust a kitchen towel with confectioners' sugar.

Step 2

Beat eggs, white sugar, and pumpkin together in a bowl until creamy.

Step 3

Sift flour, baking soda, cinnamon, cloves, and nutmeg together in a separate bowl; gradually stir into egg mixture. Stir to combine. Spread batter evenly into the prepared pan.

Step 4

Bake in the preheated oven for exactly 10 minutes.

Step 5

Immediately turn cake onto the prepared kitchen towel. Starting at a long end, roll up pumpkin cake and towel. Let rolled cake rest for 10 minutes.

Step 6

Beat cream cheese, butter, 16-ounce package confectioners' sugar, and vanilla extract together in a bowl until smooth; fold in pecans.

Step 7

Unroll cake; spread with the filling. Roll up cake (without towel). Cut off any jagged ends. Cover and refrigerate until chilled. Cut cake in half if desired; sprinkle with confectioners' sugar before serving.

Nutrition Facts

Per Serving:

207.7 calories; protein 2.4g 5% DV; carbohydrates 31.8g 10% DV; fat 8.5g 13% DV; cholesterol 36.1mg 12% DV; sodium 112.4mg 5% DV.

Cake Pops

Prep: 30 mins **Cook:** 10 mins **Additional:** 1 hr **Total:** 1 hr 40 mins **Servings:** 24 **Yield:**

24 pops

Ingredients

- 1 (12 ounce) package colored candy coating melts, divided
- 24 doughnut holes plain doughnut holes
- 24 eaches lollipop sticks
- 1 tablespoon multicolored candy sprinkles (jimmies), as desired

Directions

Step 1

Place about 1/4 cup of candy melts into a small microwave-safe bowl, and melt in the microwave at 40 percent power for 30 seconds; stir the candy coating, and continue to heat for 30 second-intervals until the coating is just warm and completely melted.

Step 2

Poke a hole halfway through a doughnut hole with a lollipop stick, then dip the end of the stick into the melted coating and reinsert into the hole. This holds the doughnut hole firmly on the stick. Stick the doughnut pop upright into a block of plastic foam, and set into refrigerator for 1 hour to firm up.

Step 3

When pops are firmly attached to their sticks, melt the remaining candy coating dots in a microwave-safe bowl on 40 percent power for 1 minute; stir, and melt for 30-second intervals until the coating is warm and smoothly melted. Dip the doughnut hole into the coating, covering it completely. Hold the dipped pop over a bowl, and sprinkle with colored candy sprinkles. Return the decorated pops to the plastic foam block to set.

Nutrition Facts

Per Serving:

131.3 calories; protein 1.7g 3% DV; carbohydrates 14.5g 5% DV; fat 7.6g 12% DV; cholesterol 3.8mg 1% DV; sodium 57.3mg 2% DV.

Pumpkin Roll with Ginger and Pecans

Prep: 35 mins **Cook:** 20 mins **Additional:** 1 day **Total:** 1 day **Servings:** 15 **Yield:** 1 pumpkin roll

Ingredients

- 3 large eggs eggs
- 1 cup white sugar
- ⅔ cup solid pack pumpkin puree
- 1 teaspoon lemon juice
- ¾ cup all-purpose flour
- 1 teaspoon baking powder
- ½ teaspoon salt
- 2 teaspoons ground cinnamon

- 1 teaspoon ground ginger
- 1 cup chopped pecans
- confectioners' sugar for dusting
- 1 (8 ounce) package cream cheese
- 4 tablespoons butter
- 1 cup confectioners' sugar
- ½ teaspoon vanilla extract
- confectioners' sugar for dusting

Directions

Step 1

Preheat oven to 350 degrees F (175 degrees C). Grease and flour a 10x15 inch jellyroll pan.

Step 2

In a large bowl, beat eggs and sugar with an electric mixer on high speed for five minutes. Gradually mix in pumpkin and lemon juice. Combine the flour, baking powder, salt, cinnamon, and ginger; stir into the pumpkin mixture. Spread batter evenly into the prepared pan. Sprinkle pecans over the top of the batter.

Step 3

Bake for 12 to 15 minutes, or until the center springs back when touched. Loosen edges with a knife. Turn out on two dishtowels that have been dusted with confectioners' sugar. Roll up cake using towels, and let cool for about 20 minutes.

Step 4

In a medium bowl, combine cream cheese, butter, 1 cup confectioners' sugar, and vanilla. Beat until smooth. Unroll pumpkin cake when cool, spread with filling, and roll up. Place pumpkin roll on a long sheet of waxed paper, and dust with confectioners' sugar. Wrap cake in waxed paper, and twist ends of waxed paper like a candy wrapper. Refrigerate overnight. Serve chilled; before slicing, dust with additional confectioners' sugar.

Nutrition Facts

Per Serving:

279.2 calories; protein 3.9g 8% DV; carbohydrates 35.1g 11% DV; fat 14.6g 23% DV; cholesterol 61.8mg 21% DV; sodium 216.6mg 9% DV.

Nickie's Apple-Pecan Cheesecake

Prep: 30 mins **Cook:** 55 mins **Additional:** 4 hrs 30 mins **Total:** 5 hrs 55 mins **Servings:** 16 **Yield:** 16 servings

Ingredients

Crust

- 1 ½ cups graham cracker crumbs
- ¼ cup melted butter
- 2 tablespoons packed brown sugar

Filling

- 4 (8 ounce) packages cream cheese, softened
- 1 cup packed brown sugar
- 1 teaspoon vanilla extract
- 1 cup sour cream
- 4 large eggs eggs

Topping

- 4 cups apples (about 3) - peeled, cored, and chopped
- ½ cup packed brown sugar
- ¾ cup chopped pecans
- 1 teaspoon ground cinnamon

Directions

Step 1

Preheat oven to 325 degrees F (165 degrees C). Line a 9x13 inch baking dish with aluminum foil, extending the foil sheets over the side of the dish.

Step 2

To make the crust, mix the graham cracker crumbs, butter, and 2 tablespoons brown sugar together in a bowl until evenly blended. Press evenly over the bottom of the prepared baking dish.

Step 3

To make the filling, beat the cream cheese, 1 cup brown sugar, and vanilla together in a mixing bowl until evenly blended. Beat in the sour cream. On low speed, add the eggs, one at a time, just until blended. Pour the mixture over the crust.

Step 4

To make the topping, place the apples in a bowl, and toss with 1/2 cup brown sugar, pecans, and cinnamon until evenly blended.

Step 5

Bake in preheated oven until center is almost set, about 55 minutes. Cool, and refrigerate 4 hours, or overnight.

Step 6

Before cutting, allow the cheesecake to sit 30 minutes at room temperature, then lift from the baking dish using the extended aluminum foil sheets, and place on a cutting board or serving plate. Remove the aluminum foil, and cut into 16 squares.

Nutrition Facts

Per Serving:

456.2 calories; protein 7.7g 15% DV; carbohydrates 37.1g 12% DV; fat 32.1g 49% DV; cholesterol 122.1mg 41% DV; sodium 263.2mg 11% DV.

Pumpkin Pie No-Bake Cheesecake

Prep: 20 mins **Additional:** 3 hrs 15 mins **Total:** 3 hrs 35 mins **Servings:** 8 **Yield:** 8 servings

Ingredients

- 1 (8 ounce) package low-fat cream cheese
- ⅓ cup white sugar
- 1 ½ tablespoons lemon juice
- 1 ½ teaspoons vanilla extract
- 1 (15 ounce) can pumpkin puree, divided

- 1 teaspoon ground cinnamon
- ½ teaspoon ground ginger
- ½ teaspoon ground nutmeg
- ½ cup heavy whipping cream
- 1 (9 inch) prepared graham cracker crust

Directions

Step 1

Place a bowl and beaters for a hand-held electric mixer into the freezer to cool, about 15 minutes.

Step 2

Mix cream cheese and sugar together in a bowl; stir in lemon juice and vanilla extract. Fold in half of the pumpkin puree; add cinnamon, ginger, and nutmeg.

Step 3

Remove the bowl and beaters from the freezer. Attach beaters to an electric mixer; pour cream into chilled bowl. Beat until stiff peaks form and cream stays in place when the bowl is tipped on its side.

Step 4

Fold remaining pumpkin puree and whipped cream into the cream cheese mixture. Spread evenly into crust; cover with plastic wrap.

Step 5

Chill in the refrigerator until set, 3 to 4 hours.

Nutrition Facts

Per Serving:

320 calories; protein 5.2g 10% DV; carbohydrates 35.3g 11% DV; fat 18.2g 28% DV; cholesterol 36.3mg 12% DV; sodium 388.8mg 16% DV.

Chocolate Buttermilk Layer Cake

Prep: 30 mins **Cook:** 20 mins **Additional:** 45 mins **Total:** 1 hr 35 mins **Servings:** 12

Yield: 12 servings

Ingredients

- ¾ cup NESTLE TOLL HOUSE Baking Cocoa, plus extra for coating pans
- 2 ¼ cups cake flour
- 2 teaspoons baking soda
- 1 teaspoon fine salt
- 1 ¼ cups buttermilk, at room temperature
- ½ cup brewed coffee or water
- 2 teaspoons vanilla extract
- 1 cup unsalted butter, at room temperature

- 2 cups superfine sugar
- 4 large eggs, at room temperature
- 2 (16 ounce) containers prepared chocolate frosting, or more if needed
- 1 (1.55 ounce) bar NESTLE CRUNCH Candy Bars, finely chopped (or more if needed)
- 24 pieces NESTLE BUTTERFINGER Bites Candy, finely chopped (or more if needed)

Directions

Step 1

Preheat oven to 350 degrees F. Grease bottoms of three 8- or 9-inch-round cake pans; line with a parchment or wax paper circle. Grease parchment, then coat lightly with small amount of cocoa, tapping out excess.

Step 2

Sift flour, cup cocoa, baking soda and salt together into a large bowl. Combine buttermilk, coffee and vanilla extract in small bowl.

Step 3

Beat butter in large mixer bowl until smooth. Beat in sugar until smooth and creamy. Beat in eggs one at a time, beating well after each addition. Scrape down sides of bowl with rubber spatula; beat again. Alternately add flour mixture in three additions with the buttermilk mixture in two additions, beginning and ending with flour mixture. Scrape down sides of bowl; beat again. Pour batter evenly into prepared pans.

Step 4

Bake for 20 to 25 minutes or until wooden pick inserted in center comes out clean. Cool in pans on wire racks for 10 minutes. Invert each layer onto wire rack; remove parchment paper, then invert right-side-up. Cool completely.

Step 5

To assemble: Level (trim tops off) the cakes if desired using a serrated knife. Place a dollop of frosting in the center of a cake pedestal or serving platter so the cake won't slip. Tear four strips of parchment paper and place in a square around the outer 3 inches of pedestal (this will help prevent getting the frosting on the pedestal). Place one cake layer over dollop of frosting. Spread about 1 cup frosting over top; sprinkle top evenly with about 1/4 cup chopped Crunch bar. Top with another cake layer; spread with about 1 cup frosting. Sprinkle with remaining chopped Crunch bar. Top with third cake layer. Cover the top and sides with a thin layer of frosting (this is the "crumb coat"; it doesn't have to be perfect). Refrigerate for 15 minutes, then cover with the remaining frosting. With hands, press chopped Butterfinger around sides of cake. After the frosting has set, gently remove strips of parchment paper. Cut cake into slices for serving.

Nutrition Facts

Per Serving:

805.4 calories; protein 6.9g 14% DV; carbohydrates 108.1g 35% DV; fat 38.5g 59% DV; cholesterol 103.7mg 35% DV; sodium 701.4mg 28% DV.

Pumpkin Patch "Dirt" Cake

Prep: 30 mins **Additional:** 1 hr **Total:** 1 hr 30 mins **Servings:** 12 **Yield:** 12 servings

Ingredients

- 1 (19.1 ounce) package chocolate sandwich cookies (such as Oreo)
- 2 (24 ounce) round cartons chocolate ice cream
- ½ cup prepared vanilla frosting
- 1 drop green food coloring
- 30 eaches mellocreme (candy corn) pumpkins

Directions

Step 1

Crush the cookies in 2 batches in a food processor. You'll need about 4 1/3 cups crumbs.

Step 2

Spread 1 1/3 cups crumbs over bottom of a 9-x-13-inch baking pan.

Step 3

Cut away cardboard packaging from 1 carton of ice cream with scissors. Slice ice cream crosswise into 1-inch-thick rounds with a long knife. Arrange slices over crumbs, cutting smaller pieces to fill gaps. Cover ice cream with another 1 1/3 cups crumbs. Repeat with second container of ice cream, and top with remaining crumbs. Freeze until firm, at least 1 hour.

Step 4

Mix frosting with enough green food coloring to make it bright green, then transfer to a pastry bag fitted with a plain tip. Arrange 3 double rows of pumpkins on top of cake and pipe vines connecting pumpkins. Freeze until ready to serve.

Nutrition Facts

Per Serving:

541 calories; protein 6.7g 13% DV; carbohydrates 82.3g 27% DV; fat 22.6g 35% DV; cholesterol 38.6mg 13% DV; sodium 322.8mg 13% DV.

Kitty Litter Cake

Servings: 20 **Yield:** 20 servings

Ingredients

- 1 (18.25 ounce) package German chocolate cake mix
- 1 (18.25 ounce) package white cake mix
- 2 (3.5 ounce) packages instant vanilla pudding mix
- 1 (12 ounce) package vanilla sandwich cookies
- 3 drops green food coloring
- 1 (12 ounce) package tootsie rolls

Directions

Step 1

Prepare cake mixes and bake according to package directions (any size pan).

Step 2

Prepare pudding according to package directions and chill until ready to assemble.

Step 3

Crumble sandwich cookies in small batches in a food processor, scraping often. Set aside all but 1/4 cup. To the 1/4 cup add a few drops of green food coloring and mix.

Step 4

When cakes are cooled to room temperature, crumble them into a large bowl. Toss with 1/2 of the remaining cookie crumbs, and the chilled pudding. You probably won't need all of the pudding, you want the cake to be just moist, not soggy.

Step 5

Line kitty litter box with the kitty litter liner. Put cake mixture into box.

Step 6

Put half of the unwrapped tootsie rolls in a microwave safe dish and heat until softened. Shape the ends so that they are no longer blunt, and curve the tootsie rolls slightly. Bury tootsie rolls randomly in the cake and sprinkle with half of the remaining cookie crumbs. Sprinkle a small amount of the green colored cookie crumbs lightly over the top.

Step 7

Heat 3 or 4 of the tootsie rolls in the microwave until almost melted. Scrape them on top of the cake and sprinkle lightly with some of the green cookie crumbs. Heat the remaining tootsie rolls until pliable and shape as before. Spread all but one randomly over top of cake mixture. Sprinkle with any remaining cookie crumbs. Hang the remaining tootsie roll over side of litter box and sprinkle with a few green cookie crumbs. Serve with the pooper scooper for a gross Halloween dessert.

Nutrition Facts

Per Serving:

351.2 calories; protein 3.4g 7% DV; carbohydrates 76.6g 25% DV; fat 7.5g 12% DV; cholesterolmg; sodium 592.9mg 24% DV.

Granny Kat's Pumpkin Roll

Prep: 20 mins **Cook:** 15 mins **Additional:** 20 mins **Total:** 55 mins **Servings:** 10 **Yield:** 10 servings

Ingredients

- ¾ cup all-purpose flour
- 1 cup white sugar
- 1 teaspoon baking soda
- 2 teaspoons pumpkin pie spice
- 1 cup pumpkin puree
- 3 large eggs eggs
- 1 teaspoon lemon juice
- 2 tablespoons confectioners' sugar
- 1 (8 ounce) package cream cheese, softened
- ¼ cup butter
- 1 teaspoon vanilla extract
- 1 cup confectioners' sugar

Directions

Step 1

Preheat oven to 375 degrees F (190 degrees C). Grease and flour a 9x13 inch jelly roll pan or cookie sheet.

Step 2

In a large bowl, mix together flour, sugar, baking soda, and pumpkin pie spice. Stir in pumpkin puree, eggs, and lemon juice. Pour mixture into prepared pan. Spread the mixture evenly.

Step 3

Bake at 375 degrees F (190 degrees C) for 15 minutes.

Step 4

Lay a damp linen towel on the counter, sprinkle it with confectioner's sugar, and turn the cake onto the towel. Carefully roll the towel up (lengthwise) with the cake in it. Place the cake-in-towel on a cooling rack and let it cool for 20 minutes.

Step 5

Make the icing: In a medium bowl, blend cream cheese, butter, vanilla, and sugar with a wooden spoon or electric mixer.

Step 6

When the cake has cooled 20 minutes, unroll it and spread icing onto it. Immediately re-roll (not in the towel this time), and wrap it with plastic wrap. Keep the cake refrigerated or freeze it for up to 2 weeks in aluminum foil. Cut the cake in slices just before serving.

Nutrition Facts

Per Serving:

315.6 calories; protein 4.9g 10% DV; carbohydrates 43.7g 14% DV; fat 14.1g 22% DV; cholesterol 92.6mg 31% DV; sodium 305.5mg 12% DV.

Chocolate Candy Bar Cake

Prep: 45 mins **Cook:** 25 mins **Total:** 1 hr 10 mins **Servings:** 12 **Yield:** 3 layer 8 inch cake

Ingredients

- 1 (18.25 ounce) package devil's food cake mix
- 1 ½ cups milk
- 3 large eggs eggs
- ¾ cup vegetable oil
- 1 (3.5 ounce) package instant vanilla pudding mix
- 1 (8 ounce) package cream cheese
- ½ cup white sugar
- 1 cup confectioners' sugar
- 1 (12 ounce) container frozen whipped topping, thawed
- 1 cup chopped pecans

- 4 (1.5 ounce) bars milk chocolate candy, coarsely chopped

Directions

Step 1

Preheat oven to 325 degrees F (165 degrees C). Grease and flour 3 (8 inch) pans.

Step 2

In a large bowl, combine cake mix, milk, eggs, oil and instant vanilla pudding mix. Beat on low speed until blended. Scrape bowl, and beat 4 minutes on medium speed. Pour batter into prepared pans.

Step 3

Bake in the preheated oven for 20 to 25 minutes, or until a toothpick inserted into the center of the cake comes out clean. Allow to cool.

Step 4

To make the frosting: In a large bowl, beat the cream cheese with the white sugar and confectioners' sugar until smooth. Fold in the whipped topping, pecans and chopped chocolate. Spread between layers and on top and sides of cake.

Nutrition Facts

Per Serving:

735.8 calories; protein 9.3g 19% DV; carbohydrates 75.2g 24% DV; fat 46.1g 71% DV; cholesterol 81.4mg 27% DV; sodium 535.4mg 21% DV.

Pumpkin Sheet Cake

Prep: 30 mins **Cook:** 30 mins **Additional:** 1 hr **Total:** 2 hrs **Servings:** 20 **Yield:** 1 - 10 x 15 inch cake

Ingredients

- 1 (15 ounce) can canned pumpkin puree
- 2 cups white sugar
- 1 cup vegetable oil
- 4 large eggs eggs
- 2 cups all-purpose flour
- 2 teaspoons baking soda
- 1 teaspoon ground cinnamon

- ½ teaspoon salt
- 1 (3 ounce) package cream cheese
- 5 tablespoons butter, softened
- 1 teaspoon vanilla extract
- 1 ¾ cups confectioners' sugar
- 3 teaspoons milk
- 1 cup chopped walnuts

Directions

Step 1

In a mixing bowl, beat pumpkin, 2 cups white sugar, and oil. Add eggs, and mix well.

Step 2

In another bowl, combine flour, baking soda, cinnamon and salt. Add these dry ingredients to the pumpkin mixture, and beat until well blended. Pour batter into a greased 15 x 10 inch baking pan.

Step 3

Bake at 350 degrees F (175 degrees C) for 25 to 30 minutes, or until cake tests done. Cool.

Step 4

In a mixing bowl, beat the cream cheese, butter or margarine, and vanilla until smooth. Gradually add 1 3/4 cups confectioners' sugar, and mix well. Add milk until frosting reaches desired spreading consistency. Frost cake, and sprinkle with nuts.

Nutrition Facts

Per Serving:

362 calories; protein 4g 8% DV; carbohydrates 42.8g 14% DV; fat 20.4g 31% DV; cholesterol 49.5mg 17% DV; sodium 282.9mg 11% DV.

Cream Cheese Pumpkin Roll

Prep: 25 mins **Cook:** 15 mins **Additional:** 2 hrs 10 mins **Total:** 2 hrs 50 mins **Servings:** 10

Yield: 1 roll

Ingredients

- 3 large eggs eggs
- 1 cup white sugar

- ⅔ cup pumpkin puree
- ¾ cup all-purpose flour
- 2 teaspoons ground cinnamon
- 1 teaspoon baking powder

- 1 teaspoon ground ginger
- ½ teaspoon ground nutmeg
- ½ teaspoon salt

Filling:

- 1 (8 ounce) package cream cheese, softened
- 1 cup confectioners' sugar

- ¼ cup butter, softened
- 1 tablespoon pumpkin puree
- 1 teaspoon vanilla extract

Directions

Step 1

Preheat oven to 375 degrees F (190 degrees C). Grease a 10x15-inch jelly roll pan and line with wax paper.

Step 2

Beat eggs and white sugar in a large bowl until well blended; stir in 2/3 cup pumpkin puree.

Step 3

Combine flour, cinnamon, baking powder, ginger, nutmeg, and salt in another bowl; stir into egg mixture until just blended. Pour mixture into prepared jelly roll pan.

Step 4

Bake in preheated oven until a toothpick inserted into the center comes out clean, about 15 minutes. Cool in the pans for 10 minutes, then turn cake out onto a clean towel. Remove and discard wax paper. Roll cake up into the towel, starting with the short end. Cool.

Step 5

Beat cream cheese, confectioners' sugar, butter, 1 tablespoon pumpkin puree, and vanilla extract in another bowl until smooth.

Step 6

Spread a large sheet of plastic wrap on a work surface. Place and unroll cake over plastic and spread with prepared filling. Re-roll cake and wrap with plastic. Refrigerate, seam-side down, until chilled, about 2 hours.

Nutrition Facts

308.1 calories; protein 4.8g 10% DV; carbohydrates 41.9g 14% DV; fat 14.1g 22% DV; cholesterol 92.6mg 31% DV; sodium 324.9mg 13% DV.

Pumpkin Spiced Dump Cake

Prep: 10 mins **Cook:** 1 hr **Total:** 1 hr 10 mins **Servings:** 12 **Yield:** 12 servings

Ingredients

- cooking spray
- 1 (15 ounce) can pumpkin puree
- 1 (12 fluid ounce) can evaporated milk
- 1 ½ cups white sugar
- 4 large eggs eggs
- 1 teaspoon vanilla extract
- ½ teaspoon ground cinnamon
- ¼ teaspoon ground nutmeg
- 1 (15.25 ounce) package yellow cake mix
- 2 cups chopped pecans
- ¾ cup butter, melted

Directions

Step 1

Preheat oven to 325 degrees F (165 degrees C). Grease a 9x13-inch baking pan with cooking spray.

Step 2

Mix pumpkin, evaporated milk, sugar, eggs, vanilla extract, cinnamon, and nutmeg together in a bowl; pour into the prepared baking pan.

Step 3

Sprinkle cake mix evenly over the pumpkin mixture; top with pecans. Drizzle melted butter on top.

Step 4

Bake in the preheated oven until golden brown, about 1 hour.

Nutrition Facts

Per Serving:

571 calories; protein 8.2g 16% DV; carbohydrates 62.2g 20% DV; fat 34.1g 53% DV; cholesterol 102.4mg 34% DV; sodium 460.6mg 18% DV.

Pumpkin Magic Cake with Maple Cinnamon Whipped Cream

Prep: 25 mins **Cook:** 50 mins **Additional:** 30 mins **Total:** 1 hr 45 mins **Servings:** 9
Yield:

1 8-inch cake

Ingredients

- 1 cup all-purpose flour
- 2 tablespoons pumpkin pie spice
- 1 teaspoon sea salt
- 1 teaspoon ground cinnamon
- 1 ½ cups lukewarm milk
- 1 cup canned pumpkin
- 2 teaspoons vanilla extract

- 4 large eggs eggs, at room temperature, separated
- 1 cup white sugar
- ¼ cup brown sugar
- 1 tablespoon water
- ½ cup unsalted butter, melted
- 1 teaspoon cream of tartar

Maple Cinnamon Whipped Cream:

- 1 ¼ cups heavy whipping cream
- ¼ cup maple syrup
- ½ teaspoon ground cinnamon
- 1 pinch sea salt

Directions

Step 1

Preheat oven to 325 degrees F (165 degrees C). Grease an 8-inch baking pan.

Step 2

Whisk flour, pumpkin pie spice, 1 teaspoon salt, and 1 teaspoon cinnamon together in a bowl.

Step 3

Combine milk, pumpkin, and vanilla extract in a bowl.

Step 4

Place egg yolks, white sugar, brown sugar, and water in the bowl of a stand mixer. Beat on high speed until creamy. Reduce speed to low; add butter. Increase speed to medium; beat until light and fluffy. Reduce speed to low and add flour mixture in 3 batches, blending thoroughly after each addition and scraping down the sides of the bowl. Stir milk-pumpkin mixture slowly into the mixture until just combined; transfer to a separate bowl.

Step 5

Clean and dry out the bowl and beaters. Beat egg whites and cream of tartar on high speed until stiff peaks form. Fold 3/4 of the egg white mixture into the pumpkin mixture using a spatula; pour into the remaining egg whites, folding mixture in slowly until batter is smooth but still light and fluffy. Pour batter into the prepared pan.

Step 6

Bake in the preheated oven until edges are set and center still jiggles slightly, about 50 minutes. Let cool completely, at least 30 minutes.

Step 7

Beat heavy cream, maple syrup, 1/2 teaspoon cinnamon, and 1 pinch salt together in a bowl using an electric mixer until soft peaks form. Spread over cooled cake.

Nutrition Facts

Per Serving:

457.3 calories; protein 6.8g 14% DV; carbohydrates 51.4g 17% DV; fat 25.9g 40% DV; cholesterol 158.3mg 53% DV; sodium 362.2mg 15% DV.

283.2 calories; protein 4.3g 9% DV; carbohydrates 42.5g 14% DV; fat 11.1g 17% DV; cholesterol 62mg 21% DV; sodium 479.3mg 19% DV.

Pumpkin Crunch Cake with Cream Cheese Frosting

Prep: 15 mins **Cook:** 50 mins **Additional:** 1 hr **Total:** 2 hrs 5 mins **Servings:** 12 **Yield:** 12 servings

Ingredients

Cake:

- 1 (29 ounce) can pumpkin puree
- 1 (12 fluid ounce) can evaporated milk
- 1 cup white sugar
- 3 large eggs eggs
- 1 teaspoon ground cinnamon
- 1 (15.25 ounce) package yellow cake mix with pudding
- 1 cup chopped nuts
- 1 cup butter, melted

Frosting:

- 1 (8 ounce) package cream cheese, softened
- 1 cup confectioners' sugar
- ¾ cup frozen whipped topping (such as Cool Whip), thawed

Directions

Step 1

Preheat oven to 350 degrees F (175 degrees C). Line a 9x13-inch baking pan with parchment paper.

Step 2

Mix pumpkin, evaporated milk, sugar, eggs, and cinnamon together in a bowl; spread in the prepared baking pan. Pour cake mix on top. Pat chopped nuts into surface. Spoon melted butter evenly over nuts.

Step 3

Bake in the preheated oven until golden brown, 50 minutes to 1 hour. Allow cake to cool completely, about 1 hour. Turn over onto a baking sheet; remove parchment paper.

Step 4

Mix cream cheese, confectioners' sugar, and whipped topping together in a bowl. Spread onto cake.

Nutrition Facts

Per Serving:

622.1 calories; protein 9.1g 18% DV; carbohydrates 67.7g 22% DV; fat 36.9g 57% DV; cholesterol 116.8mg 39% DV; sodium 627mg 25% DV.

Pumpkin Pie Cake with Yellow Cake Mix

Servings: 24 **Yield:** 1 - 9x13 inch cake

Ingredients

- 1 (29 ounce) can pumpkin puree
- 1 (12 fluid ounce) can evaporated milk
- 3 large eggs eggs
- 1 cup white sugar
- 2 teaspoons ground cinnamon
- 1 teaspoon ground nutmeg
- ½ teaspoon ground ginger
- ½ teaspoon ground cloves
- 1 (18.25 ounce) package yellow cake mix
- 1 cup butter
- 1 cup chopped walnuts

Directions

Step 1

Preheat oven to 350 degrees F (175 degrees C). Line a 9 x 13 inch pan with parchment paper.

Step 2

In a large bowl, combine pumpkin, evaporated milk, eggs, sugar, cinnamon, nutmeg, ginger and cloves. Mix until smooth and pour into a 9x13 inch pan.

Step 3

Sprinkle dry cake mix over pumpkin mixture, then sprinkle chopped nuts and pat down gently. Melt butter or margarine and drizzle over cake.

Step 4

Bake at 350 degrees F (175 degrees C) for approximately 45 to 60 minutes. (Be sure to check the cake after 45 minutes because oven temperatures vary.)

Step 5

After cake cools, turn it upside down so the top of the cake will be the crust. Remove the parchment paper. Top with dessert topping (optional) before serving.

Nutrition Facts

Per Serving:

268 calories; protein 4g 8% DV; carbohydrates 30.5g 10% DV; fat 15.3g 24% DV; cholesterol 48.6mg 16% DV; sodium 303.2mg 12% DV.

Pumpkin Upside Down Cake

Prep: 20 mins **Cook:** 1 hr **Total:** 1 hr 20 mins **Servings:** 16 **Yield:** 1 - 9x13 inch cake

Ingredients

- 1 (29 ounce) can pumpkin
- 1 cup white sugar
- 3 large eggs eggs
- 1 (12 fluid ounce) can evaporated milk
- 1 tablespoon pumpkin pie spice
- 1 (18.25 ounce) package yellow cake mix
- 1 cup butter, melted
- 2 cups frozen whipped topping, thawed

Directions

Step 1

Preheat the oven to 350 degrees F (175 degrees C). Line a 9x13 inch baking pan with parchment paper or aluminum foil.

Step 2

In a large bowl, stir together the pumpkin, sugar and eggs. Mix in the evaporated milk and pumpkin pie spice; pour into the prepared pan.

Step 3

Sprinkle the dry cake mix over the pumpkin and then drizzle melted butter over the cake mix.

Step 4

Bake for 1 hour in the preheated oven, or until a knife inserted into the cake comes out clean. Cool, then invert onto a serving dish. Serve with whipped topping.

Nutrition Facts

Per Serving:

383 calories; protein 5g 10% DV; carbohydrates 46.7g 15% DV; fat 20.5g 32% DV; cholesterol 72.9mg 24% DV; sodium 457mg 18% DV.

Pumpkin Cheesecake I

Prep: 20 mins **Cook:** 50 mins **Total:** 1 hr 10 mins **Servings:** 16 **Yield:** 2 - 8 inch pie pans

Ingredients

- 2 (8 ounce) packages cream cheese
- ¾ cup white sugar
- 1 (15 ounce) can pumpkin puree
- 1 ¼ teaspoons ground cinnamon
- ½ teaspoon ground ginger
- ½ teaspoon ground nutmeg
- 2 large eggs eggs
- ¼ teaspoon salt
- 2 8" pie crust (blank)s prepared 8 inch pastry shells

Directions

Step 1

Preheat oven to 350 degrees F (175 degrees C).

Step 2

Beat together the cream cheese and the sugar, add the pumpkin and the spices. Beat in eggs one at a time. Add salt. Beat until creamy. Pour the batter evenly into the two pastry shells.

Step 3

Bake at 350 degrees F (175 degrees C) for 50 minutes or until the knife inserted in the center comes out clean. Let cool then top with whipped topping, if desired.

Nutrition Facts

Per Serving:

218 calories; protein 3.8g 8% DV; carbohydrates 18.8g 6% DV; fat 14.6g 23% DV; cholesterol 54mg 18% DV; sodium 274mg 11% DV.

Midnight Moon Cake

Servings: 12 **Yield:** 1 -9 inch round cake

Ingredients

- ½ cup shortening
- 1 ¼ cups white sugar
- 2 large eggs eggs
- 1 cup hot water
- ½ cup unsweetened cocoa powder
- 1 ½ cups sifted all-purpose flour
- ½ teaspoon salt
- 1 teaspoon baking soda
- 1 teaspoon baking powder
- 1 teaspoon vanilla extract
- 1 ½ cups confectioners' sugar
- 1 teaspoon lemon zest
- 2 fluid ounces lemon juice

Directions

Step 1

Preheat oven to 350 degrees F (175 degrees C). Grease and line with parchment paper one 9 inch round cake pan.

Step 2

Cream shortening, add white sugar gradually and cream until fluffy. Blend in the well beaten eggs.

Step 3

In a separate bowl, slowly add hot water to cocoa and mix until smooth, dissolving cocoa completely.

Step 4

In a third bowl, sift together the flour, salt, baking soda, and baking powder; add to creamed mixture alternately with the cocoa mixture. Blend in vanilla. Pour batter into one 9 inch round pan.

Step 5

Bake at 350 degrees F (175 degrees C) for 30 to 35 minutes or until cake tester comes out clean. Let cake cool then ice with Lemon Icing.

Step 6

To Make Icing: Combine confectioner's sugar with enough lemon juice to make the icing spreadable without being runny or stiff (about 1/4 cup). Stir in the grated zest. Pour icing over top of cake. See the full moon.

Nutrition Facts

Per Serving:

294.1 calories; protein 3.4g 7% DV; carbohydrates 50.3g 16% DV; fat 10g 15% DV; cholesterol 31mg 10% DV; sodium 255.4mg 10% DV.

The Popcorn Cake

Prep: 10 mins **Cook:** 10 mins **Additional:** 10 mins **Total:** 30 mins **Servings:** 14 **Yield:** 1 - 10 inch tube pan

Ingredients

- 14 cups popped popcorn
- 1 cup semisweet chocolate chips
- 1 cup peanuts
- ½ cup margarine
- ½ cup peanut butter
- 5 cups miniature marshmallows

Directions

Step 1

Line a 10 inch tube pan or other 12 cup pan with aluminum foil.

Step 2

In a very large bowl, combine popcorn, chocolate chips and peanuts and mix well.

Step 3

In a medium saucepan over low heat, melt margarine. Stir in peanut butter. Stir in marshmallows and continue stirring until marshmallows melt and the mixture is smooth. Remove from the heat. Stir marshmallow mixture into popcorn mixture until well coated.

Step 4

Press mixture into prepared pan. Allow to cool completely before removing and cutting into slices to serve.

Nutrition Facts

Per Serving:

356 calories; protein 6.4g 13% DV; carbohydrates 30.8g 10% DV; fat 24.6g 38% DV; cholesterolmg; sodium 259.3mg 10% DV.

Marie-Claude's Orange Cake

Prep: 1 hr 15 mins **Cook:** 30 mins **Total:** 1 hr 45 mins **Servings:** 12 **Yield:** 12 servings

Ingredients

- ⅜ cup vegetable oil
- 1 cup white sugar
- 2 large eggs eggs
- ½ cup plain yogurt
- 2 fruit, (2-5/8" dia, sphere)s oranges, zested and juiced
- 1 ½ cups all-purpose flour
- 1 teaspoon baking powder

Directions

Step 1

Preheat the oven to 375 degrees F (190 degrees C).

Step 2

In a medium bowl, mix together the vegetable oil, sugar and eggs. Stir in yogurt and orange zest. Combine the flour and baking powder; stir into the mixture just until blended. Pour the dough into a greased 9x13 inch baking pan.

Step 3

Bake for 30 minutes in the preheated oven, or until a knife inserted into the cake comes out clean. Poke holes in the cake with a knife, and pour the juice from the oranges over the cake slowly until it has all been absorbed.

Nutrition Facts

Per Serving:

213.3 calories; protein 3.5g 7% DV; carbohydrates 32.8g 11% DV; fat 8g 12% DV; cholesterol 31.6mg 11% DV; sodium 59.8mg 2% DV.

Pumpkin Roll with Toffee Cream Filling and Caramel Sauce

Servings: 12 Yield: 12 servings

Ingredients

- ¾ cup cake flour
- 1 ½ teaspoons ground cinnamon
- 1 ¼ teaspoons ground ginger
- ¾ teaspoon ground allspice
- 6 large egg yolks egg yolks
- 6 large egg whites egg whites
- ⅓ cup white sugar
- ⅓ cup packed light brown sugar
- ⅔ cup solid pack pumpkin puree
- ⅛ teaspoon salt
- ¼ cup confectioners' sugar for dusting
- 2 tablespoons dark rum
- 1 teaspoon unflavored gelatin
- 1 cup heavy whipping cream
- 3 tablespoons confectioners' sugar
- 10 tablespoons crushed toffee candy
- 1 (16 ounce) jar caramel ice cream topping, warmed
- ½ cup crushed toffee candy

Directions

Step 1

Preheat oven to 375 degrees F (190 degrees C). Spray a 15x10 inch baking sheet with vegetable oil spray. Sift flour, cinnamon, ginger and allspice into small bowl. Set aside.

Step 2

In a large bowl, beat egg yolks, 1/3 cup white sugar and 1/3 cup brown sugar until very thick, about 3 minutes with an electric mixer. On low speed, beat in pumpkin, then flour mixture. Using clean, dry beaters, in a large bowl, beat egg whites and salt until stiff but not dry. Fold egg whites into batter in 3 additions.

Step 3

Spread into prepared pan. Bake at 375 degrees F (190 degrees C) for 15 minutes, or until a toothpick inserted into cake comes out clean.

Step 4

Place smooth (not terry cloth) kitchen towel on work surface; dust generously with powdered sugar. Cut around pan edges to loosen cake. Turn cake out onto kitchen towel. Fold towel over 1 long side of cake. Starting at 1 long side, roll cake up in towel. Arrange cake seam side down and cool completely, about 1 hour.

Step 5

To make the filling: Pour 2 tablespoons rum into small heavy saucepan and sprinkle gelatin over. Let stand until gelatin softens, about 10 minutes. Stir over low heat just until gelatin dissolves, then remove from heat. In a large bowl, beat chilled whipping cream and 3 tablespoons powdered sugar until stiff peaks form. Beat in gelatin mixture. Fold in 6 tablespoons English toffee pieces.

Step 6

Unroll cake, sprinkle with 4 tablespoons English toffee pieces. Spread filling over. Starting at 1 long side and using kitchen towel as aid, roll up cake to enclose filling. Place cake seam side down on platter. (Can be prepared 1 day ahead.) Cover with foil and refrigerate.

Step 7

Trim ends of cake on slight diagonal. Dust cake with powdered sugar. Spoon some of the warm caramel sauce over top of cake. Sprinkle with 1/2 cup toffee. To serve, cut cake crosswise into 1 inch thick slices. Serve with remaining sauce.

Nutrition Facts

Per Serving:

428.7 calories; protein 5.2g 10% DV; carbohydrates 62.6g 20% DV; fat 17.7g 27% DV; cholesterol 147.8mg 49% DV; sodium 335.8mg 13% DV.

Pumpkin Upside-Down Cake

Prep: 15 mins **Cook:** 1 hr **Additional:** 1 hr 30 mins **Total:** 2 hrs 45 mins **Servings:** 24

Yield: 1 9x13-inch baking pan

Ingredients

- 1 (16 ounce) can pumpkin puree
- 1 (12 fluid ounce) can evaporated milk
- 1 cup white sugar
- 3 large eggs eggs
- 2 teaspoons ground cinnamon
- 1 (15.25 ounce) package yellow cake mix
- 1 cup chopped pecans
- 1 cup butter, melted
- 12 ounces nondairy whipped topping
- 1 (8 ounce) package cream cheese, softened
- 1 cup white sugar

Directions

Step 1

Preheat oven to 350 degrees F (175 degrees C). Line a 9x13-inch baking pan with parchment paper.

Step 2

Mix pumpkin puree, evaporated milk, 1 cup sugar, eggs, and cinnamon together in a bowl; pour into the prepared baking pan. Sprinkle cake mix over pumpkin mixture and top with pecans. Drizzle butter over pecan layer.

Step 3

Bake in the preheated oven until a toothpick inserted into the center comes out clean, about 1 hour. Cool cake in the pan, at least 30 minutes. Invert cake onto a flat plate.

Step 4

Mix whipped topping, cream cheese, and 1 cup white sugar together in a bowl; spread over the cake. Chill in the refrigerator, 1 to 2 hours. Cut into 1-inch squares.

Nutrition Facts

Per Serving:

344.7 calories; protein 4.1g 8% DV; carbohydrates 39.6g 13% DV; fat 20g 31% DV; cholesterol 58.8mg 20% DV; sodium 271.5mg 11% DV.

Spiderweb Pumpkin Cheesecake

Prep: 20 mins **Cook:** 50 mins **Additional:** 30 mins **Total:** 1 hr 40 mins **Servings:** 12
Yield:

12 servings

Ingredients

- 1 ¼ cups chocolate wafer crumbs
- ¼ cup butter, melted
- 3 (8 ounce) packages cream cheese, softened
- ¾ cup white sugar
- 3 large eggs eggs
- 1 ½ cups canned pumpkin pie filling
- 1 tablespoon cornstarch
- 1 cup sour cream
- 2 (1 ounce) squares semisweet chocolate
- 2 teaspoons vegetable oil

Directions

Step 1

Preheat oven to 350 degrees F (175 degrees C).

Step 2

Mix chocolate wafer crumbs and melted butter in a bowl; press onto the bottom of a 9-inch springform pan.

Step 3

Beat cream cheese and sugar with an electric mixer in a large bowl until smooth. Beat in eggs, one at a time, until just blended. Stir in pumpkin pie filling and cornstarch; pour over chocolate wafer crust.

Step 4

Bake in preheated oven until center is just set, 50 to 55 minutes.

Step 5

Spread sour cream over top of warm cheesecake; let cool.

Step 6

Melt chocolate and oil in a microwave-safe bowl in a microwave for 1 minute; stir until completely melted. Drizzle chocolate onto sour cream topping in a spiral pattern, starting from the center; draw a toothpick outward, from center to edges, through circles to form a web. Remove side of pan and serve.

Nutrition Facts

454.8 calories; protein 7.9g 16% DV; carbohydrates 35.5g 12% DV; fat 32.6g 50% DV; cholesterol 126.9mg 42% DV; sodium 358.6mg 14% DV.

Double Layer Pumpkin Pie Cheesecake

Prep: 20 mins **Additional:** 4 hrs **Total:** 4 hrs 20 mins **Servings:** 8 **Yield:** 8 servings

Ingredients

- 1 (8 ounce) package cream cheese, softened
- 1 tablespoon milk
- 1 tablespoon white sugar
- 1 (8 ounce) container whipped topping (such as Cool Whip), thawed and divided
- 1 (6 ounce) graham cracker crust (such as Nabisco Honey Maid)
- 1 (15 ounce) can pumpkin puree
- 1 cup milk
- 2 (3.4 ounce) packages instant vanilla pudding mix
- 1 teaspoon ground cinnamon
- ½ teaspoon ground ginger
- ¼ teaspoon ground cloves

Directions

Step 1

Beat cream cheese, 1 tablespoon milk, and sugar together in a large bowl with a whisk until blended. Stir in half of whipped topping; spread into crust.

Step 2

Whisk pumpkin puree, 1 cup milk, pudding mix, cinnamon, ginger, and ground cloves together in a bowl until mixture is thick and blended. Spread over cream cheese mixture.

Step 3

Chill in the refrigerator until set, about 4 hours. Remove from the refrigerator; top with remaining whipped topping before serving.

Nutrition Facts

Per Serving:

421.2 calories; protein 5g 10% DV; carbohydrates 50.9g 16% DV; fat 23.1g 36% DV; cholesterol 33.4mg 11% DV; sodium 696.3mg 28% DV.

Trick or Treat Cheesecake

Prep: 20 mins **Cook:** 50 mins **Additional:** 9 hrs **Total:** 10 hrs 10 mins **Servings:** 12 **Yield:**

12 servings

Ingredients

- cooking spray

Crust:

- 25 cookies chocolate sandwich cookies (such as Oreo), crushed
- ⅓ cup white sugar
- ⅓ cup melted butter

Filling:

- 2 (8 ounce) packages cream cheese, softened
- 1 (14 ounce) can sweetened condensed milk
- 3 large eggs eggs
- 20 mini chocolate-coated caramel-peanut nougat candy bars (such as Snickers), cut into quarters
- 2 teaspoons vanilla extract

Directions

Step 1

Preheat oven to 300 degrees F (150 degrees C). Place a shallow pan 1/2-full with water on the lower oven rack to minimize cracking in the cheesecake. Spray the inside of a 9-inch springform pan with cooking spray and line with parchment paper.

Step 2

Mix chocolate sandwich cookies, sugar, and butter together in a bowl; press into the bottom of the prepared pan.

Step 3

Beat cream cheese and sweetened condensed milk together in a separate bowl using an electric mixer until smooth; beat in eggs, 1 at a time, until just blended. Stir candy bars and vanilla extract into cream cheese mixture; pour over crust.

Step 4

Bake in the preheated oven until edges are set and center is still slightly soft, about 50 minutes. Turn off oven, leaving door open, and cool cheesecake in oven, at least 1 hour. Run a knife or spatula around the edges to loosen cheesecake; refrigerate in the pan until set, 8 hours or overnight.

Nutrition Facts

Per Serving:

490.4 calories; protein 9.3g 19% DV; carbohydrates 48.5g 16% DV; fat 29.8g 46% DV; cholesterol 114.2mg 38% DV; sodium 343.4mg 14% DV.

Frankenstein Ice Cream Cake

Prep: 30 mins **Additional:** 6 hrs 30 mins **Total:** 7 hrs **Servings:** 16 **Yield:** 1 loaf cake

Ingredients

- ½ gallon mint chocolate chip ice cream
- 2 cups heavy whipping cream
- ½ cup white sugar
- 1 pouch whipped cream stabilizer (such as Dr. Oetker Whip It)
- 2 teaspoons vanilla extract
- 1 drop green food coloring, or as desired
- 2 cups crushed chocolate sandwich cookies (such as Oreo)
- ½ cup melted butter
- 1 tablespoon hot fudge sauce, or as needed
- 2 tablespoons chocolate sprinkles, or as desired
- 2 cookies chocolate sandwich cookies (such as Oreo)

Directions

Step 1

Put ice cream in the refrigerator to soften while you make whipped cream frosting.

Step 2

Beat cream in a bowl using an electric mixer until stiff peaks almost form. Add white sugar, whipped cream stabilizer, vanilla extract, and green food coloring to whipped cream; beat until stiff peaks form.

Step 3

Scoop softened ice cream into a large bowl; stir until a uniform consistency is reached. The ice cream shouldn't be completely melted, but firm enough to hold form. Scoop ice cream into the loaf pan and spread evenly using a spatula, trying to avoid creating air bubbles.

Step 4

Mix crushed cookies and melted butter together in a bowl. Pat cookie mixture the ice cream for the "hair"; freeze for 5 hours. Run a knife along the edges of the pan and carefully flip it upside-down over a cake platter. Return cake to the freezer until firm, at least 30 minutes.

Step 5

Spread whipped cream evenly over the top and sides of cake. Freeze cake until solid, about 1 hour more.

Step 6

Spoon hot fudge sauce onto the cake creating "eyes", a "mouth", and "hairline"; top hot fudge areas with sprinkles. Place 1 cookie on each side of the bottom of the cake for the "neck bolts". Freeze cake until ready to eat.

Nutrition Facts

Per Serving:

541.9 calories; protein 6.3g 13% DV; carbohydrates 42g 14% DV; fat 39.2g 60% DV; cholesterol 150.4mg 50% DV; sodium 174.8mg 7% DV.

Halloween Layer Cake

Prep: 30 mins **Cook:** 30 mins **Total:** 1 hr **Servings:** 24 **Yield:** 2 - 9 inch round cakes

Ingredients

- 1 ¾ cups cake flour
- 1 teaspoon baking soda
- 1 teaspoon salt
- 1 ½ cups white sugar
- ⅓ cup shortening
- 1 cup buttermilk
- 3 large egg whites egg whites
- 4 (1 ounce) squares unsweetened chocolate, melted
- 1 teaspoon butter
- ⅓ cup butter, softened
- 1 ½ tablespoons orange zest
- 1 teaspoon lemon zest
- ¼ teaspoon salt
- 1 egg yolk
- 4 cups sifted confectioners' sugar
- 1 tablespoon orange juice
- 2 teaspoons lemon juice

Directions

Step 1

Preheat oven to 350 degrees F (175 degrees C). Line the bottoms of two 8 or 9 inch round cake pans with parchment paper.

Step 2

Sift together the flour, baking soda, salt, and white sugar.

Step 3

Beat shortening until light and fluffy. Mix in dry ingredients. Add 3/4 cup of buttermilk and mix until all flour is dampened. Then beat with electric mixer. Add egg whites, melted chocolate, and remaining buttermilk, beat well and pour batter into prepared pans.

Step 4

Bake at 350 degrees F (175 degrees C) for 30 minutes. When cake is cool frost between layer and over top and sides with Golden Orange Frosting. Mark outlines of Halloween cats and bats by lightly pressing paper cut-outs into frosting, then removing paper. Melt 1 square unsweetened chocolate with 1 tsp. butter. Using a brush, fill in the outlines with the chocolate mixture.

Step 5

To Make Golden Orange Frosting: Cream together butter, orange rind, lemon rind, and salt. Add egg yolk and mix well. Add confectioners sugar, alternately with orange juice and

161

lemon juice, beating well after each addition. Makes 2 cups frosting, or enough to cover tops and sides of two 9 inch layers.

Nutrition Facts

Per Serving:

249.2 calories; protein 2.4g 5% DV; carbohydrates 43.6g 14% DV; fat 8.4g 13% DV; cholesterol 16.2mg 5% DV; sodium 212.5mg 9% DV.

Dairy-Free Halloween Black Cake

Prep: 15 mins **Cook:** 20 mins **Total:** 35 mins **Servings:** 8 **Yield:** 1 9-inch cake pan

Ingredients

- 1 ½ cups all-purpose flour
- 1 cup white sugar
- ¾ cup chocolate chips
- ⅔ cup unsweetened cocoa powder
- 2 teaspoons baking soda
- 1 teaspoon salt

- 1 cup cold brew coffee with grounds
- ¾ cup pumpkin puree
- 2 tablespoons vegetable oil
- 2 teaspoons vanilla extract
- 2 tablespoons white vinegar

Directions

Step 1

Preheat oven to 350 degrees F (175 degrees C).

Step 2

Mix flour, sugar, chocolate chips, cocoa powder, baking soda, and salt together in a 9-inch cake pan. Add cold brew, pumpkin puree, oil, and vanilla extract and mix thoroughly. Stir vinegar in until just combined.

Step 3

Bake in the preheated oven until a toothpick inserted into the center comes out clean, 20 to 30 minutes.

Nutrition Facts

Per Serving:

315.3 calories; protein 4.8g 10% DV; carbohydrates 58.7g 19% DV; fat 9.4g 15% DV; cholesterolmg; sodium 665.1mg 27% DV.

Halloween Cheesecake

Prep: 15 mins **Cook:** 40 mins **Additional:** 1 hr 30 mins **Total:** 2 hrs 25 mins **Servings:** 10

Yield: 1 9-inch cheesecake

Ingredients

Crust:

- 16 cookies chocolate sandwich cookies (such as Oreo)
- 5 tablespoons butter, melted
- 3 tablespoons white sugar

Filling:

- 2 (8 ounce) packages cream cheese, softened
- ½ cup white sugar
- 2 large eggs eggs
- ½ cup sour cream
- 1 teaspoon vanilla extract

Directions

Step 1

Preheat the oven to 350 degrees F (175 degrees C). Butter a 9-inch springform pan.

Step 2

Process cookies in a food processor until reduced to coarse crumbs. Reserve 1 tablespoon for decoration; combine the rest with butter and sugar. Spread mixture onto the bottom of the prepared pan, pressing down firmly to form a crust.

Step 3

Bake in the preheated oven until set, 8 to 10 minutes. Remove; reduce oven temperature to 325 degrees F (163 degrees C).

Step 4

Beat cream cheese and sugar together using an electric mixer until creamy, about 2 minutes. Add eggs one at a time, mixing well after each addition. Add sour cream and vanilla extract. Blend well. Pour filling into the cooled crust.

Step 5

Bake in the preheated oven until center is nearly set, about 30 minutes. Turn off oven and leave cheesecake inside to cool, at least 30 minutes. Continue cooling in the refrigerator for at least 1 hour. Decorate with reserved cookie crumbs.

Nutrition Facts

Per Serving:

375.2 calories; protein 5.9g 12% DV; carbohydrates 27g 9% DV; fat 27.8g 43% DV; cholesterol 106.8mg 36% DV; sodium 270.9mg 11% DV.

Chocolate Magic Cake

Prep: 20 mins **Cook:** 50 mins **Additional:** 30 mins **Total:** 1 hr 40 mins **Servings:** 10
Yield: 10 servings

Ingredients

- ⅔ cup unsweetened cocoa powder
- ⅓ cup all-purpose flour
- 2 teaspoons instant espresso powder
- ¾ teaspoon sea salt
- 4 large eggs eggs at room temperature, separated

- 1 cup white sugar
- 1 tablespoon water
- ½ cup unsalted butter, melted
- 2 teaspoons vanilla extract
- 2 cups whole milk, lukewarm
- 1 teaspoon cream of tartar

Directions

Step 1

Preheat oven to 325 degrees F (165 degrees C). Grease an 8-inch baking pan.

Step 2

Whisk cocoa powder, flour, espresso powder, and salt together in a bowl.

Step 3

Combine egg yolks, white sugar, and water in the bowl of a stand mixer. Beat on high speed until eggs are light and creamy, about 2 minutes. Reduce speed to low and add butter and vanilla extract. Increase speed to medium; beat until light and fluffy, about 1 minute. Reduce speed to low and add the cocoa mixture in 3 batches, mixing thoroughly after each addition and scraping down the sides of the bowl. Stir milk slowly into the batter until well combined. Pour chocolate batter into a separate bowl.

Step 4

Clean and dry out bowl and beaters. Beat egg whites and cream of tartar together on high speed until stiff peaks form. Fold 3/4 of the egg white mixture into the chocolate batter using a spatula; pour back into the egg white bowl, folding mixture in slowly until batter is smooth but still light and fluffy. Pour batter into the prepared pan.

Step 5

Bake in the preheated oven until edges are set and center still jiggles slightly, about 50 minutes. Let cake cool completely, at least 30 minutes.

Nutrition Facts

Per Serving:

248.6 calories; protein 5.8g 12% DV; carbohydrates 29g 9% DV; fat 13.6g 21% DV; cholesterol 103.7mg 35% DV; sodium 182.4mg 7% DV.

Potato Chocolate Cake

Prep: 1 hr **Cook:** 45 mins **Additional:** 15 mins **Total:** 2 hrs **Servings:** 24 **Yield:** 1 - 9x13 inch pan

Ingredients

- 1 cup margarine
- 2 cups white sugar
- 4 large eggs eggs
- 2 (1 ounce) squares unsweetened chocolate, melted
- 1 teaspoon vanilla extract

- 1 cup prepared instant mashed potatoes
- 2 cups sifted all-purpose flour
- 1 teaspoon baking soda
- 1 teaspoon salt
- ¾ cup buttermilk

Directions

Step 1

Preheat oven to 375 degrees F (190 degrees C). Grease and flour a 9x13 inch pan. Sift together the flour, baking soda and salt. Set aside.

Step 2

In a large bowl, cream together the margarine and sugar until light and fluffy. Beat in the eggs one at a time. Stir in the melted chocolate, vanilla and mashed potatoes. Beat in the flour mixture alternately with the buttermilk, mixing just until incorporated.

Step 3

Pour batter into prepared pan. Bake in the preheated oven for 45 minutes, or until a toothpick inserted into the center of the cake comes out clean. Allow to cool.

Nutrition Facts

Per Serving:

204.9 calories; protein 2.9g 6% DV; carbohydrates 26.8g 9% DV; fat 10.1g 16% DV; cholesterol 32.5mg 11% DV; sodium 271.8mg 11% DV.

White Chocolate Bubbling Cauldrons

Prep: 1 hr **Cook:** 30 mins **Additional:** 10 mins **Total:** 1 hr 40 mins **Servings:** 6 **Yield:** 6 8-ounce ramekins

Ingredients

- 1 pound bittersweet chocolate, chopped
- 1 (12 ounce) package black confectioners' coating (such as black Wilton Candy Melts)
- 1 cup unsalted butter, softened
- ½ cup white sugar
- 3 large eggs eggs, room temperature
- 3 large egg yolks egg yolks, room temperature
- 1 cup all-purpose flour
- 1 cup ground toasted pecans
- 1 teaspoon vanilla extract
- 1 (12 ounce) package green confectioners' coating (such as green Wilton Candy Melts)
- 1 (12 ounce) package white confectioners' coating (such as white Wilton Candy Melts)
- ¾ cup heavy whipping cream
- 2 ounces bittersweet chocolate, grated
- 6 pretzels chocolate-covered pretzel sticks

Directions

Step 1

Preheat oven to 350 degrees F (175 degrees C). Generously butter six 8-ounce ramekins and place on baking sheet.

Step 2

Melt 1 pound chopped bittersweet chocolate in a plastic or glass bowl in microwave oven on low, stirring every 30 seconds, or in the top of a double-boiler over gently simmering water. Remove melted chocolate from heat and set aside to cool. It should be room temperature but still fluid.

Step 3

Melt black confectioners' coating in a separate large plastic or glass bowl in microwave oven on low, stirring every 30 seconds, until coating is melted, warm, and smooth. Keep candy warm.

Step 4

Beat butter and sugar in a bowl using an electric mixer fitted with a whisk attachment on high speed until mixture is light and fluffy, about 5 minutes. Add eggs one at a time, allowing each egg to blend into the butter mixture before adding the next. Beat in egg yolks one at a time. Continue mixing until batter is thick and lemon-colored, about 3 minutes.

Step 5

Pour cooled melted chocolate into butter mixture and mix on low speed, stopping to scrape down sides of bowl, until fully combined. Beat flour, ground pecans, and vanilla extract into chocolate mixture and continue to mix just until batter comes together. Divide batter among prepared ramekins.

Step 6

Bake in preheated oven for 15 minutes. Remove tray from oven. Carefully place 2 or 3 green candy pieces and 1 white candy piece (or more white than green, if desired) in the center of each half-baked cake. Return cakes to oven and bake for another 10 to 15 minutes, or until a knife inserted in the side comes out clean (do not pierce the centers). Let cakes cool in ramekins for 10 minutes.

Step 7

Melt 2 or 3 pieces of the green candy in a small microwave-safe bowl in microwave set on low, stirring every 30 seconds, until green candy is warm and smooth. Let cool until room temperature but still fluid. Whip the heavy cream in a bowl and gently fold cooled green candy melts into the whipped cream.

Step 8

Gently unmold cakes onto baking sheet. Carefully dip cakes into black candy coating, or pour it over the cakes to coat. Sprinkle grated chocolate onto a serving platter and place cakes onto the grated chocolate. Spoon a dollop of green whipped cream on top of each cake. Pierce each cake with a chocolate-covered pretzel stick, allowing the bubbling cauldrons to ooze their green and white candy filling. Serve immediately.

Nutrition Facts

Per Serving:

2117.8 calories; protein 25.4g 51% DV; carbohydrates 193.1g 62% DV; fat 141.7g 218% DV; cholesterol 356.9mg 119% DV; sodium 275.1mg 11% DV.

Super Easy Halloween Cake

Prep: 10 mins **Cook:** 25 mins **Total:** 35 mins **Servings:** 24 **Yield:** 1 9x13-inch pan

Ingredients

- 1 (18.25 ounce) package yellow cake mix
- 1 (15 ounce) can pumpkin puree
- 2 large eggs eggs
- 1 cup semisweet chocolate chips

Directions

Step 1

Preheat oven to 350 degrees F (175 degrees C). Grease a 9x13-inch baking pan.

Step 2

Beat cake mix, pumpkin puree, and eggs together in a bowl using an electric mixer until batter is smooth, about 2 minutes. Fold chocolate chips into batter; pour into the prepared baking pan.

Step 3

Bake in the preheated oven until a toothpick inserted into the center comes out clean, 25 to 30 minutes.

Nutrition Facts

Per Serving:

138.6 calories; protein 2g 4% DV; carbohydrates 22.7g 7% DV; fat 5.1g 8% DV; cholesterol 15.9mg 5% DV; sodium 190.9mg 8% DV.

Smart Cookie's Spiderweb Pumpkin Cheesecake

Prep: 20 mins **Cook:** 1 hr 20 mins **Additional:** 7 hrs **Total:** 8 hrs 40 mins **Servings:** 12

Yield: 1 (10-inch) cheesecake

Ingredients

Gingersnap and Pecan Crust:

- cooking spray
- 48 eaches gingersnap cookies
- ½ cup pecan pieces
- ½ cup salted butter, melted

Pumpkin Cheesecake:

- 4 (8 ounce) packages cream cheese, at room temperature
- 1 ½ cups white sugar
- 4 eaches eggs, at room temperature
- 2 teaspoons vanilla extract
- 1 cup canned pumpkin puree
- 1 ½ teaspoons pumpkin pie spice blend

Directions

Step 1

Preheat the oven to 350 degrees F (175 degrees C). Spray a 10-inch springform pan with cooking spray and wrap the outside with foil.

Step 2

Pulse gingersnap cookies into fine crumbs in a food processor. Transfer to a medium mixing bowl. Pulse pecans in the same food processor bowl until finely ground. Add to the cookie mixture and mix in melted butter.

Step 3

Press the cookie and pecan mixture into the bottom and halfway up the sides of the springform pan.

Step 4

Bake in the preheated oven until golden brown on the edges, about 10 minutes. Cool on a wire rack. Reduce the oven temperature to 300 degrees F (150 degrees C).

Step 5

Beat cream cheese with sugar in the bowl of a stand mixer fitted with the paddle attachment, stopping occasionally to scrape the sides of the bowl, until smooth and creamy, about 3 minutes. Add eggs 1 at a time, beating just until combined and scraping the sides of the bowl after each addition. Beat in vanilla extract.

Step 6

Pour about 1/2 of the batter into a different bowl and set aside.

Step 7

Add pumpkin puree and pumpkin spice to the batter in the stand mixer bowl and mix until combined.

Step 8

Transfer 1/4 cup of the plain batter into a piping bag or plastic storage bag. Spread the rest over the pie crust. Top with the pumpkin cheesecake batter.

Step 9

Pipe remaining plain batter into 5 concentric circles on the top of the cheesecake. Drag the tip of a toothpick or small knife out from the center of the batter to the edge, wiping it down between each pull, to create a spider web effect.

Step 10

Place the springform pan in the bottom of a roasting pan; fill roasting pan halfway up with warm water to create a water bath.

Step 11

Carefully transfer cheesecake to the oven and bake until edges are set, top is no longer shiny, and center is still a little jiggly, about 1 hour and 10 minutes.

Step 12

Turn the oven off and prop the door open at least 4 inches. Leave the cheesecake in the oven for an additional 30 minutes.

Step 13

Remove cheesecake from the oven and water bath. Run a knife around the edge to prevent sticking and cool on a cooling rack for 30 minutes more. Cover loosely and chill for at least 6 hours, or overnight.

Step 14

Run a knife around the edge of the pan and carefully remove the sides of the springform pan. Slice and serve.

Nutrition Facts

Per Serving:

606.4 calories; protein 9.3g 19% DV; carbohydrates 48.1g 16% DV; fat 43.2g 66% DV; cholesterol 157mg 52% DV; sodium 439.9mg 18% DV.

Pumpkin Cake I

Prep: 15 mins **Cook:** 1 hr **Additional:** 5 mins **Total:** 1 hr 20 mins **Servings:** 12 **Yield:**

1 10-inch bundt cake

Ingredients

- 1 cup vegetable oil
- 3 large eggs eggs
- 1 (15 ounce) can pumpkin puree
- 1 teaspoon vanilla extract
- 2 ½ cups white sugar
- 2 ½ cups all-purpose flour
- 1 teaspoon baking soda
- 1 teaspoon ground nutmeg
- 1 teaspoon ground allspice
- 1 teaspoon ground cinnamon
- 1 teaspoon ground cloves
- ¼ teaspoon salt
- 1 cup chopped walnuts

Directions

Step 1

Preheat oven to 350 degrees F (175 degrees C). Grease one 10-inch bundt or tube pan.

Step 2

Blend oil, beaten eggs, pumpkin and vanilla together.

Step 3

Sift the flour, sugar, baking soda, ground nutmeg, ground allspice, ground cinnamon, ground cloves and salt together. Add the flour mixture to the pumpkin mixture and mix until just combined. If desired, stir in some chopped nuts. Pour batter into the prepared pan.

Step 4

Bake in preheated oven until a toothpick inserted in the middle comes out clean, about 1 hour. Let cake cool in pan for 5 minutes, then turn out onto a plate and sprinkle with confectioners' sugar.

Nutrition Facts

Per Serving:

517.3 calories; protein 6.2g 12% DV; carbohydrates 66.4g 21% DV; fat 26.6g 41% DV; cholesterol 46.5mg 16% DV; sodium 257.7mg 10% DV.

Rosemary-Pumpkin Seed Brittle

YIELDS:**12** servings TOTAL TIME:**0** hours **55** mins

INGREDIENTS

- 2 c. granulated sugar
- 1/2 c. (1 stick) unsalted butter, sliced
- 1/3 c. golden syrup
- 1/2 tsp. baking soda
- 2 1/2 c. roasted, salted pepitas
- 1 tbsp. chopped fresh rosemary
- 1/4 tsp. freshly ground black pepper
- Large-flake sea salt (such as Maldon)

DIRECTIONS

1. Line a rimmed baking sheet with parchment paper. Combine sugar, 1/2 cup water, butter, and golden syrup in a large saucepan. Bring to a boil over medium-high heat. Cook, without stirring, until caramel is light brown and registers 300°F on a candy thermometer, 10 to 15 minutes.

2. Remove from heat and carefully stir in baking soda (mixture will bubble up). Quickly stir in pepitas, rosemary, and pepper. Immediately scrape brittle onto prepared baking sheet and spread into a thin, even layer. Sprinkle with salt. Cool completely, 35 to 45 minutes. Break into pieces.

Mummy Pumpkin Hand Pies

YIELDS:**12** servings TOTAL TIME:**3** hours **45** mins

INGREDIENTS

- 2 1/2 c. all-purpose flour, spooned and leveled, plus more for work surface
- 3 tbsp. plus 2 teaspoons granulated sugar, divided, plus more for sprinkling
- 1 tsp. plus a pinch kosher salt, divided
- 1 c. (2 sticks) cold unsalted butter, cut into pieces

- 3 oz. cream cheese, at room temperature
- 1/2 c. canned pure pumpkin
- 1 large egg plus 1 egg yolk, divided
- 1/2 tsp. pumpkin pie spice
- 1/2 tsp. pure vanilla extract
- 24 edible candy eyes

DIRECTIONS

1. Pulse flour, 2 teaspoons sugar, and 1 teaspoon salt in a food processor, 4 to 5 times. Add butter and pulse until it resembles a coarse meal with several pea-size pieces remaining, 12 to 15 times. Add 5 tablespoons ice-cold water, 1 tablespoon at a time, pulsing until dough just begins to come together (add up to an additional tablespoon of water, if needed). Divide dough into 2 piles; knead together and wrap each with plastic wrap. Use plastic to flatten and press dough into loose rectangles. Refrigerate until firm, 2 hours.
2. Beat cream cheese until smooth, about 1 minute. Add pumpkin, egg yolk, pie spice, vanilla, pinch of salt, and remaining 3 tablespoons sugar with an electric mixer on medium speed until smooth, 2 to 3 minutes.
3. Line 2 baking sheets with parchment paper. Working with one piece of dough at a time on a lightly floured work surface, roll dough to 1/4-inch thickness. Cut into 6 three-by-four-inch rectangles. Transfer to prepared baking sheets. Repeat with remaining dough. Top rectangles with a rounded tablespoonful of pumpkin mixture, spreading lightly and leaving a 1/2-inch border around edges.
4. Knead dough scraps together and reroll. Cut into thin strips about 1/4 inch wide and 5 inches long. Top hand pies with several overlapping strips to create a mummy. Seal edges with your fingertips and trim excess.
5. Whisk together egg and 1 tablespoon water in a bowl. Brush strips lightly with egg wash and sprinkle with sugar. Chill 20 minutes.
6. Preheat oven to 400°F. Bake until golden brown, 20 to 25 minutes. Cool 20 minutes. Place candy eyes on mummies.

Spiced Pumpkin-Molasses Cake

INGREDIENTS

- Cooking spray
- 3 c. cake flour, spooned and leveled
- 1 tbsp. pumpkin pie spice
- 1 tsp. baking soda
- 1 tsp. baking powder
- 1 tsp. kosher salt

- 1 c. molasses
- 1 c. canned pure pumpkin
- 3/4 c. buttermilk
- 1/2 c. vegetable oil
- 1 large egg
- Confectioners' sugar

DIRECTIONS

1. Preheat oven to 350°F. Lightly grease a 10-inch round cake pan. Whisk together flour, pie spice, baking soda, baking powder, and salt in a bowl; make a well in center of mixture. Whisk together molasses, pumpkin, buttermilk, oil, and egg in a second bowl. Pour wet ingredients into well of dry ingredients, and whisk just until combined. Transfer to prepared pan.
2. Bake until a wooden pick inserted in center comes out clean, 50 to 55 minutes. Cool cake in pan on a wire rack 10 minutes, then invert onto rack to cook completely.
3. Just before serving, dust with confectioners' sugar, using a festive stencil made from parchment

Pumpkin-Spiced Buns with Spiderweb Glaze

YIELDS:**12** TOTAL TIME:**2** hours **40** mins

INGREDIENTS

- 1/2 c. warm whole milk (100°F to 110°F)
- 2 (1/4-ounce) packages active dry yeast
- 2/3 c. packed light brown sugar, divided
- 4 3/4 c. all-purpose flour, spooned and leveled, plus more for work surface
- 1 1/2 tsp. kosher salt
- 2 tsp. pumpkin pie spice, divided

- 14 tbsp. (1 3/4 sticks) unsalted butter, at room temperature, divided
- 1 c. canned pure pumpkin, divided
- 2 large eggs, at room temperature
- 2 c. confectioners' sugar
- 6 oz. cream cheese, at room temperature
- 1 tsp. pure vanilla extract

DIRECTIONS

1. Lightly grease a bowl. Place milk in a second bowl and sprinkle with yeast. Let stand until foamy, 4 to 5 minutes (if yeast does not foam, discard and start again). Add 1/3 cup brown sugar and 1 cup

flour. Beat, with a dough hook, on low speed with an electric mixer until combined, 1 to 2 minutes. Beat in salt, 1 teaspoon pumpkin pie spice, and 6 tablespoons butter until smooth, 1 minute. Beat in 3/4 cup pumpkin until smooth, 1 to 2 minutes. Add eggs, one at a time, beating until blended after each addition. Gradually beat in remaining 3 3/4 cups flour just until combined, 1 minute.

2. Increase mixer speed to medium and beat until dough forms a loose ball and begins to pull away from top of bowl, about 1 minute (dough will still stick to bottom of bowl). Continue to beat until dough is smooth and elastic, 3 to 5 minutes. Place dough in prepared bowl and turn to coat. Cover with a clean dish towel and let rise in a warm place (80°F to 85°F) until doubled in size, 45 minutes to 1 hour, or refrigerate overnight.

3. Stir together remaining 8 tablespoons butter and 1/4 cup pumpkin in a bowl. Stir together remaining 1/3 cup brown sugar and 1 teaspoon pumpkin pie spice in a second bowl.

4. Punch down dough and turn out onto a well-floured work surface. Roll to a 12-by-16-inch rectangle. Spread butter mixture over dough, leaving a 1/2-inch border around edges. Sprinkle with brown sugar mixture, pressing gently to help adhere. Roll up dough, starting at one long side. Trim both ends of dough.

5. Line a large rimmed baking sheet with parchment paper. Using a serrated knife, cut dough into 12 equal slices. Arrange on prepared baking sheet. Cover with a clean dish towel and let rise in a warm place until puffed, about 30 to 40 minutes.

6. Preheat oven to 350°F. Bake until golden brown and cooked through, 20 to 25 minutes. Cool on a wire rack, 10 minutes.

7. Whisk together confectioners' sugar, cream cheese, and vanilla in a bowl until smooth. Transfer to a zip-top bag. Cut a 1/4-inch hole in one corner of bag. Pipe glaze on top of buns in a spiderweb pattern. Serve warm.

Spider Cookie Truffles

YIELDS:**36** TOTAL TIME:**2** hours **30** mins

INGREDIENTS

- 36 chocolate sandwich cookies
- 1 (8-ounce) package cream cheese, cut into pieces, at room temperature
- 2 (12-ounce) bags semisweet chocolate chips, melted
- Edible candy eyeballs
- Black string licorice, cut into 2-inch pieces

DIRECTIONS

1. Line a baking sheet with wax paper. Process cookies in a food processor until fine crumbs form, about 30 seconds. Add cream cheese and pulse until combined, 15 to 20 times. Scoop mixture into 1 1/4-inch balls and place on prepared baking sheet. Freeze until firm, 1 hour.

2. Dip cookies in chocolate; return to baking sheet. Decorate with edible candy eyeballs and black string licorice. Refrigerate until set, 1 hour.

Coffin Sandwich Cookies

YIELDS:**34** servings TOTAL TIME:**3** hours **45** mins

INGREDIENTS

For the Cookies:

- 1/3 c. cornstarch
- 2 tbsp. unsweetened cocoa powder
- 3/4 tsp. kosher salt
- 1 c. (2 sticks) unsalted butter, softened

- 1 c. packed light brown sugar
- 1/2 c. molasses
- 2 large eggs
- 5 c. all-purpose flour, spooned and leveled

For the White Chocolate Bones:

- 1/2 c. white chocolate candy melts

For the Buttercream Filling:

- 1/2 c. (1 stick) unsalted butter, softened
- 1 1/2 c. sifted confectioners' sugar
- 1/4 tsp. pure vanilla extract

- Pinch kosher salt
- Red food coloring
- Orange food coloring

For the Royal Icing

- 2 c. confectioners' sugar
- 2 tbsp. meringue powder
- Black food coloring

DIRECTIONS

1. Make cookies: Preheat oven to 375°F. Line 4 baking sheets with parchment paper. Whisk together cornstarch, cocoa, and salt in a bowl.
2. Beat butter and sugar with an electric mixer on medium speed until light and fluffy, 2 to 4 minutes. Add molasses and beat until incorporated, 1 minute. Beat in eggs, one at a time, scraping the bottom and sides of the bowl after each addition. Reduce mixer speed to medium-low and beat in cornstarch mixture. Beat in flour just until incorporated. Divide dough into two pieces and wrap in plastic wrap; flatten. Chill at least one hour and up to 2 days.
3. Roll dough to 3/8-inch thickness on a floured work surface. Cut coffin shapes with a 3-inch coffin cookie cutter; transfer to prepared baking sheets. Bake until cookies are set around the edges but still a little soft in the center, 8 to 9 minutes.
4. Make white chocolate bones: Melt candy melts according to package directions. Transfer to a zip-top bag and snip a small hole in one corner. Fill the bone mold with melted candies. Chill until firm, 20 to 30 minutes. Tap out of molds.

5. Make filling: Beat butter with an electric mixer on medium speed until smooth and creamy, 1 to 2 minutes. Add confectioners' sugar, 1/2 cup at a time, mixing well and scraping down sides of bowl occasionally. Beat in vanilla and salt. Use red and orange food coloring to dye a deep orange color.
6. Make royal icing: Combine confectioners' sugar and meringue powder in a bowl. Add 1 1/2 tablespoons water and stir to combine.

Hats and Bats Chocolate-Peanut Butter Tarts

YIELDS:**20** servings TOTAL TIME:**3** hours **5** mins

INGREDIENTS

- 1/2 c. smooth peanut butter
- 1/2 c. confectioners' sugar
- 1/3 c. mini chocolate chips
- 2 c. all-purpose flour, spooned and leveled, plus more for work surface
- 1/4 c. unsweetened cocoa powder
- 3 tbsp. granulated sugar

- 1/2 tsp. kosher salt
- 1/2 c. (1 stick) cold unsalted butter, cut into small pieces
- 1 package (8 ounces) cold cream cheese, cut into small pieces
- Store-bought white frosting
- White sanding sugar, for decorating

DIRECTIONS

1. Stir together peanut butter and confectioners' sugar in a bowl until smooth and a dough forms. Stir in chocolate chips.
2. Pulse together flour, cocoa powder, granulated sugar, and salt in a food processor, 3 to 4 times. Add butter and pulse until butter is the size of peas, 5 to 6 times. Add cream cheese and pulse until dough forms, 10 to 12 times. (Add 1 to 2 tablespoons water if needed to help dough form.) Divide dough into two pieces and wrap in plastic wrap; flatten. Chill at least one hour and up to 2 days.
3. Preheat oven to 350°F. Line two baking sheets with parchment paper. Roll out dough to 1/8-inch thick on a lightly floured work surface. Cut shapes with 3-inch witch hat and bat cookie cutters; place half of each shape, 1/2-inch apart, on prepared baking sheet. Top with peanut butter filling leaving a small border around the edge. Brush edges with water and place a duplicate cutout on top. Crimp edges with a fork.
4. Bake until cooked through, 9 to 10 minutes. Transfer to wire racks and cool completely. Place a small amount of white frosting in a ziptop bag, snip a very small hole in one corner. Pipe eyes on bats and a band on the witch hats. Sprinkle with sanding sugar.

Spooky Forest Pudding Cups

YIELDS:**10** TOTAL TIME:**3** hours **50** mins

INGREDIENTS

- 1 1/2 c. sugar
- 1/2 c. unsweetened cocoa powder
- 1/3 c. cornstarch
- 1/2 tsp. kosher salt
- 3 1/2 c. whole milk
- 6 large egg yolks
- 8 oz. semisweet chocolate, chopped
- 4 tbsp. unsalted butter
- 4 tbsp. pure vanilla extract
- 20 whole chocolate sandwich cookies, plus 12 crushed
- 1 1/2 c. chocolate candy melts
- 4- or 6-inch bamboo skewers
- Chocolate sprinkles, optional
- Candy pumpkins, for decorating

DIRECTIONS

1. Whisk together sugar, cocoa, cornstarch, and salt in a medium saucepan. Whisk in milk and eggs. Cook over medium heat, whisking, until mixture just begins to bubble and thicken, 5 to 7 minutes. (Make sure to stir the bottom and inside corners of the pan to prevent scorching.) Remove from heat. Add chocolate, butter, and vanilla. Stir until chocolate is melted and mixture is smooth.
2. Place 1 whole cookie on the bottom of 10 juice glasses (about 6 ounces each). Top with half of the pudding, dividing evenly. Top with a second cookie. Top each glass with remaining pudding, dividing evenly. Top with crushed cookies, dividing evenly; cover and chill.
3. Place tree template under a sheet of parchment on a baking sheet. Melt candy melts according to package directions. Transfer to a heavy-duty zip-top bag and cut a small hole in one corner. Pipe a line of melted chocolate on the trunks of the trees and place the bamboo skewers on top. Pipe chocolate over the bamboo skewer and over the rest of the lines on the template to create trees (this can be done loosely—there is no need to follow the template exactly). Sprinkle the branches with chocolate sprinkles. Chill until set.
4. Insert chocolate trees into glasses of pudding and decorate with candy pumpkins.

Towering Haunted House Cake

YIELDS:**30** servings TOTAL TIME:**5** hours **0** mins

INGREDIENTS

For the Cake (Make Twice):

- 1 3/4 c. all-purpose flour, spooned and leveled
- 2 c. granulated sugar
- 3/4 c. unsweetened cocoa powder
- 2 tsp. baking soda
- 1/2 tsp. baking powder
- 1 tsp. kosher salt
- 3 large eggs
- 2/3 c. vegetable oil
- 1 tsp. pure vanilla extract
- 1 c. milk, warm

For the Vanilla Buttercream and Decoration:

- 2 1/2 c. unsalted butter (5 sticks), at room temperature
- 7 1/2 c. sifted confectioner's sugar
- 1 1/2 tsp. pure vanilla extract
- Pinch kosher salt
- 17 chocolate sandwich cookies, crushed, divided
- Black food coloring
- 1 c. black candy melts
- Black fondant
- Silver luster dust
- White fondant
- Wilton bones and skulls sprinkles, for top of windows and door
- Black and Gray Sixlets, for roof and balcony
- Green sprinkles, for moss
- Green licorice or sour strings, for plants
- Black and gunmetal dragées, for above windows and door and along house corners
- Silver & white lollipops, for door trim

DIRECTIONS

1. **Make cake:** Preheat oven to 350°F. Grease a 9- by 13-inch pan and line the bottom with parchment paper. Grease parchment.
2. Whisk together flour, sugar, cocoa, baking soda, baking powder, and salt with an electric mixer on medium speed until combined, about 1 minute. Add eggs, oil, vanilla, and milk. Whisk on medium-low until smooth, about 1 minute. Increase speed to medium and beat for 2 minutes.
3. Spread batter into prepared pan. Bake, rotating once, until a toothpick inserted in the center comes out clean, 35 to 40 minutes. Cool in pan on a wire rack, 15 minutes. Turn out onto wire rack, right side up, and cool completely. Make a second cake. Wrap cooled cakes in plastic wrap and chill for 1 hour and up to 2 days.
4. **Make buttercream:** Beat butter with an electric mixer on medium speed until smooth and creamy, 1 to 2 minutes. Beat in confectioners' sugar, 1/2 cup at a time, mixing well and scraping down sides of bowl occasionally. Beat in vanilla and salt. (Use within 2 hours or refrigerate for up to 1 week. Before using, bring to room temperature and beat until smooth.)
5. Transfer 1 2/3 cups buttercream to a separate bowl, stir in 10 crushed cookies. Color remaining buttercream gray with black food coloring; transfer 1 cup to a zip-top bag and snip a small hole in one corner
6. Set fence template on a baking sheet; top with parchment paper. Melt black candy melts per package directions; transfer to a zip-top bag and snip a very small hole in 1 corner. Pipe melted candy on to parchment, following template; chill.
7. Cut cake according to template. Place 1 base layer on a platter; frost top with about 2/3 cup cookie buttercream. Repeat with remaining base layer; frosting only the left- hand side. Place second-story layer on frosting; frost top with about 1/3 cup frosting; top with remaining second story layer. Place tower pieces next to the second story, frosting between the layers. Top with roof pieces, frosting between layers. Frost outside with gray buttercream. Use a cake comb to create siding texture.
8. Roll black fondant to about 1/8-inch thickness. Using templates, cut windows and door; gently press a butter knife onto the windows to create panes. Brush windows and door lightly with luster dust; attach to house. Roll together some black and white fondant and make small marbled stones for the walkway.

9. Using the gray frosting in the piping bag as "glue," decorate the roof, windows, and all outside with candies. Add the Chocolate Fence. Use remaining 7 crushed cookies to create a path.

Marshmallow Ghost Brownies

YIELDS:**12 - 16** servings TOTAL TIME:**2** hours **50** mins

INGREDIENTS

For the Brownies:

- Cooking spray
- 1 c. plus 2 tablespoons all-purpose flour, spooned and leveled
- 1 1/2 tsp. pumpkin pie spice
- 1/4 tsp. baking powder
- 1/2 tsp. kosher salt
- 1 c. semisweet chocolate chips

- 9 tbsp. (1 stick plus 1 tablespoon) unsalted butter
- 1/4 c. unsweetened cocoa powder
- 1 1/2 c. sugar
- 3/4 c. pumpkin puree
- 3 large eggs
- 1 tsp. pure vanilla extract

For the Marshmallow Ghosts:

- 1 1/4 tsp. unflavored gelatin (part of 1 envelope)
- 1/2 c. granulated sugar
- Store-bought black piping frosting

DIRECTIONS

Make the Brownies:

1. Preheat oven to 350°F. Line a 9- by 13-inch pan with parchment paper, leaving a 2-inch overhang on the 2 long sides. Grease paper.
2. Whisk together flour, pie spice, baking powder, and salt in a bowl. Melt chocolate chips, butter, and cocoa in a small saucepan over medium heat, stirring occasionally, until smooth, 2 to 3 minutes. Whisk together sugar, pumpkin puree, eggs, and vanilla in a separate bowl. Add butter mixture to sugar mixture and stir to combine. Add flour mixture and stir to combine. Transfer to prepared pan.
3. Bake until a toothpick inserted in the center comes out with a few moist crumbs attached, 20 to 22 minutes. Transfer to a wire rack and cool completely in pan. Run a knife along the two short sides of the pan and lift brownies from pan using parchment. Remove parchment and transfer brownies to a serving platter.

Make the Marshmallow Ghosts:

1. Sprinkle gelatin over 1/4 cup cold water in a bowl to soften.
2. Combine sugar and 1/4 cup water in a small saucepan. Cook over medium-high heat, stirring, until sugar is dissolved, 1 to 2 minutes. When water comes to a boil, stop stirring, and wash down sides of

the pan with a wet pastry brush to remove any undissolved sugar and prevent crystals from forming. Boil until the temperature reaches 238°F on a candy thermometer, 4 to 6 minutes.

3. Add sugar mixture to gelatin. Whisk with an electric mixer on medium speed for 3 minutes. Increase speed to high and whisk until soft peaks form, 8 to 10 minutes. Transfer marshmallow to a heavy-duty zip-top bag with a small hole cut in one corner (or a piping bag fitted with a #12 plain tip).

4. Immediately pipe ghost shapes on brownies. Let dry 1 hour. Pipe black frosting eyes and mouths. Brownies can be stored in an airtight container for 1 day.

5. The marshmallows are best made in a small saucepan. If the sugar mixture does not reach the bulb on your candy thermometer, simply tilt the pan to bring it up to the level.

Black-Bottom Brownies

YIELDS:**16** servings TOTAL TIME:**1** hour **0** mins

INGREDIENTS

Brownies

- 3/4 c. (1 1/2 sticks) unsalted butter, cut into pieces, plus more for pan
- 8 oz. bittersweet chocolate, chopped
- 1 tsp. pure vanilla extract
- 1 1/4 c. sugar
- 1/2 c. unsweetened cocoa powder
- 1/2 tsp. instant espresso powder
- 1/4 tsp. kosher salt
- 4 large eggs
- 1 c. all-purpose flour, spooned and leveled

Cheesecake topping

- 8 oz. (1 package) cream cheese, at room temperature
- 1 large egg, at room temperature
- 2 tbsp. sugar
- 1 tsp. pure vanilla extract

DIRECTIONS

1. Place a baking sheet on the middle rack of oven and preheat to 350°F. Butter an 8- by 8-inch baking pan. Line bottom and sides with parchment paper, leaving a 2-inch overhang on 2 sides; butter paper.

2. **Make the brownie:** Melt butter in a medium saucepan over medium heat; remove from heat. Add chocolate, and stir until melted and smooth. Stir in vanilla. Add sugar and stir until mixture is smooth and shiny. Stir in cocoa, espresso, and salt; cool 10 minutes.

3. Whisk eggs into chocolate mixture until incorporated. Add flour and stir until smooth. Transfer 1/4 cup batter to a bowl; set aside. Transfer remaining batter to prepared pan.

4. **Make the cheesecake topping:** Beat cream cheese with an electric mixer on medium speed until smooth, 1 to 2 minutes. Reduce mixer speed to low. Beat in egg, sugar, and vanilla until fully

incorporated, stopping to scrape down sides as necessary, 30 seconds to 1 minute. Spread over brownie batter.

5. Dollop reserved chocolate batter on top of cream cheese layer and gently swirl with a butter knife. Place the pan on top of the hot baking sheet and bake until a toothpick inserted in the center comes out with moist crumbs attached, 35 to 40 minutes. Cool in pan on a wire rack.

6. Use paper to lift brownies from pan. Remove paper and cut brownies into shapes with a witch hat cookie cutter or into 16 bars.

"Poison" Candy Apples

YIELDS:**12** PREP TIME:**0** hours **40** mins TOTAL TIME:**1** hour **0** mins

INGREDIENTS

- 12 baby Granny Smith apples
- 12 wooden candy apple sticks or dowels
- 1 1/2 c. sugar

- 1/2 c. light corn syrup
- 1 tsp. black gel paste food coloring

DIRECTIONS

1. Wash and dry apples thoroughly. Place on a baking sheet and poke firmly with dowels. Line a second baking sheet with buttered parchment paper, and set aside.

2. Place a candy thermometer in a medium saucepan and add sugar, 3/4 cups water, and corn syrup. Place over medium heat; whisk until sugar is dissolved. Let the temperature rise without stirring until it reaches the hard-crack mark at 310 degrees F. Remove pan from heat. Carefully remove thermometer, and add food coloring.

3. Swirl pan to mix in the color completely. Swipe and twirl the apple through the candy, shake off excess, and place on buttered baking sheet. Repeat with remaining apples.

Spiced Chocolate Bat Cookies

YIELDS:**1** dozen PREP TIME:**0** hours **45** mins TOTAL TIME:**2** hours **30** mins

INGREDIENTS

- 2 1/2 c. flour
- 1/2 c. dark chocolate powder
- 1/2 tsp. ground cardamom
- 1/2 tsp. ground cinnamon
- 1/2 tsp. fine sea salt
- 1/2 tsp. baking soda
- 1/2 tsp. baking powder

- 3/4 c. dark brown sugar
- 1 1/2 stick unsalted butter
- 1 large Egg
- 1/2 c. unsulphered molasses
- Silver edible sugar pearls
- granulated sugar

DIRECTIONS

1. In a large bowl whisk together first 7 ingredients until well combined; set aside.
2. Place sugar and butter in a large bowl; beat using the paddle attachment of an electric mixer. Add egg and beat until pale and fluffy, about 4 minutes. Add molasses, and mix to combine. Add flour mixture and beat until just combined, about 1 minute.
3. Divide dough in half. Place each between two pieces of parchment paper, and roll to a 3/8-inch-thick disk. Refrigerate 1 hour.
4. Heat oven to 325 degrees F. Dust countertop with cocoa powder.
5. Transfer dough to countertop and cut cookie shaped with a 6-inch bat-shaped cutter (see note) or desired size (adjust baking time accordingly). Repeat with remaining dough. Place 1 inch apart on parchment paper–lined baking sheets.
6. Bake about 12 minutes, rotating baking sheets halfway through baking, until cookies are crisp. Lightly press 2 sugar pearls into each cookie for eyes. Let cookies cool for 5 minutes on baking sheets; transfer to wire rack to cool completely.
7. Use a pastry brush to lightly coat the tops of the bat wings with water. Sprinkle with sugar and allow to set.

Peanut Butter Acorns

YIELDS:**1** dozen PREP TIME:**0** hours **15** mins COOK TIME:**0** hours **10** mins TOTAL TIME:**0** hours **35** mins

INGREDIENTS

- 3/4 c. smooth natural peanut butter
- 3/4 c. sugar
- 1 tsp. vanilla
- 1 large Egg

- 1 tbsp. flour
- 1/2 c. Mini chocolate chips
- 48 chocolate kisses

DIRECTIONS

1. Heat oven to 350 degrees F. Beat first 5 ingredients in a bowl using an electric mixer until well combined.
2. Spoon dough by rounded 1/4 teaspoonfuls onto an unlined baking sheet. Flatten each piece into a dome shape.
3. Bake about 10 minutes or until golden around edges, rotating baking sheet halfway through baking. Let cool for 5 minutes on baking sheets.
4. Microwave 1/4 cup mini chips in a small heat-proof bowl on high for 30 seconds, stirring at 10-second intervals. Dip the bottom of each chocolate kiss in melted chocolate, and place on the flat side of each cookie. Use the same method to affix a mini chip "stem" to the top of each cookie, completing the acorn.

Meringue Ghost Tartlets

YIELDS:**8** PREP TIME:**2** hours **0** mins COOK TIME:**0** hours **20** mins TOTAL TIME:**2** hours **30** mins

INGREDIENTS

Graham Cracker Crust

- 8 large graham cracker planks
- c. sugar
- 6 tbsp. melted butter

Chocolate Ganache

- 1/2 c. heavy cream
- 4 oz. bittersweet chocolate

Meringue Ghosts

- 1 1/2 c. sugar
- 6 large egg whites
- 1 tsp. cocoa powder

DIRECTIONS

1. Heat oven to 350 degrees F.
2. **To make Graham Cracker Crust:** Crush graham crackers into pieces. Transfer to the bowl of a food processor; add sugar. Process until crackers form a very fine crumb. Add butter, and pulse to combine.
3. Pack graham cracker mixture into 8 (2 1/2-inch) mini tart pans; transfer to a baking sheet, and bake 20 minutes or until the edges of the tartlets darken slightly. Let cool.
4. **To make Chocolate Ganache:** Heat cream in a small saucepan over low heat until barely simmering. Remove from heat, add chocolate, and whisk well until very smooth. Spoon into graham crusts.
5. **To make Meringue Ghosts:** Heat 3 inches of water in a saucepan over medium-high heat. Bring to a boil, and reduce heat to low. Place sugar and egg whites in a heat-proof bowl. Place bowl over the water and whisk to combine the sugar and egg whites. Stir constantly until sugar is dissolved and mixture is hot to the touch. (Rub a bit between your fingers. If it feels gritty, the sugar has not dissolved.)
6. Remove bowl from the stove and beat egg white mixture with the whisk attachment of an electric mixer until shiny stiff peaks form. Transfer meringue to a plastic pastry bag, snip the end to about 1 1/2 inches wide, and pipe 4-inch-tall ghost shapes onto the ganache.
7. Use a small paint brush dipped in cocoa to form the eyes and mouth. Serve immediately.

Chocolate Pumpkin Witch Cupcakes

YIELDS:**12** PREP TIME:**0** hours **40** mins TOTAL TIME:**1** hour **30** mins

INGREDIENTS

Chocolate Pumpkin Cupcakes

- c. cocoa powder
- 1 c. all-purpose flour
- 3/4 tsp. baking soda
- 3/4 tsp. fine sea salt
- 1/2 tsp. ground cinnamon
- 1/2 tsp. ground ginger
- tsp. ground allspice
- 1 c. brown sugar

- 11 tbsp. unsalted butter
- 3 large eggs
- 3/4 c. pumpkin puree
- 1 tsp. vanilla extract
- Hazelnut Cream Cheese Frosting
- 6 oz. black candy melts
- 12 pointy sugar ice-cream cones
- Black paper cupcake liners

Hazelnut Cream Cheese Frosting

- 1 package cream cheese
- 2 stick unsalted butter
- 1 c. confectioners' sugar

- 1/4 c. hazelnut chocolate cream spread
- 1 tsp. vanilla

DIRECTIONS

1. Heat oven to 350 degrees F.
2. Whisk first 7 ingredients in a medium bowl to combine. In a large bowl, beat sugar and butter using an electric mixer until light and fluffy. Add eggs and pumpkin puree, and beat to combine. Stir in vanilla. Add flour mixture, and beat until well combined.
3. Line a 12-cup muffin pan with paper liners. Divide mixture among prepared muffin cups, filling each 3/4 full.
4. Bake for 20 to 25 minutes or until a toothpick inserted in the center of a cupcake comes out clean.
5. Line a baking sheet with parchment paper. Microwave candy melts in a heat-proof bowl on high for 30 seconds, stirring at 10 second intervals. Use a pastry brush to cover the ice cream cones with the candy melt. Set on baking sheet to dry. Cut a 1 3/4 inch diameter hole in the center of a paper cupcake liner. Place over candy-coated ice-cream cone to form the brim of the witch's hat.
6. Frost cupcakes with Hazelnut Cream Cheese Frosting. Top each with a witch's hat.
7. **To make the Hazelnut Cream Cheese Frosting:** Place all ingredients in a large bowl. Beat until light and fluffy using the whisk attachment of an electric mixer.

Cereal Bar Hay Bales

YIELDS:**6** PREP TIME:**0** hours **35** mins TOTAL TIME:**0** hours **45** mins

INGREDIENTS

- 5 tbsp. butter
- 2 packets shredded wheat
- 15 oz. marshmallows
- 6 c. puffed rice cereal
- 6 licorice laces

DIRECTIONS

- Butter an 8-inch square pan. Crush shredded wheat in a bowl to make fine splinters.
- Melt butter in a large saucepan over medium-low heat. Add marshmallows and stir to melt completely. Stir in rice cereal. Use a rubber spatula to toss mixture and coat cereal completely.
- Turn mixture out into the prepared pan; use the spatula to flatten the mixture into the pan.
- Remove square of cereal treats from pan to cutting board. Cut in half horizontally, and then make 2 evenly spaced vertical cuts to form 6 rectangles.
- While the bars are still warm, pat the sides with crushed shredded wheat. Wrap each bale with licorice laces.

Almond Shortbread Owls

YIELDS:**2** dozen PREP TIME:**0** hours **45** mins COOK TIME:**0** hours **20** mins TOTAL TIME:**2** hours **0** mins

INGREDIENTS

- 1 1/2 c. Sliced almonds
- 2 c. all-purpose flour
- Zest of one lemon
- 1/2 tsp. fine sea salt
- 1 c. unsalted butter
- 1 c. confectioners' sugar
- 3/4 tsp. almond extract
- 1/4 c. chocolate chips
- 1/4 c. Whole Almonds
- 2 tbsp. shelled sunflower seeds

DIRECTIONS

1. Heat oven to 350 degrees F. Use a coffee grinder or food processor to grind 3/4 cups sliced almonds into a fine meal. In a large bowl, whisk ground almonds with flour, zest, and salt; set aside.
2. Combine butter, sugar, and extract in a large bowl and beat, using an electric mixer, until smooth. Add flour mixture, and stir until combined. Divide dough in half. Flatten each piece into a 1/2-inch-thick slab and wrap tightly with plastic wrap; refrigerate 1 hour or until firm.
3. Cut circles out of dough using a 2 1/2-inch diameter round cookie cutter. Place 2 inches apart on parchment paper-lined baking sheets. Use scraps of dough to make 1/4 teaspoon rounded balls of dough for the eyes. Lightly press two balls onto the top of each circle and place a whole almond on

its side between them for the beak. Insert a chocolate chip in each dough ball to make the pupil. Use sunflower seeds to make the owls' toes. Overlap 3 sliced almonds on each side for wings.

4. Bake about 20 minutes, rotating baking sheets halfway through baking, until the edges of cookies are lightly golden. Let cool on baking sheet for about 5 minutes; transfer to a wire rack to cool completely.

Nancy's Brown Butter-Hazelnut Blondies

YIELDS:**16** servings PREP TIME:**0** hours **25** mins TOTAL TIME:**2** hours **0** mins

INGREDIENTS

- 3/4 c. (1 1/2 sticks) unsalted butter, plus more for pan
- 1 1/2 c. all-purpose flour, spooned and leveled
- 1 1/4 tsp. Kosher salt

- 1 tsp. baking powder
- 1 1/2 c. packed dark brown sugar
- 1 1/2 tsp. pure vanilla extract
- 2 large eggs
- 1 1/2 c. coarsely chopped toasted hazelnuts

DIRECTIONS

1. Preheat over to 375°F. Line bottom and sides of a 9- by 9-inch baking pan with aluminum foil, leaving a 2-inch overhang on 2 sides; butter foil. Whisk together flour, salt, and baking powder in bowl.
2. Cook butter in a small saucepan over medium-high heat, stirring often, until fragrant and deep golden brown, 6 to 8 minutes. Transfer to a bowl, and let cool 10 minutes. Whisk in sugar and vanilla. Whisk in eggs, one at a time, whisking until blended after each addition. Whisk in flour mixture. Fold in toasted hazelnuts. Transfer to prepared pan.
3. Bake until wooden pick inserted in center comes out with a few moist crumbs clinging, 24 to 26 minutes. Cool completely in pan on wire rack. Use foil to lift blondies from pan. Remove foil, and cut blondies into 16 squares.

Magnifying Glass Cookies

YIELDS:**24** PREP TIME:**1** hour **0** mins TOTAL TIME:**3** hours **0** mins

INGREDIENTS

- 2 1/4 c. cups all-purpose flour, spooned and leveled, plus more for working
- 3/4 tsp. Kosher salt
- 3/4 c. (1 1/2 sticks) unsalted butter, at room temperature
- 3/4 c. sugar

- 2 tsp. pure vanilla extract
- 1/2 tsp. pure almond extract
- 1 large egg, beaten
- 1 c. finely crushed pineapple Lifesavers candy

- 1/2 c. finely crushed green apple Lifesavers candy

DIRECTIONS

1. Whisk together flour and salt in a bowl. Beat butter, sugar, and extracts on medium-high speed with an electric mixer until light and fluffy, 1 to 2 minutes. Beat in egg until blended. Reduce mixer speed to low, and gradually add flour mixture to butter mixture, beating just until flour is incorporated.
2. Divide dough in half, and flatten into 2 disks. Wrap in plastic wrap, and chill at least 2 hours or up to 3 days.
3. Preheat oven to 325°F. Line three baking sheets with parchment paper. Working with one disk at a time, on a lightly floured work surface, roll dough to 1/4-inch thickness. Use a 5 3/4-inch-long magnifying glass-shaped cookie cutter to cut as many cookies as possible; place on prepared baking sheets. Use a 2-inch round cutter to remove center from each cookie; reroll scraps, and repeat process. Freeze 10 minutes. Stir together candies in a bowl.
4. Bake until golden brown around edges, 10 to 12 minutes. Cool 3 minutes. Sprinkle crushed candies in center of each cookie, dividing evenly. Bake until candies melt, 2 to 3 minutes; swirl with a toothpick to mix colors. Cool completely on baking sheets on a wire rack.

Something-to-Hide Devil's Food Cupcakes

YIELDS:**12** PREP TIME:**1** hour **0** mins TOTAL TIME:**2** hours **0** mins

INGREDIENTS

- 1/4 c. unsweetened cocoa powder
- 6 tbsp. strong coffee
- 1 1/4 c. all-purpose flour, spooned and leveled
- 1/2 tsp. Kosher salt
- 1/2 tsp. baking powder
- 1/4 tsp. baking soda
- 1 c. sugar
- 1/2 c. (1 stick) unsalted butter, at room temperature
- 2 large eggs, at room temperature
- 1 tsp. pure vanilla extract
- 1/2 c. sour cream, at room temperature
- 1 c. blue and yellow chocolate candies (such as M&M's and Sixlets), plus more for decorating
- Cream Cheese Buttercream
- Yellow food coloring

DIRECTIONS

1. Preheat oven to 350°F. Line a 12-cup standard muffin tin with paper liners. Stir together cocoa and coffee until smooth; let cool. Whisk together flour, salt, baking powder, and baking soda in a bowl.
2. Beat sugar and butter on medium speed with an electric mixer until light and fluffy, 2 to 4 minutes. Add eggs, one at a time, beating until blended after each addition. Beat in vanilla. Reduce mixer speed to low, and beat in flour mixture and sour cream, alternately, beginning and ending with flour mixture, just until flour is incorporated. Beat in cocoa mixture.

3. Spoon batter into prepared tin, dividing evenly. Bake until a toothpick inserted in center comes out clean, 24 to 26 minutes. Cool completely in tin on a wire rack.
4. Use a tablespoon measure to scoop out a hole in the top of each cupcake. Fill with candies, dividing evenly. 5. Tint Cream Cheese Buttercream to desired shade with food coloring, and frost cupcakes. Decorate with additional candies.

Follow-the-Footprints Malted Sheet Cake

YIELDS:**12 - 16** servings PREP TIME:**0** hours **30** mins TOTAL TIME:**2** hours **30** mins

INGREDIENTS

- Baking spray
- 4 1/2 c. cake flour, spooned and leveled
- 2/3 c. malted milk powder
- 1 tbsp. baking powder
- 1 1/2 tsp. Kosher salt
- 2 1/4 c. sugar
- 1 1/2 c. (3 sticks) unsalted butter, at room temperature

- 5 large eggs, at room temperature
- 1 tbsp. pure vanilla extract
- 1 1/2 c. Buttermilk
- Cream Cheese Buttercream
- Footprint template, cocoa powder, and Candy Pearls, for decoration

DIRECTIONS

1. Preheat oven to 325°F. Spray a 9- by-13-inch baking pan. Whisk together flour, malted milk powder, baking powder, and salt in a bowl.
2. Beat sugar and butter on medium speed with an electric mixer until light and fluffy, 4 to 6 minutes. Add eggs, one at a time, beating until blended after each addition. Beat in vanilla. Reduce mixer speed to low, and beat in flour mixture and buttermilk, alternately, beginning and ending with flour mixture, just until flour is incorporated.
3. Transfer batter to prepared pan. Bake until a toothpick inserted in the center comes out clean, 55 minutes to 1 hour. Cool in pan on a wire rack 15 minutes, then invert onto a rack to cool completely.
4. Place cake on a platter, and frost with Cream Cheese Buttercream; refrigerate 15 minutes. Place template on cake, and dust with cocoa powder. Place Candy Pearls around cake base.

Basic Sugar Cookie Dough

YIELDS:**1** PREP TIME:**0** hours **25** mins TOTAL TIME:**0** hours **25** mins

INGREDIENTS

- 2 3/4 c. all-purpose flour
- 1/2 tsp. baking powder
- 1/4 tsp. Kosher salt

- 1 c. unsalted butter
- 3/4 c. granulated sugar
- 1 large Egg

- 1 1/2 tsp. pure vanilla extract

DIRECTIONS

1. In a large bowl, whisk together the flour, baking powder and salt.
2. Using an electric mixer, beat the butter and sugar until light and fluffy, about 3 minutes. Beat in the egg and then the vanilla.
3. Reduce the mixer speed to low and gradually add the flour mixture, mixing just until incorporated.
4. Heat oven to 350 degrees F. Line 2 baking sheets with parchment paper. Using floured cookie cutters, cut out cookies and place them on the prepared sheets. Reroll, chill and cut the scraps.
5. Bake, rotating the positions of the pans halfway through, until the cookies are lightly golden brown around the edges, 10 to 12 minutes. Let cool on the sheets for 5 minutes, then transfer to wire racks to cool completely.

Apple-Cardamom Cakes with Apple Cider Icing

CAL/SERV:**178** YIELDS:**24** PREP TIME:**0** hours **35** mins COOK TIME:**0** hours **25** mins TOTAL TIME:**1** hour **0** mins

INGREDIENTS

- 2 1/4 c. flour
- 1 tsp. baking soda
- 1/2 tsp. salt
- 1 tsp. ground cardamom
- 2 eggs
- 1 1/2 c. sugar
- 1 1/2 tsp. vanilla extract
- 1 c. Applesauce
- 1/2 c. butter
- 2 tbsp. butter, melted
- 1/2 c. sour cream
- 1 1/2 tsp. lemon zest
- 1 1/2 c. peeled and chopped Granny Smith apple
- 1 1/4 c. confectioners' sugar
- 3 tbsp. apple cider

DIRECTIONS

1. Heat oven to 400 degrees F. Butter and flour 24 3 1/2-ounce cake molds or 2 12-cup cupcake tins and set aside.
2. Sift the flour, baking soda, salt, and cardamom together and set aside.
3. Beat the eggs and sugar together, using a mixer set on medium-high speed, until the mixture forms a thick ribbon when the beaters are lifted from the bowl. Reduce speed to low and mix in the vanilla and applesauce. Add 1/2 cup of the melted butter, sour cream, and zest and beat until combined. Gradually add the flour mixture and mix until smooth.
4. Fold in the apples and divide the batter among the prepared molds (about 1/4 cup per mold). Bake until a skewer inserted in the center of the cake tests clean -- 20 to 25 minutes.
5. Cool for 5 minutes in the pan on a wire rack. Unmold the cakes and cool completely on the rack.

6. Stir the remaining melted butter, confectioners' sugar, and apple cider together in a medium bowl until smooth and drizzle over the cooled cakes and let the icing set before serving.

Cookie Cutter Ginger Crisps

CAL/SERV:**30** YIELDS:**14** dozen COOK TIME:**0** hours **8** mins TOTAL TIME:**1** hour **0** mins

INGREDIENTS

- 1 c. butter
- 1/2 c. brown sugar
- 1/2 c. sugar
- c. molasses
- c. light corn syrup
- 4 1/2 c. sifted flour
- 1 1/2 tsp. ground cinnamon
- 1 1/2 tsp. ground ginger
- 1 tsp. salt
- 1 tsp. baking soda
- 1/2 tsp. ground cloves

DIRECTIONS

1. Heat oven to 350 degrees F.
2. Beat butter and sugars together, using a mixer on medium speed, until light and fluffy. Beat in molasses and corn syrup until well combined. Add in the remaining ingredients and stir until a smooth dough forms. Chill for 30 minutes.
3. Roll out on a lightly floured surface to less than 1/8-inch thick. Cut with floured cutters. Bake on greased cookie sheet for 8 minutes.

How to Make Pumpkin Mousse

CAL/SERV:**531** YIELDS:**16** TOTAL TIME:**8** hours **30** mins

INGREDIENTS

- 5 large egg yolks
- 1 c. sugar
- 3 1/2 c. heavy cream
- 15 oz. Canned pumpkin
- 2 tsp. vanilla extract
- 1 1/2 tsp. ground cinnamon
- 1/2 tsp. ground ginger
- 1/4 tsp. ground nutmeg
- 1/4 tsp. salt
- 2 tbsp. dark rum
- 1 tsp. powdered gelatin
- 3 oz. shaved dark chocolate

DIRECTIONS

1. Fill a large bowl halfway with ice water and set aside.
2. Whisk the yolks, 3/4 cup plus 2 tablespoons sugar, and 3/4 cup cream together in a medium saucepan. Heat while stirring continuously with a rubber spatula or wooden spoon over medium-low heat, until thickened and the mixture coats the spatula -- about 10 minutes. Transfer to a medium bowl and set over the ice bath. Stir to cool.
3. Add pumpkin, vanilla, spices, and salt to the egg mixture. Stir 1 tablespoon rum and 1 teaspoon gelatin together in a small bowl. Heat the remaining tablespoon rum, and stir in to the gelatin mixture until dissolved. Gently whisk into the pumpkin mixture. Beat 1/2 cup cream to stiff peaks, and fold into pumpkin mixture. Pour into a shallow dish, cover and chill until cold and thick enough to fall from a spoon in heavy dollops -- about 8 hours or up to overnight.
4. Beat the remaining cream and sugar to stiff peaks. Alternately layer the pumpkin mousse and whipped cream in a glass serving dish. Sprinkle the chocolate shavings between top two layers. Serve chilled.

Maple Cupcakes

CAL/SERV:**222** YIELDS:**18** TOTAL TIME:**0** hours **45** mins

INGREDIENTS

- 2 1/2 c. all-purpose flour
- 2 tsp. baking powder
- 1 tsp. baking soda
- 1/2 tsp. salt
- 3/4 tsp. ground ginger
- 1 stick unsalted butter
- 1/2 c. light-brown sugar
- 2 large eggs
- 1 1/4 c. maple syrup
- 2 tsp. vanilla extract
- 1/2 c. Buttermilk
- 1/2 c. walnuts or pecans

DIRECTIONS

1. Heat oven to 350 degrees F. Sift together the flour, baking powder, baking soda, salt, and ginger. Set aside. Beat the butter and sugar together using a mixer set on medium speed in a large bowl until fluffy. Beat in the eggs, syrup, and vanilla. Stir in flour mixture by thirds, alternating with the buttermilk. Stir in nuts. Fill 18 lined muffin cups and bake until a tester comes out clean, about 20 minutes. Cool completely. Ice with Maple-Butter Frosting.

Upside-Down Pear Tartlets

CAL/SERV:**340** YIELDS:**6** TOTAL TIME:**0** hours **50** mins

INGREDIENTS

- 1 3/4 lb. D'Anjou pears
- 4 tbsp. butter

- 1 c. sugar
- 1 sheet puff pastry

DIRECTIONS

2. Heat oven to 400 degrees F. Peel, core, and cut the pears into 1/2 inch wedges. Melt half the butter in a skillet. Add pears and cook over medium-high heat until juices release and begin to turn golden on edges. Drain juices and reserve the pears.
3. Place sugar in a large skillet over high heat until sugar melts, bubbles, and turns amber. Add remaining 2 tablespoons butter and pears, being careful as the caramel will sputter. Turn to coat pears using a heatproof rubber spatula. Remove pan from heat and spoon pear slices into the cups of a jumbo muffin tin (3/4-cup capacity). Arrange to form a 1-inch layer.
4. Cut the pastry (it should be about 1/8-inch thick) into six 2 1/2-inch rounds. Discard or reserve scraps for another use. Top the pears in each muffin cup with a piece of puff pastry and bake until pastry puffs and is golden brown — about 25 minutes. Cool on wire rack.
5. Run a spoon around the edges of each tartlet. Remove and serve pear side up. Serve warm.

Sweet Popcorn Balls

YIELDS:**1**

INGREDIENTS

- 12 c. popped popcorn
- 3 c. mixed dried fruit such as golden raisins, cherries, and chopped apricots and figs
- 1 1/4 c. granulated sugar
- 3/4 c. brown sugar
- 1 c. corn syrup
- 1/2 c. water

DIRECTIONS

1. Toss popcorn and dried fruit together in a large, lightly oiled, heatproof bowl. Oil 2 waxed paper-lined baking pans and a long metal fork. Set aside.
2. Bring sugar, brown sugar, corn syrup, and water to a boil over medium-high heat in a medium saucepan fitted with a candy thermometer. Reduce heat to medium and cook until mixture reaches 260 degrees F.
3. Carefully pour the syrup over the popcorn mixture. Stir with the fork to distribute. Let sit for 1 to 2 minutes.
4. With well-oiled hands, form 3-inch balls, place on pans, and cool completely. Store in an airtight container for up to 4 days.

Marbled Chocolate Bark

CAL/SERV:**358** YIELDS:**8** PREP TIME:**0** hours **15** mins TOTAL TIME:**4** hours **0** mins

INGREDIENTS

- 8 oz. semisweet chocolate
- 8 oz. white chocolate
- 1/2 c. Sliced almonds
- 1/2 c. dried cranberries

DIRECTIONS

1. Line a large baking sheet with nonstick foil. Melt chocolates in separate microwavable bowls on high 2 minutes, stirring once or twice, until almost melted. Let stand 1 minute; stir until completely melted and smooth.
2. Alternately spoon melted chocolates onto prepared baking sheet and carefully spread out into a 14 x 10-in. rectangle. With an offset spatula, swirl chocolates together to create a marbled effect. Scatter almonds and cranberries evenly over chocolate. Let stand at room temperature until firm and set (or refrigerate for 1 hour to set). Break into large pieces.

Turtle Corn

CAL/SERV:**355** YIELDS:**1**

INGREDIENTS

- 16 c. fresh-popped popcorn
- 1/2 tsp. salt
- 8 oz. dark baking chocolate
- 1 tsp. Vegetable shortening
- 1 c. sugar

- 1 c. light corn syrup
- 1 c. cream
- 1/4 lb. butter
- 2 tsp. butter

DIRECTIONS

1. Coat an 11- by 17-inch baking pan with 2 teaspoons butter. Toss the popcorn and salt together and spread the popcorn in an even layer in baking pan. Set aside.
2. Place the chocolate and vegetable shortening in a double boiler or a heat-proof dish set over a pot of simmering water and stir occasionally until melted. Set aside and keep warm.
3. Combine the sugar, corn syrup, cream, and butter in a medium saucepan. Bring the mixture to a simmer and cook until the caramel reaches the firm-ball stage and reads 249 degrees F on a candy thermometer. Immediately remove from the heat and pour the caramel over the popcorn in fat ribbons.
4. Let the caramel cool. Pour the chocolate in fat ribbons over the popcorn, taking care not to completely cover the caramel. Cool completely before slicing into 3 1/4-inch squares. Store, in an airtight container, for up to 3 days.

Peanut Butter Monsters

PREP TIME 30 minutes **TOTAL TIME** 30 minutes

Ingredients

- 6 Tablespoons butter, softened
- 1/2 cup creamy peanut butter
- 1/4 cup marshmallow cream
- 1/2 teaspoon vanilla
- pinch of salt

- 2 cups powdered sugar
- 1 bag green candy melts
- 30 large candy eyes
- purple sprinkles

Instructions

1. Beat together the butter, peanut butter, marshmallow, vanilla, and salt until creamy.
2. Slowly beat in the powdered sugar. Roll the mixture into 30 even balls. Place in the refrigerator for at least an hour.
3. Melt the candy melts according to the package directions. Use a toothpick to dip the peanut butter balls in the melted candy. Place on a piece of parchment paper and pull the toothpick out. Use the toothpick to cover the hole and to drag across the melted candy to create a fur effect.
4. Press a candy eye in the front and add sprinkles to the top. Let set.

EASY HALLOWEEN CUPCAKES

prep time 15 minutes **cook time** 18 minutes **total time** 33 minutes **servings** 24 cupcakes

INGREDIENTS

Chocolate Cupcakes

- 3 large eggs
- 3/4 cup full fat sour cream
- 3/4 cup canola or vegetable oil
- 1 tablespoon vanilla extract
- 1 box (15.25 ounces) Super Moist Chocolate Fudge Cake Mix

- 1 package (3.4 ounces) chocolate pudding mix, dry
- 1/2 cup warm water (you can also use leftover coffee or add in some espresso for a heightened chocolate flavor)
- 1/2 cup walnuts, finely chopped
- 1/3 cup miniature chocolate-chips

Cream Cheese Frosting

- 1/2 cup unsalted butter at room temperature
- 1 package (8 ounces) full-fat cream cheese, at room temperature

- 1/2 teaspoon vanilla bean paste (or use 1 teaspoon pure vanilla extract)
- 1/8 teaspoon fine sea salt
- 3 cups powdered sugar

Decorating

- GHOST: miniature chocolate chips and #24 tip
- PURPLE MONSTER: purple food coloring, edible eyes, and #17 tip
- GREEN MONSTER: green food color, edible eyes, toothpicks, miniature marshmallows, and #17 tip

INSTRUCTIONS

1. Preheat the oven to 350 degrees F and line a cupcake pan with liners. Set aside.
2. In a large bowl, whisk the eggs with a fork. Add in the sour cream, canola oil, and vanilla extract. Stir until completely combined.
3. In another large bowl, add in the cake mix and pudding mix. Stir. Add in the chocolate chips and walnuts and stir until they are lightly coated in the dry ingredients. Add dry to wet. Add in the water and mix until just combined.
4. Fill cupcake liners 3/4ths the way full (batter should yield 24 cupcakes). Bake for 18-23 minutes or until a fork when inserted in the center of a cupcake comes out clean.
5. Remove and allow to completely cool before frosting.

Frosting

1. Meanwhile, prepare the frosting. Using a hand mixer, cream together the room temperature butter and cream cheese on medium-high speed until completely smooth. Mix in vanilla extract and sea salt. With mixer running on low speed, slowly add powdered sugar and beat until well blended and smooth. Chill the frosting while the cupcakes finish cooling.
2. Frost completely cooled cupcakes with cream cheese frosting and decorate to look like Halloween creatures: FOR THE GHOST: Pipe the cream cheese frosting (using a plain #24 piping tip) onto the cupcake in an upside-down cone shape. Place two mini chocolate chips near the top of the frosting for the eyes!
3. FOR THE GREEN MONSTER: Dye the cream cheese frosting green and using a #17 tip create short quick actions (while applying pressure) to add "fur" to the cupcake. Add edible eyes wherever you want on top!
4. FOR THE PURPLE MONSTER: Dye the cream cheese frosting purple and using a #17 tip create short quick actions (while applying pressure) to add "fur" to the cupcake. Using the frosting, pipe a short action on two marshmallows and attach 2 edible eyes. Using toothpicks, attach the marshmallows to the cupcakes.
5. Halloween cupcakes best enjoyed within 1-2 days.

CANDY CORN ICEBOX CAKE

Prep Time: 4 hours **Cook Time:** 0 minutes **Total Time:** 4 hours **Yield:** 12-14 Slices 1x

INGREDIENTS

- 12 oz (339g) cream cheese, room temperature
- 3/4 cup (155g) sugar
- 1/2 cup + 2 tbsp (150ml) milk, divided
- 1 tbsp vanilla extract

- 2 1/2 cups (600ml) heavy whipping cream, cold
- 1 1/4 cups (144g) powdered sugar
- Five 4.7 oz boxes Walkers Shortbread Triangles

TOPPING

1. 3/4 cup (180ml) heavy whipping cream, cold
2. 6 tbsp (43g) powdered sugar
3. 1 tsp vanilla extract

INSTRUCTIONS

1. Prepare a 9-inch springform pan by lining the sides with parchment paper that sticks about an inch above the sides of the pan.
2. To make the mousse, beat cream cheese and sugar for together in a large mixer bowl until smooth.
3. Add 2 tablespoons of milk and the vanilla extract to the cream cheese mixture and beat until smooth. Set the cream cheese mixture aside and make the whipped cream.
4. Add the heavy whipping cream and powdered sugar to a large mixer bowl fitted with the whisk attachment and whip on high until stiff peaks form.
5. Carefully fold whipped cream into cream cheese mixture.
6. Divide the cream cheese mixture evenly between 3 bowls. Leave one bowl as is (white), then color one yellow and the other orange. I like to use gel icing color – you don't have to use as much to get a strong color and it won't thin out the mixture.
7. Place the remaining 1/2 cup of milk in a small bowl. Place a single layer of shortbread cookies into the bottom of the pan, dipping each into the milk before adding.
8. Top the cookies with the yellow filling and spread into an even layer.
9. Place another layer of shortbread cookies on top of the yellow layer, dipping them in the milk first.
10. Top the cookies with the orange filling and spread into an even layer.
11. Place another layer of shortbread cookies on top of the orange layer, dipping them in the milk first Spread the final layer of white filling evenly on top of the cookies.
12. Refrigerate cake until firm, 4-5 hours or overnight.
13. Once firm, remove the springform pan sides from the cake and set on a serving plate.
14. Make the whipped cream topping. Add the heavy whipping cream, powdered sugar and vanilla extract to a large mixer bowl fitted with the whisk attachment and whip on high until stiff peaks form.
15. Pipe swirls of whipped cream around the edge of the cake and top it with some candy corn. Refrigerate until ready to serve.

Loaded Cream Cheese Halloween Brownies

prep time 10 MINUTES YIELD: 9 SERVINGS **cook time** 45 MINUTES **total time** 55 MINUTES

INGREDIENTS

Brownies

- 1/2 cup unsalted butter (1 stick)
- 6 ounces dark or bittersweet chocolate, chopped (I use 72%)
- 2 large eggs
- 3/4 cup granulated sugar
- 1 tablespoon McCormick Pure Vanilla Extract
- 1 tablespoon brewed coffee (leftover or cold coffee is okay), optional but recommended
- 1 teaspoon instant espresso granules, optional but recommended
- 3/4 cup all-purpose flour
- 1/2 teaspoon salt, or to taste

Cream Cheese Topping

- 8 ounces brick-style cream cheese, softened
- 1 large egg
- 1/4 cup granulated sugar
- 10 drops Yellow McCormick Assorted Food Color, or as needed
- 5 drops Red McCormick Assorted Food Color, or as needed
- 12 sandwich cookies (such as Oreos), chopped (I chop each cookie in 6 to 9 pieces)
- 1/2 cup semi-sweet chocolate chips

INSTRUCTIONS

Make the Brownies

1. Preheat oven to 350F. Line an 8-inch square pan with aluminum foil leaving overhang and spray with cooking spray, or grease and flour the pan; set aside.
2. To a large microwave-safe bowl, add the butter, chocolate, and heat on high power to melt, about 2 minutes. Stop to check and stir after 1 minute. Heat in 15-second increments until chocolate has melted and mixture can be stirred smooth. Allow mixture to cool momentarily before adding the eggs so they don't scramble.
3. Add the eggs, sugar, vanilla, optional coffee, optional espresso granules (neither make brownies taste like coffee and both enhance and round out the chocolate flavor), and whisk vigorously to combine.
4. Add the flour, salt, and stir until smooth and combined without overmixing.
5. Turn batter out into prepared pan, smoothing the top lightly with a spatula as necessary; set aside.

Make the Cream Cheese Topping

1. To a medium bowl, add the cream cheese, egg, sugar, and beat with a handheld electric mixer on high speed for about 2 minutes, or until mixture is smooth. Stop to scrape down the sides of the bowl as necessary.
2. Add the Yellow Food Color, Red Food Color, and mix to incorporate. As needed, add additional drops of food color to achieve the desired shade of orange. Remember to add slowly because you can't un-do it once you add it.

3. Turn mixture out over the brownie layer in heaping tablespoon-sized dollops, leaving a bare 1/2-inch perimeter around the edges (the cream cheese is prone to burning if you add it right up to the edge so leave some space). Take your time and evenly smooth the dollops together to form an solid layer.

4. Evenly sprinkles the sandwich cookies, chocolate chips, and bake for about 43 to 45 minutes, or until brownies are done. The toothpick test is tricky since you'll hit melted chocolate chips and soft cream cheese, but test a few patches and when inserting the toothpick into the deepest brownie layer, it should feel 'thick' and set and not runny.

5. Allow brownies to cool uncovered on a wire rack for about 2 hours.

6. Cover with foil and refrigerate for at least 3 to 4 hours (I prefer overnight) before slicing and serving. The cream cheese needs to be chilled and set before slicing.

boo! chocolate peanut butter bars

prep time 20 minutes cook time 10 minute total time 30 minutes servings bars calories 296 kcal

INGREDIENTS

- 1/2 cup honey
- 1/2 cup real maple syrup
- 1 cup creamy peanut butter
- 6 cups corn flakes

- 8-12 ounces semi-sweet or dark chocolate, melted
- 6 ounces white chocolate, melted
- black sprinkles, for decorating (optional)

INSTRUCTIONS

4. Line a 9x13 inch baking pan with parchment paper.

5. In a large, microwave safe bowl, melt together the honey, maple, and peanut butter until smooth, about 30 second to 1 minute. Stir in the corn flakes, tossing well to combine. Spread the mix out into the prepared pan, packing it in tightly.

6. Melt the chocolate chips and pour the melted chocolate over the bars, spreading in and even layer.

7. To make the ghosts. Melt the white chocolate, then spoon a small dollop (1 teaspoon for small ghosts and 1 tablespoon for large ghosts) of white chocolate onto the chocolate, making sure each ghost is 1 inch apart from each other. Using a wooden skewers or the end of a skinny spoon, gently drag the white chocolate into a ghost shape, don't worry about making these perfect, the more imperfect they look, the better.

8. Insert 2 small sprinkles for eyes or use additional melted chocolate.

9. Transfer the bars to the fridge and chill 1 hour or until set. Using a sharp knife, cut around the ghost, creating irregular shapes. Keep in the fridge until ready to serve. BOO!

Mummy and Monster Dirt Cups

Yield 4 -6 servings, depending on size

INGREDIENTS

- Walkers Mini Shortbread Fingers or regular Shortbread Fingers
- White candy melts or almond bark about 1 cup for 4 mummies
- Green candy melts about 1 cup for 4 monsters
- Sugar eyeballs
- Chocolate pudding mix plus the milk called for to make the pudding
- Crushed chocolate cookies I used Walkers Chocolate Scottie Dogs

INSTRUCTIONS

TO MAKE THE MONSTERS AND MUMMIES:

1. Lay cookies out on a parchment paper or wax paper lined cookie sheet.
2. Melt candy according to package directions, adding some shortening or oil to help aid in melting if needed. Place melted candy in a sandwich bag and cut off one tip. Pipe the candy over the cookies, making them look like monsters or mummies, as shown. Add eyeballs as desired. Chill to set.

TO ASSEMBLE THE DIRT CUPS:

1. Make pudding according to package directions. Place in serving cups. Top with crushed chocolate cookies. Add a monster or mummy cookie to each serving. (You can use glass dishes as I've shown, or use plastic cups for easy clean up.)
2. Store in refrigerator. Do not place the cookies in the pudding until you're ready to serve them.

BLOODY TRUFFLES

prep time1 HR chilling time1 HR total time1 HR SERVINGS: truffles

INGREDIENTS

- 1 box cake mix, any flavorprepared according to package directions
- 1 cup prepared frosting
- 48 Amarena cherries optional
- 24 oz white candy coating
- Royal icing knives axes, or similar edible weapons
- Red gel food coloring

INSTRUCTIONS

1. Prepare the cake mix according to the directions on the package, and bake it in a 9x13-inch cake pan. Once baked, allow the cake to cool completely.
2. Crumble the cake into a large bowl and work it with your hands until it is in small pieces.
3. Spoon three-quarters of the frosting into the bowl and stir with a rubber spatula until the mixture is well-combined. It should be moist and hold together if you squeeze a ball of cake between your fingers, but not too wet or greasy. If the cake mixture is still a bit dry and crumbly, add more frosting to get it to the desired consistency—the exact amount you need will depend on the texture of the cake you started with.

4. Using a small cookie or candy scoop, scoop out 1-inch balls of cake and roll between your palms until they are round. You should get about 36 balls from this recipe.
5. **Cherry Variation**: If you want a cherry filling, drain 48 Amarena cherries and gently pat them dry. Flatten out a ball of cake truffle mix on your palm, and place a cherry in the center. Gently press the cake mixture around the cherry, and roll it between your palms so it's completely covered.
6. Place the cakes balls on a baking sheet covered with parchment or waxed paper, and refrigerate them until firm, at least 1 hour. Longer is fine, and even overnight works well.
7. Place the candy coating in a medium microwave-safe bowl and microwave it until melted, stirring after every 30 seconds to prevent overheating.
8. Using dipping tools or a fork, submerge a cake ball in the melted candy coating. Remove it from the coating let the excess drip back into the bowl. Replace the dipped truffle on the baking sheet. While the coating is still wet, firmly press a royal icing knife or axe into the truffle. Repeat until all of the truffles are dipped and decorated.
9. Once all of the cake balls are dipped, refrigerate the candies to set the coating completely, about 20 minutes. Take a clean paintbrush and brush some red gel food coloring around the tops of the truffles where the royal icing decorations are.
10. These Bloody Truffles are best served at room temperature, and can be stored in an airtight container in the refrigerator for up to a week.

Jack Skellington Cheesecakes

Prep Time 30 mins **Cook Time** 15 mins **Total Time** 45 mins

Ingredients

Crust:

- 2 cups chocolate graham cracker crumbs
- 5 tablespoons light brown sugar
- 8 tablespoons butter, melted

Cheesecake Filling:

- 16 ounces 2 blocks cream cheese, softened
- 2/3 cup sugar
- 2 large eggs
- 2/3 cup sour cream
- 1 teaspoon vanilla extract or vanilla bean paste

Chocolate Ganache:

- 3 ounces dark chocolate, finely chopped or chips
- 3 tablespoons heavy whipping cream

Instructions

1. Preheat your oven to 350 Fahrenheit.
2. Stir together the chocolate graham cracker crumbs, brown sugar, and melted butter.
3. Press about 2 tablespoons of the crumbs into 18 paper-lined muffin cups.
4. Beat cream cheese on medium speed, scraping down the bowl, as needed, until creamy and smooth.
5. Add sugar and beat until light and fluffy.
6. Add egg and vanilla and beat until creamy.
7. Stir in the sour cream.
8. Equally divide cheesecake filling among the 18 muffin cups, spooning about 2 tablespoons of filling into each.
9. Bake on the middle rack in the oven for 15-18 minutes until the cheesecakes no longer look wet, but the center still jiggles.
10. Remove and set on a cooling rack.
11. Allow to cool for about an hour.
12. Combine chocolate and heavy whipping cream in a small glass measuring cup.
13. Heat in the microwave on high power for 40 seconds.
14. Let the cup sit in the microwave for 3 minutes then remove and stir until melted.
15. If needed, heat for 10 more second bursts of power, stirring after each until melted.
16. Allow this chocolate ganache to cool until slightly thickened.
17. Pour into a pastry bag or squeeze bottle fitted with a #3 round tip.
18. Pipe two eyes, two nostrils, and a mouth onto each cheesecake to make them look like Jack Skellington.

Mummy Cookies Recipe

Prep Time 5 minutes **Cook Time** 10 minutes **Refrigerate** 30 minutes **Total Time** 15 minutes
Servings 26 **Calories** 317 kcal

Ingredients

- 26 Vienna Fingers vanilla cookies
- 2 bags white candy coating
- 52 Mini M&Ms

Instructions

1. Begin by melting candy coating as directed on package.
2. Place cookie in melted candy using a fork and making sure all sides are coated. Set on waxed paper and repeat for all cookies.
3. Let candy coating set (in the fridge for half hour) or on the counter for at least 1 hour.
4. Melt more candy coating and place in a ziploc bag. Snip edge and drizzle over cookies. Add mini M&Ms as eyes. Let set. ENJOY!

Halloween Pumpkin Cookies

Prep Time: 20 minutes Cook Time: 13 minutes Resting Time: 1 hour Total Time: 33 minutes
Servings: 13 cookies Calories: 330kcal

Ingredients

Cookie dough

- 2 oz unsalted butter (room temperature, 57 g)2 oz unsalted butter (room temperature, 57 g)
- 2/3 cup light brown sugar (134 g)2/3 cup light brown sugar (134 g)
- 1/2 cup pumpkin puree (120 g)1/2 cup pumpkin puree (120 g)
- 1 large egg1 large egg
- 1 teaspoon pure vanilla extract1 teaspoon pure vanilla extract

- 1 1/2 cup all-purpose flour (195 g)1 1/2 cup all-purpose flour (195 g)
- 1/2 teaspoon baking soda1/2 teaspoon baking soda
- 1 teaspoon baking powder1 teaspoon baking powder
- 1/4 teaspoon kosher salt1/4 teaspoon kosher salt
- 1/4 teaspoon pumpkin pie spice1/4 teaspoon pumpkin pie spice

Topping

- 1 tablespoon granulated sugar1 tablespoon granulated sugar
- 1/4 teaspoon pumpkin pie spice1/4 teaspoon pumpkin pie spice
- 13 Butterfinger peanut butter skulls13 Butterfinger peanut butter skulls
- Extra melted butterExtra melted butter

Instructions

1. Add brown sugar and softened butter to a medium mixing bowl and beat with the paddle attachment until combined and fluffy, about 1 minute. Add pumpkin puree, egg, vanilla, and beat for another minute until thoroughly combined.
2. In a small bowl, whisk together flour, baking soda, baking powder, salt, and pumpkin pie spice until evenly distributed. Add the flour mixture to the pumpkin mixture with the mixer on low speed, and mix until just combined.
3. Scrape the side and bottom of the bowl to ensure everything is well mixed. Allow the dough to rest in the refrigerator for at least 1 hour or overnight.
4. Take the dough out of the fridge and divide into 13 portions, about 1 1/2 oz each. For precise measurement, use a kitchen scale. Grease your hands with melted butter and roll the dough into balls. Set them on a parchment lined baking sheet about 2 inches apart. Place the baking sheet back into the refrigerator.
5. Preheat the oven to 375°Mix granulated sugar and pumpkin pie spice together for topping and set aside.

6. When the oven is ready, take a baking sheet with the cookie dough out of the fridge. Grease the bottom of a measuring cup with melted butter and flatten the dough balls. It may be a little sticky still, slide the measuring cup from side to side to remove it from the cookie dough instead of lifting straight up. Sprinkle the sugar mixture over each cookie generously and bake for 13 minutes.
7. Let the cookies cool on the baking sheet for 8 minutes. Press a Butterfinger skull into the middle of the slightly cooled cookies. Place the cookie tray in the freezer immediately to stop the candy from melting further.

Halloween Candy Bark

PREP TIME10 mins FREEZE10 mins TOTAL TIME20 mins SERVINGS24 CALORIES42 kcal
YIELD: 24 TREATS

INGREDIENTS

- 1 lb vanilla candy bark candy melts, or white chocolate
- mini pretzel twists
- chocolate sandwich cookies with orange filling
- candy corn
- assorted sprinkles
- additional candies of your choice

INSTRUCTIONS

1. Prepare a baking sheet by lining it with a silicone liner or parchment paper; set aside. Chop or break any larger candies, cookies, or pretzels; set aside.
2. Melt the vanilla candy bark (or white chocolate) as directed on package. If heating in the microwave, use 50% power to prevent overheating the candy/chocolate. Pour about half of the melted chocolate onto the lined baking sheet, then spread about 1/4 inch thick.
3. Working quickly, add an assortment of pretzels, cookie pieces, and candy corn (or other candies) in a single layer. Pour the remaining melted chocolate on top of the pretzels and cookies, then add additional toppings, including sprinkles. Set aside and allow the chocolate to cool fully. You can place the entire baking sheet in the freezer for 10 minutes to speed up the process.
4. Once the chocolate is fully set and cool, break the candy bark into pieces. Store Halloween Candy Bark in an airtight container for up to a week.

Halloween Oreo Stuffed Rice Krispie Treats

PREP TIME10 minutes **TOTAL TIME**10 minutes

Ingredients

- 1 - 16 ounce bag mini marshmallows (8 cups)
- 6 Tablespoons butter
- 8 cups Cocoa Krispies
- 24 Halloween Oreos
- 1 -10 ounce bag dark chocolate melts
- sprinkles and candy eyes

Instructions

1. Line a 9x13 pan with foil. Use soft butter to lightly coat the bottom of the pan.
2. Place the marshmallows and butter in a large pot over low to medium heat. Stir until melted and creamy.
3. Stir in the rice krispies cereal until everything is coated.
4. Press half the cereal mixture into the bottom of the prepared pan using parchment paper.
5. Place the 24 cookies on top leaving a little bit of room around each on.
6. Spoon the rest of the cereal mixture on top and press down with more parchment paper. Make sure to get some for the cereal down in between each cookie. Let cool.
7. Melt the bag of chocolate melts according to the package directions. Pour on top of the cooled treats and spread out evenly. Top with sprinkles and candy eyes before it sets.
8. Let the chocolate set, then cut the rice krispies treats into 24 squares. Store in a tightly sealed container.

GHOST POPCORN BALLS

yield: 8-10 BALLS DEPENDING ON THE SIZE additional time: 1 HOUR total time: 1 HOUR

Ingredients

- 16 cups popped popcorn (about 1 standard size bag of popcorn)
- one 10 oz bag of mini marshmallows
- 1/2 stick butter (1/4 cup)
- 1 package Wilton bright white candy melts
- candy eye balls (I used regular sized ones)

Instructions

1. Place the popcorn in a large bowl (or 2 large bowls to make mixing easier).
2. In a large pot over medium heat, melt the mini marshmallows and butter. Stir occasionally until smooth.
3. Pour the melted mixture over the popcorn (dividing between 2 bowls if you divided the popcorn). Stir with a spatula until the popcorn is coated.
4. Butter your hands and begin to form the popcorn into balls. You can make taller balls like the shape of a ghost, or whatever you prefer.

5. Place the balls on a baking sheet lined with a silicone mat or parchment paper. Allow the balls to cool and firm up. (30 minutes to 1 hour)
6. Melt the white candy melts according to the package. You can add vegetable shortening or vegetable oil to help thin out the chocolate if desired. Dip the tops of the popcorn balls into the melted chocolate and return to the baking sheet. Allow the chocolate to set for 1-2 minutes before adding candy eye balls to each ball. You can try to add the eyes right away, but they may slide off if the chocolate is too hot.
7. Allow the chocolate to set before serving. If you'll be serving them the next day, place them in a tupperware container.
8. You can display them in a fun way! You can display them in a large tray on top of halloween colored m&ms with some fake spiders added in!

Mini Monster Chocolate Whoopie Pies with Orange Cream Filling

Prep Time15 mins Cook Time10 mins Total Time25 mins Servings: 60 whoopie pies
Calories: 141kcal

Ingredients

Mini Monster Chocolate Whoopie Pies

- 4 cups flour
- 1-1/3 cups cocoa
- 2-1/2 teaspoons baking soda
- 1 tablespoon salt
- 1 cup butter softened

- 2 cups brown sugar
- 2 eggs
- 2 tablespoons coffee prepared
- 2 teaspoons vanilla
- 2 cups chocolate milk

Orange Cream Filling

- 1 cup butter softened
- 4 cups powdered sugar
- 1/4 cup milk

- 2-3 drops orange food coloring
- candy eyes

Instructions

Mini Monster Chocolate Whoopie Pies

1. Preheat oven to 350 degrees.

2. In a large bowl, add flour, cocoa, baking soda, and salt.
3. Whisk dry ingredients together to combine. Set aside.
4. In the bowl of an electric mixer, add butter and sugar.
5. Cream together on medium speed until light and fluffy.
6. Add egg, coffee and vanilla to bowl.
7. Mix together on medium speed until thoroughly combined.
8. Add half of flour mixture to mixing bowl.
9. Mix on low speed until almost fully combined, being careful not to over mix.
10. step.
11. Add half of chocolate milk to mixing bowl and mix together on low speed until combined.
12. Repeat three previous steps again so that all of the flour mixture and chocolate milk are added and combined.
13. Using a tablespoon scoop, scoop batter onto parchment or silicone mat lined baking sheet, leaving approximately 2" around each cake.
14. Bake at 350 degrees for 8-10 minutes or until cakes spring back to the touch. Cool halves completely.

Orange Cream Filling

1. Add butter and half of the powdered sugar in the bowl of an electric mixer.
2. Cream together on medium speed until light and fluffy.
3. Add remaining powder sugar.
4. Cream together on medium speed until fully combined.
5. Add milk and food coloring to mixing bowl.
6. Mix together on medium speed until food coloring is completely incorporated and frosting is light and fluffy.

Assemble Whoopie Pies

1. Fill large pastry bag with orange cream frosting and pipe on the bottom of one whoopie pie half.
2. Top frosting covered half with another pie half to create whoopie pie.
3. Dot the back of candy eyes with frosting to adhere to whoopie pie to create face.

SPIDER OREO POPS

prep time 20 minutes **total time** 20 minutes **servings** 20 -25 pops

INGREDIENTS

- 1 package of your favorite Oreos
- 1 bag (12 ounces) milk chocolate chips
- 48 edible candy eyeballs
- 1 bag string black licorice laces
- Optional: vegetable oil or shortening -- makes the chocolate easier to work with

- Lollipop sticks
- Parchment Paper

INSTRUCTIONS

1. Line a large tray with parchment paper and set aside. Gently separate the oreos by slowly twisting them apart. (Some will break, it's okay, just try to be gentle)
2. Separate the milk chocolate into 3 parts (this is to keep it from getting hard while you decorate) and place each section in a microwave safe bowl.
3. Into each bowl of chocolate chips add about 1/2 teaspoon vegetable oil or shortening (more if needed to thin it even more).
4. Melt in 20 second bursts in the microwave (Microwave 20 seconds, stir 20 seconds, etc.)
5. Be patient when melting and stir well in between bursts to avoid burning the chocolate.
6. Dip one end of the lollipop stick into the melted chocolate and press that side into the cream side of the oreo. Cut the licorice laces into even pieces about an inch long. Press 4 cut licorice laces into the cream of the right side of the oreo and 4 more cut licorice laces into the cream on the left of the oreo.
7. Place the other half of the oreo on top and gently press and hold. Let harden.
8. Gently spoon melted chocolate over the top of the oreos being careful to avoid the licorice (its okay if some chocolate gets on the licorice).
9. Gently place two edible eyes into the melted chocolate and set the finished (but still wet) oreos onto the prepared tray lined with parchment paper (if you don't use parchment paper they won't come up nicely).
10. Allow to harden at room temperature.

Halloween Muddy Buddies

Ingredients

- 9 cups Rice Chex cereal
- 1 cup semisweet chocolate chips
- ½ cup peanut butter
- ¼ cup butter
- 1 teaspoon vanilla extract
- 1 ½ cups powdered sugar
- 1 cup Kit Kats cut into small pieces
- ½ cup candy corn Hershey's fun size
- candy skulls
- sprinkles
- edible eyeballs

Instructions

1. In a large bowl, microwave chocolate chips, peanut butter and butter for 1 minute; stir. Return to microwave for 30 seconds or until mixture is smooth.
2. Stir in vanilla extract.
3. Combine chocolate mixture with Chex cereal. Stir until evenly coated.
4. Combine cereal and powdered sugar; mix until well coated.
5. Add candy, sprinkles and eyeballs.
6. Store in airtight container

RICE KRISPIE TREAT MUMMIES

Prep Time: 10 MINUTES Servings: 6

INGREDIENTS

- 6 snack-size rice krispie treats6 snack-size rice krispie treats
- 3 cup white chocolate chips3 cup white chocolate chips
- black edible piping gel or icing (found near cake decorating supplies)black edible piping gel or icing (found near cake decorating supplies)
- optional: red food coloringoptional: red food coloring

INSTRUCTIONS

1. Unwrap rice krispie treats and set aside. Place white chocolate chips in a microwave-safe bowl and microwave on half power for 2 minutes. Stir and return to microwave for 20 seconds at a time (still on half power) stirring after each until chocolate is completely melted and smooth.
2. Dip rice krispie treats in the chocolate being sure to coat the front and sides (the back side can remain uncovered). Place uncovered-side-down on a foil-lined plate or small baking sheet.
3. Repeat process with remaining rice krispie treats. Transfer plate/baking sheet to fridge or freezer to cool for 2-3 minutes.
4. While treats are cooling, spoon melted white chocolate into a small zip lock bag. Remove treats from fridge/freezer. Use scissors to snip off a tiny bit of one bottom corner of the chocolate-filled bag, then drizzle chocolate in a random pattern over the treats to create the look of mummy wrapping. Return treats to fridge or freezer for 1-2 minutes.
5. Pipe two dots onto each rice krispie treat to create mummy eyes. (Optional step, dip a Q-tip in red food coloring and dap two dots onto the rice krispie treats before adding the eyes to create a creepy "bloodshot" look.) Serve or store in airtight container up to 1 week.

Chocolate Monster Cookies

Prep Time: 1 hour Cook Time: 15 minutes Total Time: 1 hour 15 minutes

Ingredients

ganache:

- 1 1/2 cups chocolate (coarsely chopped (I used 60% Ghirardhelli))1 1/2 cups chocolate (coarsely chopped (I used 60% Ghirardhelli))
- 1 cup heavy cream1 cup heavy cream
- 2 tablespoons unsalted butter (room temperature)2 tablespoons unsalted butter (room temperature)

Also needed:

- one jumbo marshmallow for teethone jumbo marshmallow for teeth

Instructions

how to make the ganache:

1. Place coarsely chopped chocolate in a medium sized heat safe bowl and set aside.
2. In a small saucepan over medium heat bring the heavy cream to a boil. You just want to get it to the point of a boil and then remove it from the heat as soon as it does.
3. Pour the scalded heavy cream over the chocolate and let stand for 2-3 minutes undisturbed until chocolate has softened.
4. Slowly whisk the mixture until smooth and add the room temperature butter. Whisk until butter is melted and incorporated.
5. Either add ganache to pastry bag or place plastic wrap directly on the surface of the ganache and allow to cool at room temperature for 2-4 hours.

To assemble monster cookies:

1. Match cookie pairs according to size. Put the first cookie face down. Pipe on some ganache, making it thicker on one side. Place top cookie on ganache and press down on only one side to give the illusion of an open mouth.
2. Use additional ganache on top to make your eyes stick.
3. Cut out small teeth from the marshmallow. Get creative!
4. Store in an airtight container if not eaten right away.

Strawberry Ghosts

Prep time 45 mins **Total time**45 mins Serves: 24

Ingredients

- 1 (16 oz) package Vanilla CANDIQUIK Coating
- 24 Fresh strawberries
- Mini chocolate chips

Instructions

1. Melt Candiquik in tray according to directions on package.
2. Place a large piece of wax or parchment paper on a flat surface.
3. Dip strawberries in melted Candiquik Coating, remove and allow the excess coating to pour off onto the wax paper to form the "tail" of the ghost; slide the strawberry back and set on wax paper to dry.
4. Before coating has set, place two mini chocolate chips on as the eyes. For the mouth, cut off the tip of a mini chocolate chip and place on the strawberry with the bottom side facing up.

Candy Corn Pudding Pops

Servings: 4 people Calories: 149 kcal

Ingredients

- Small box 3.3 oz Instant Jello Pudding – White Chocolate Flavor for white layer
- Large Box 5.1 oz Instant Jello Pudding - Vanilla Flavor for yellow and orange layer
- Honey
- Red and Yellow food coloring
- 4 cups of milk

Instructions

1. Prepare White Chocolate Jello by mixing pudding mix with 1 1/2 cups of cold milk.
2. Note: This is less milk than the box directions call for. This makes the pudding pops richer and creamier.
3. Stir in 1 teaspoon of honey and transfer pudding mixture to a large plastic baggie.
4. Prepare Vanilla Pudding by mixing pudding mix with 2 1/2 cups of cold milk.
5. Again, a little less than the box calls for.
6. Stir in two teaspoons of honey and divide pudding into two bowls.
7. Color one bowl with yellow food coloring, adding just a few drops at a time.
8. Next, color the other bowl orange by combing yellow and red food coloring.
9. Transfer the yellow and orange pudding to a plastic baggie.
10. Snip corner of plastic baggies and squeeze pudding into popsicle molds.
11. Start with white layer and finish with yellow.
12. Tap mold on counter between layers to reduce air bubbles and level the layers.
13. Freeze pudding pops 2-3 hours or overnight.

Graveyard Chocolate Cheesecake Dip

Prep Time: **20m** Yield: **6 - 8 servings**

INGREDIENTS

Chocolate Cheesecake Dip

- 1 package cream (8 ounce) cheese, room temperature
- 1/4 cup (1/2 stick) unsalted butter, room temperature
- 5 tablespoons cocoa powder
- 2 tablespoons Imperial Sugar Light Brown Sugar
- 1/2 teaspoon vanilla extract
- 1/4 teaspoon kosher salt
- 2 tablespoons milk

- 2 cups, plus 2 tablespoons sifted Imperial   Sugar Confectioners Powdered Sugar

To Decorate and Serve

- 10 crushed chocolate cream sandwich cookies
- Vanilla sandwich cookies, such as Milanos
- Black decorating icing
- Candy corn and pumpkins
- Graham crackers, apple slices, and/or pretzels, for serving

DIRECTIONS

1. In a medium bowl, beat together cream cheese and butter until smooth. Sift in cocoa powder, then add brown sugar, vanilla extract, salt, and milk. Beat on low speed until the cocoa powder is incorporated, then increase speed to high until very well combined. Sift in powdered sugar 1/2 cup at a time, beating slowly after each addition to incorporate. Increase speed to high and beat until smooth and light, about 3 minutes. Transfer dip to a serving dish and smooth top with a spatula.
2. Spread crushed chocolate cookies over top of dip to form "dirt." With decorating icing, write "RIP" on vanilla wafer cookies, then stand upright in dip to form "tombstones." Scatter candy corn and candy pumpkins over top to decorate. Serve with graham crackers, sliced apples, and/or pretzels as desired.

Pumpkin Spice Rice Krispie Treats

SERVINGS 12 to 15 treats (using a 9 x 9 inch pan)

Ingredients

- Nonstick cooking spray
- 3 Tablespoons unsalted butter
- 1/4 cup pumpkin puree
- 1 10 oz. bag mini marshmallows
- 1/4 teaspoon vanilla extract
- 1/2 teaspoon ground cinnamon
- 1/4 teaspoon ground nutmeg
- 1/8 teaspoon ground cloves
- 1/8 teaspoon salt
- 6 cups crispy rice cereal
- 2 oz. pure white chocolate white chocolate candy melts, melted, optional

Instructions

1. Choose your desired size baking pan (I used a 9x9, but for thinner treats use 11x7 or 13x9) and spray generously with nonstick cooking spray. Set aside.
2. In a large saucepan (I used a 5.5 qt. Dutch oven), melt butter over medium heat. Stir in pumpkin puree and cook until warmed through. Fold in marshmallows, stirring frequently until melted. Remove from heat and stir in vanilla, cinnamon, nutmeg, cloves and salt.
3. Let marshmallow mixture cool at room temperature for 20 minutes (cooling helps avoid soggy treats). Add the crispy rice cereal and stir until combined.

4. Pour mixture into prepared baking pan, spread out evenly and gently press down with a rubber spatula. Refrigerate to set for at least 1 hour. Cut into squares and drizzle with melted white chocolate, if desired.
5. Store in an airtight container up to one week.
6. Enjoy!

HALLOWEEN CANDY BARK

PREP TIME: 5 MINUTES TOTAL TIME: 10 MINUTES SERVINGS: 16 CALORIES: 233

INGREDIENTS

- 1 package of vanilla or chocolate almond bark I've used candiquik too
- 1 cup orange candy melts
- Optional toppings: Candy corn crushed OREO's, Candy eyeballs, crushed pretzels, M&M's, sprinkles, nuts, any other leftover Halloween candy

INSTRUCTIONS

1. Lay out a large sheet of wax paper and get all of your toppings ready.
2. Melt the chocolate in the microwave according to package directions. Then pour chocolate onto wax paper. Smooth with a spatula.
3. Melt orange melts in the microwave according to package directions. Place spoonfuls onto the chocolate and then swirl with a toothpick.
4. Top with your toppings immediately. Let cool and then break into pieces or cut with a large knife.

HALLOWEEN MARSHMALLOW POPS

yield: 12 servings prep time: 5 minutes total time: 5 minutes

INGREDIENTS

- 12 Campfire Giant Roasters
- 1 10-ounce bag candy melts
- assorted sprinkles

INSTRUCTIONS

1. Line a baking sheet with parchment paper or a silicone baking mat.
2. Insert a lollipop stick into each Campfire Giant Roaster.
3. Melt candy melts according to package directions.

4. Working with one marshmallow at a time, spoon the melted candy over the sides of a marshmallow and allow the excess to drip back into the bowl. Immediately coat with festive sprinkles. Place marshmallow on prepared baking sheet until the candy coating is set.
5. Repeat with remaining marshmallows.

Movie Night Caramel Corn

Ingredients

- 2 bags popped popcorn
- 1 cup brown sugar
- 1/2 cup light Karo Syrup
- 1/2 cup butter
- 1/2 teaspoon salt

- 1/2 teaspoon baking soda
- 1 teaspoon vanilla
- 1/2 cup white chocolate
- 1 tablespoon coconut oil or crisco
- sprinkles

Instructions

1. Preheat oven to 250 degrees. Generously spray a large shallow pan with nonstick cooking spray.
2. In a large saucepan, combine brown sugar, karl syrup, butter and salt on medium heat.
3. Continue stirring until mixture begins to boil.
4. Once boiling, stop stirring and cook for an additional 5 minutes.
5. Pour popped popcorn into shallow pan.
6. Remove pan from heat and add vanilla and baking soda while stirring.
7. Carefully pour caramel over popcorn and stir to coat all popcorn.
8. Bake in preheated oven for 1 hour, but stirring the popcorn every 15 minutes.
9. Allow to cool (popcorn will harden once cooled) then break apart.
10. Melt white chocolate and crisco or coconut oil in the microwave for 1 minute.
11. Remove from microwave and stir. If it is not smooth, reheat in intervals of 15 seconds, stirring in between each interval.
12. Pour melted chocolate into a sandwich bag and snip the corner. Drizzle chocolate over popcorn then sprinkle with sprinkles.
13. Store in an air tight container for up to 1 week.

Melted Witch Bark Recipe

Prep Time 5 minutes **Cook Time** 10 minutes **Total Time** 15 minutes **Servings** 8 melted witches
Calories 251 kcal

Ingredients

- 1 bag Wilton Candy Melts vibrant green
- 1/2 cup mini chocolate chips divided

- 8 pretzel sticks
- 8 mini Reese's Peanut Butter Cups
- 8 Halloween Oreos
- 8 Hershey's Hugs

Instructions

1. Begin by laying out parchment paper on a cookie sheet.
2. Get pretzels sticks, Reese's, Oreos, Hugs, mini chips out and ready so they are easy to grab.
3. Place 1 cup candy melts in a small pot and melt on low heat stirring constantly. Once all melted spoon out onto parchment paper and spread into a circle. We made ours about 4 inches in diameter.
4. Quickly add remaining mini chips to a small pot and melt on low heat stirring constantly. Spoon a tiny amount onto your green circles and use a toothpick to swirl around.
5. Add Oreos as hat in the corner. Add Hugs by dipping into excess melted chocolate and adding to the top of the Ore. Add mini chips for eyes.
6. Stick pretzels in your mini Reese's and place on the opposite side of the Oreo.
7. Let set until ready to eat or package.

Bloody Cups for Halloween (Vegan & Gluten-Free)

PREP TIME15 mins COOK TIME10 mins TOTAL TIME25 mins SERVINGS8 CALORIES97 kcal

INGREDIENTS

- 1 cup frozen raspberries
- 1 tablespoon rice syrup or maple syrup or agave syrup
- 1 cup + 3/4 cup (150g + 100g) vegan baking chocolate (or chocolate chips)

INSTRUCTIONS

1. Heat the frozen raspberries in a small pot on medium-high heat until soft, mash the raspberries until there are no large chunks anymore & add the rice syrup. Give it a mix and set aside to cool.
2. In a double boiler, melt 1 cup of the chocolate. Meanwhile place 8 muffin liners in a muffin pan.
3. Place about 1 1/2 teaspoon of melted chocolate in the muffin liners and tilt them, so the chocolate spreads to the sides. Repeat for all the muffin liners and place it into the fridge for a few minutes (until the chocolate hardens).
4. Melt 3/4 cup of vegan chocolate in the double boiler. Meanwhile add about a teaspoon of the raspberry filling into the chocolate coated muffin liners (place it in the middle). Once the chocolate has melted, pour it over the raspberry filling. Tilt it a bit so the top is covered with the chocolate completely. Let it harden in the fridge for about 5 minutes.
5. Once the chocolate is hard, carefully remove the cupcake liners and enjoy.

PUMPKIN CHEESECAKE TRUFFLE MUMMIES (NO BAKE)

Prep Time: 20 MINUTES Chill Time: 30 MINUTES Total Time: 50 MINUTES
Servings: 14

INGREDIENTS

- 1 1/2 cups gingersnap cookie crumbs1 1/2 cups gingersnap cookie crumbs
- 1/4 cup canned pumpkin puree1/4 cup canned pumpkin puree
- 1/3 cup graham cracker crumbs1/3 cup graham cracker crumbs
- 3 tablespoons powdered sugar3 tablespoons powdered sugar
- 1/4 teaspoon ground cinnamon1/4 teaspoon ground cinnamon

- 1/8 teaspoon salt1/8 teaspoon salt
- 3 ounces cream cheese, softened3 ounces cream cheese, softened
- 1/2 cup white chocolate chips1/2 cup white chocolate chips
- white chocolate chips or white dipping chocolate (like CandiQuik)white chocolate chips or white dipping chocolate (like CandiQuik)
- red food coloringred food coloring

INSTRUCTIONS

1. In a large bowl combine gingersnap crumbs, pumpkin puree, graham cracker crumbs, powdered sugar, cinnamon, salt, and cream cheese. Mix until smooth. Melt 1/2 cup white chocolate chips and mix into truffle mixture.
2. Cover and chill until dough is solid enough to roll into balls - about 1 hour in the fridge or 30 minutes in the freezer. When cold enough, roll mixture into 12-14 balls. Place a toothpick in each ball.
3. Melt remaining white chocolate chips or white dipping chocolate in a small bowl. Use toothpicks to dip each truffle ball into the white chocolate, being sure to coat all sides. Gently shake off excess chocolate. Place chocolate-covered truffle balls on a baking sheet or plate lined with wax paper, parchment paper, or foil. Chill for 3-5 minutes until chocolate hardens.
4. Drizzle more white chocolate over the truffles. Soak the end of a Q-tip in red food cloring. Dap 2 dots of food coloring to make the mummy eyes. Handle carefully so you don't wipe off the eyes. Store chilled in airtight container.

Mummy Pumpkin Cookies

Prep Time: 40 minutes Cook Time: 20 minutes Yield: 9 mummies 1x

Ingredients

For the Crust :

- 1 cup (2 sticks) unsalted butter cut into cubes-chilled
- 2 and 1/2 cups all-purpose flour
- 1 teaspoon salt

- 1 teaspoon sugar
- 4 Tablespoons ice water
- (or you can use 1 package Refrigerated Pie Crust (2 crusts))

For filling and topping:

- 3/4 cup reduced pumpkin puree (place 1 cup pumpkin puree on several layers of paper towel, wrap and press to soak excess moisture until you get 3/4 cup pumpkin puree)
- 2 oz cream cheese -slightly softened
- 2 tablespoons packed light-brown sugar
- 2 tablespoons granulated sugar
- 1 teaspoon ground cinnamon

- 1/2 teaspoon ground ginger
- 1/4 teaspoon of nutmeg
- 1/8 teaspoon allspice
- 1 egg yolk
- 1/2 teaspoon vanilla extract
- 1 egg white-lightly beaten
- 1/2 tablespoon water
- 2 tablespoon sugar
- 1 teaspoon cinnamon

Instructions

1. To make the crust pulse together in a food processor flour, salt and sugar, then add butter and pulse until look like a coarse meal (don't over-process, just pulse until butter is no longer in large pieces). Add chilled water 1-2 tablespoon at the time and pulse several times(if it doesn't come together in clumps add remaining water). If you don't have a food processor you can make the dough using two fork or pastry blender. Gather dough onto working surface, divide into two portions, shape each into 5-inch disk, cover with plastic wrap and chill 1 hour.
2. To make the pumpkin pie filling in a bowl stir together cream cheese, granulated sugar and brown sugar to blend. Add reduced pumpkin puree to cream cheese mixture along with cinnamon, ginger, nutmeg and allspice. Mix in egg yolk and vanilla extract. Cover bowl and chill until ready to assemble the cookies.
3. Preheat oven to 375 F and line large baking sheet with parchment paper, set aside.

To assemble the mummies:

1. Roll out first disk of the dough onto a floured surface to about 13 x 11-inch rectangle . If the edges start to crack a little when rolling, seal them and continue rolling. Trim edges to get straight edges, then cut into rectangles(I made nine 4×3 rectangles, but you can make them smaller or larger, what ever you prefer) Roll out second dough disc and cut into 1/2 inch stripes.
2. Arrange the rectangles, spaced apart on prepared baking sheet and spread heaping 1 1/2-2 tablespoons of pumpkin pie filling onto each rectangle, leaving rim on all sides uncoated. Brush uncoated edges with the mixture of lightly beaten egg white and 1 Tbsp water. Top with strips to create mummy look, then seal edges with your fingertips, and trim the excess of the stripes. Brush the stripes with egg whites and sprinkle with mixture of 2 Tbsp sugar and 1 tsp. cinnamon.
3. Bake until golden brown about 20 minutes.
4. Stick candy eyes onto cooled mummies.

Pumpkin Candy Cups for Halloween

yield: 8-10 candy cups

Ingredients

- 12 oz orange melting chocolate wafers
- Small round water balloons
- 1/4 cup milk melting chocolate wafers
- 5 cups assorted Halloween candy, like Pumpkin Spice Malted Milk Balls,Candy Corn, Monster Mash Mix Jelly Beans, Mellocreme Pumpkins, and Halloween Jordan Almonds

Directions

1. Place the orange melting wafers in a microwave-safe bowl. Microwave them in 30-second increments, stirring after every 30 seconds, until melted and smooth. The texture should be on the thinner side–it should flow nicely from a spoon. If it seems thick or clumpy, stir in a spoonful or two of shortening, until it flows freely. Set aside to cool until it is barely warm. If you try to make these candy cups when the melted wafers are hot, the balloons will explode and it will be a huge mess!
2. While you wait for the wafers to cool, blow up the balloons until they're the size you want your candy cups to be, and tie them off. This recipe yields 8-10 candy cups (depending on how large you make them) but you should blow up a few extra balloons just in case.
3. When the coating is still melted but no longer very warm to the touch, hold a balloon by the knot and dip it in the melted coating until it comes halfway up the sides of the balloon. Rotate it around so that the sides are evenly coated. Remove the balloon from the coating and let the excess drip back into the bowl.
4. Place the dipped balloon on a baking sheet covered in parchment or waxed paper. Repeat with the remaining coating and balloons.
5. Once all the balloons are dipped, refrigerate the tray to set the coating, for about 20 minutes.
6. To remove the balloons from the candy shell, hold the balloon tightly right below the knot. Cut a small hole above your fingers, and carefully loosen your grip so that a small amount of air can escape. Gently let the air out of the balloon slowly and steadily. Use your other hand to help pull the balloon away from the side of the candy as it deflates. When most of the air has left the balloon, very gently peel it away from the bottom of the candy. Repeat until all of the balloons are removed.
7. If you'd like, you can use a paring knife to level the tops of the cups and remove any uneven edges. You can also just run your finger along the top to smooth any ridges down.
8. Melt the chocolate melting wafers. Pour them into a plastic bag and snip a very small hole in the corner, or use a parchment paper cone. Draw simple pumpkin faces on the side of your candy cups. (Alternately, you can use food markers specifically designed for candy–they are commonly available at craft stores like Michaels.)
9. Fill the candy cups with a mix of your favorite Halloween candy. Enjoy! Cups can be stored at cool room temperature for several months–the candy coating has a long shelf life.

BROWNIE CUPCAKES

YIELD 20 CUPCAKES **PREP TIME** 15 MINUTES **COOK TIME** 18 MINUTES
ADDITIONAL TIME 10 MINUTES **TOTAL TIME** 43 MINUTES

INGREDIENTS

- Brownie Mix
- White Cake mix
- Cupcake Liners

INSTRUCTIONS

1. Mix up a batch of brownies.
2. Mix up a box of White Cake Mix and color it with orange food coloring.
3. Add a spoonful of brownie mix to the cupcake liners. The brownie batter should only go about 1/3 of the way up the cupcake liner. You want more cake batter than brownie batter.
4. Then cover the brownie batter with the orange cake batter.
5. Bake the cupcakes as you normally would, 15-20 minutes in a 350 degree oven.
6. Make a batch of our Best Buttercream Frosting to top your Brownie Cupcakes.
7. Add Halloween Sprinkles

Pumpkin Patch Dirt Cups

INGREDIENTS

- 1 box Instant Chocolate Pudding
- 3 cups milk
- 2 packages Oreos
- 1 package Green Sour Straws Candy
- 1 package Pumpkin Candies

INSTRUCTIONS

1. Make the pudding by following directions on the box (whisk together pudding mix and 3 cups cold milk).
2. Use a food processor to crush the Oreos until smooth.
3. Layer the Oreos and chocolate pudding in a clear cup. Oreos, pudding, Oreos, pudding, and top with Oreos.
4. Top with a Green Sour Straw candy cut in half (the pumpkin vine) and three pumpkin candies.
5. Serve with a spoon!

Marbled Candy Apples

Prep Time: 20 minutes Cook Time: 10 minutes Total Time: 30 minutes Calories: 563kcal

Ingredients

- 6 Granny Smith apples6 Granny Smith apples
- 3 cups sugar3 cups sugar
- 1 cup water1 cup water
- 1/2 cup light corn syrup1/2 cup light corn syrup
- 1 teaspoon vanilla extract1 teaspoon vanilla extract
- White food coloringWhite food coloring
- 2 additional colors of food coloring, we used teal and green gel
- coloring2 additional colors of food coloring, we used teal and green gel coloring
- Candy thermometerCandy thermometer
- Parchment paperParchment paper
- 6 lollipop sticks, for dipping and twigs if you want to go with a fall look.6 lollipop sticks, for dipping and twigs if you want to go with a fall look.

Instructions

1. Prep your apples by washing and drying them. Take the stems off and put the lollipop sticks in as far as they can go. Put your apples near the stove so they're close by when you need them. Prep a cookie sheet with parchment to keep close as well.
2. In medium a sauce pan, mix the sugar, water and corn syrup. Attach the candy thermometer to the side of the pot, but make sure it's not touching the bottom of the pan. Heat over medium high heat and let bubble without mixing, until it reaches 302 degrees.
3. Once it reaches that temperature, immediately take off of the heat and with a heat-proof rubber spatula.
4. Mix in the vanilla extract and the white food coloring until combined.
5. Quickly add a few drops of the two other colors.
6. Use a wooden skewer to gently stir the colors, but don't mix.
7. Just lightly move the colors around. Tip the pot to one side and dip the apple in the candy, coating it on all sides.
8. When you pull the marbled candy apple out of the sugar, give it a second to drip off the bottom, then place it on the parchment paper to cool and harden.

Mini Caramel Pumpkin Pies

yield: 24 prep time: 20 MINUTES cook time: 35 MINUTES total time: 55 MINUTES

Ingredients

- 1 cup pumpkin puree
- 1/2 cup granulated sugar

- 2 tsp cornstarch
- 1 tsp vanilla
- 1/2 tsp ground cinnamon
- 1/4 tsp ground nutmeg
- 1/8 tsp ground cloves
- 1/8 tsp salt
- 1 egg, beaten
- 1/2 cup evaporated milk
- 1/4 cup caramel ice cream topping
- 2 pie crusts, I used Pillsbury refrigerated
- 2 tbsp butter, melted
- Orange sanding sugar sprinkles
- 2 green Laffy Taffy Ropes, or other green chewy candy cut into 24 pieces

Instructions

1. Whisk together pumpkin puree, sugar, cornstarch, vanilla, cinnamon, nutmeg, cloves and salt.
2. Whisk in the beaten egg.
3. Whisk in the evaporated milk and caramel.
4. Roll out the pie crusts and cut about twenty-four 2 3/4 inch circles.
5. Brush the pie crust circles with melted butter and sprinkle with orange sanding sugar, if desired.
6. Press into a silicone mini bundt pan or mini muffin pan and add about one tablespoon of the caramel pie filling to each one.
7. Bake at 350 degrees for 30-35 minutes.
8. Allow the mini caramel pumpkin pies to cool completely before carefully removing them from the pan. Gently press them upward from the bottom of the pan.
9. Before serving, add a green stem cut from green chewy candy.

Candy Corn Pretzel Hugs

Prep Time: 5 minutes **Cook Time:** 4 minutes **Total Time:** 20 minutes **Yield:** as many as you want

YIELD: 12 JACK SKELLINGTON OREO POPS

Ingredients

- circle or square-shaped pretzels
- Hershey's Kisses Hugs (or any flavor Kiss)
- candy corn

Instructions

1. Preheat oven to 250°F (121°C).
2. Line baking sheet with parchment paper or a silicone baking mat. Align pretzels on the sheet. Unwrap Hugs and place one on each pretzel. Stick in the oven until the hug begins to melt down. Mine takes about 4 minutes.
3. While the Hugs are melting in the oven, get your candy corn ready because you will have to move quickly once the pretzels are out of the oven.

4. Remove pretzel hugs from oven and gently press a candy corn down on each one. The Hug should flatten out when you press the candy corn on it. If it is not flattening out, place the pretzel hugs back in the oven for 30 more seconds.
5. Let the pretzel hugs cool completely and let the chocolate set for about 10 minutes in the refrigerator.

JACK SKELLINGTON OREO POPS

PREP TIME15 minutes **COOK TIME**5 minutes **TOTAL TIME**20 minutes

INGREDIENTS

- 12 Oreos
- White chocolate candy coating/White chocolate candy melts
- Black Edible Marker (I use the AmeriColor Black Edible Markers now)

- MATERIALS
- Lollipop Sticks
- Black Ribbon
- Baking Sheet lined with Foil

INSTRUCTIONS

1. Melt the candy melts according to package directions. Pour into a short glass.
2. Add a dab of chocolate to the end of the lollipop stick and stick a lollipop stick into the cream filling of each Oreo. Lay Oreo pops onto the foil lined baking sheet.
3. Stick into the freezer for 1 minute. (This step is optional but it helped me keep the Oreos on the Stick)
4. Remove Oreo pops from freezer.
5. Dip the Oreos into the white chocolate one at a time. Covering each one and tapping off the excess chocolate. Place back onto the foil lined baking sheet.
6. Place into the fridge for 5 minutes or until chocolate is hard.
7. Remove Oreo pops from fridge.
8. Using an edible marker, draw Jack Skellington's face onto each pop. If you have trouble with the marker "drying out" while you're drawing the faces, lightly wet a paper towel and press the tip of the marker onto the wet paper towel and then continue to draw the faces. (I've been using AmeriColor Black Edible Markers for about a month now and love them)
9. Tie on Jack's bow to finish the pops.

HALLOWEEN PRETZEL TREATS ~ CANDY SPIDERWEBS

Prep Time: 20 minutes **Cook Time**: 10 minutes **Total Time**: 30 minutes **Servings**: 9 to 12 webs (per 16-ounce package of candy coating) **Calories**: 289kcal

INGREDIENTS

- Wax paperWax paper
- Pretzel sticksPretzel sticks
- 16 ounces vanilla/white chocolate candy coating16 ounces vanilla/white chocolate candy coating
- Halloween sprinklesHalloween sprinkles
- 1/2 cup chocolate chips1/2 cup chocolate chips

INSTRUCTIONS

1. Use an approximately 8-inch diameter bowl to trace circles onto wax paper. Cut out and place wax paper circles on cookie sheets and arrange 8 pretzel sticks on each circle so that they are touching in the center and radiating outwards.

2. Melt the candy coating according to package directions (do not overheat). Stir until smooth and transfer to a gallon-sized heavy-duty/freezer plastic bag. Snip a 1/4-inch hole in the corner of the bag and pipe a flat circle in the center of the pretzels where they meet. Starting at the center and working outwards, make a spiraling line across the pretzels until a spiderweb look is achieved. Stop before reaching the tips of the pretzels so that they stick out a bit beyond the outermost ring. Pipe over the outermost ring several times in order to make it thicker, so that the sprinkles have a place to adhere.

3. Pour sprinkles in a bowl and use a small spoon to carefully pour sprinkles over the thick outer ring of the spiderweb.

4. Place chocolate chips in a microwave safe bowl and heat in 30-second increments, stirring well in between, until chocolate is melted and smooth. Transfer melted chocolate to a small plastic baggie and snip a tiny hole in the corner of the bag. In the center of each spider web, make a spider by starting with the legs. Draw a thin plus sign (+) topped with an X, which should end up looking like 8 small legs. Fill in a small circle of chocolate on top for the spider's body. Place two tiny sprinkles on top for eyes.

5. Allow webs to dry for several hours until completely set. Carefully peel spiderwebs from wax paper (if you are able to do so without breaking), or serve directly from wax paper circles.

Eerie eyeball pops

Prep:30 mins **Cook:**5 mins plus chilling **Makes 10**

Ingredients

- 100g/4oz madeira cake
- 100g Oreo cookie
- 100g bar milk chocolate, melted
- 200g bar white chocolate, melted

223

- few Smarties and icing pens, to decorate
- You will also need
- 10 wooden skewers
- ½ small pumpkin or butternut squash , deseeded, to stand pops in

Method

STEP 1

Break the Madeira cake and cookies into the bowl of a food processor, pour in the melted milk chocolate and whizz to combine.

STEP 2

Tip the mixture into a bowl, then use your hands to roll into about 10 walnut-sized balls. Chill for 2 hrs until really firm.

STEP 3

Push a skewer into each ball, then carefully spoon the white chocolate over the cake balls to completely cover. Stand the cake pops in the pumpkin, then press a Smartie onto the surface while wet. Chill again until the chocolate has set. Before serving, using the icing pens, add a pupil to each Smartie and wiggly red veins to the eyeballs.

Halloween slash cake

Prep: 45 mins **Cook:** 30 mins plus cooling **Serves 16**

Ingredients

- 140g unsalted butter , plus extra for the tin
- 100ml grapeseed oil , or another flavourless oil
- 200ml milk
- 3 tbsp yogurt
- 1 tsp vanilla extract
- 2 large eggs , at room temperature
- 250g light muscovado sugar
- 250g plain flour
- 3 tsp baking powder
- 50g cocoa powder
- ¾ x 340g jar strawberry jam
- 1¼ kg ready-to-roll white fondant icing
- For the buttercream
- 600g icing sugar , sifted, plus extra for dusting
- 300g butter , softened
- red food colouring

Method

STEP 1

Heat the oven to 180C/160C fan/gas 4. Butter and line the bases of two 20cm sandwich tins. Melt the butter in a pan, then remove from the heat and beat in the oil, milk, yogurt, vanilla and eggs. Whisk the dry ingredients together with a large pinch of salt, squishing any lumps of sugar with your fingers. Tip the wet ingredients into the dry, then whisk until smooth.

STEP 2

Divide the batter between the tins and bake for 25-30 mins on the same shelf of the oven until risen and a skewer inserted into the middle comes out clean. Leave to cool for 10 mins in the tins, then transfer to a rack to cool completely.

STEP 3

To make the buttercream, beat together the sugar, butter and a few drops of the red food colouring. Add 2-3 tbsp of boiling water if needed to soften the mixture, until you end up with a smooth, spreadable icing.

STEP 4

Trim the cakes flat if needed, then halve each through the middle using a large serrated knife. Put one cake layer on a board or plate, spread over a thin layer of the buttercream and dot over a third of the jam. Top with another cake layer and repeat with the buttercream, jam and cake, finishing with a layer of cake. Use most of the remaining buttercream to ice the cake all over, reserving a small amount.

STEP 5

Roll the fondant icing out on a surface dusted with icing sugar until large enough to cover the top and sides of the cake. Carefully lift it up onto the cake and smooth down to help it to stick. Use a sharp knife to cut slashes into the icing, then drizzle a little of the reserved buttercream mixed with some water into each to look like blood.

Spider biscuits

Prep: 25 mins **Cook:** 12 mins Plus cooling and setting **Makes 20**

Ingredients

- 70g butter, softened
- 50g peanut butter
- 150g golden caster sugar
- 1 medium egg
- 1 tsp vanilla extract

- 180g plain flour
- ½ tsp bicarbonate of soda
- 20 peanut butter cups, Rolos or Maltesers
- 100g milk chocolate, chopped
- icing eyes, or make your own

Method

STEP 1

Heat oven to 180C/160C fan/gas 4 and line two baking sheets with parchment. Using an electric hand whisk, cream the butter, peanut butter and sugar together until very light and fluffy, then beat in the egg and vanilla. Once combined, stir in the flour, bicarb and ¼ tsp salt.

STEP 2

Scoop 18-20 tbsps of the mixture onto the trays, leaving enough space between each to allow for spreading. Make a thumbprint in the centre of the cookies. Bake for 10-12 mins or until firm at the edges but still soft in the middle – they'll harden a little as they cool. Leave to cool on the tray for a few mins before topping each biscuit with a peanut butter cup, Rolo or Malteser. Transfer to a wire rack to cool completely.

STEP 3

Heat the chocolate in the microwave in short bursts, or in a bowl set over a pan of simmering water, until just liquid. Scrape into a piping bag and leave to cool a little. Pipe the legs onto each spider, then stick two eyes on each. Leave to set. Will keep for three days in an airtight container.

Grasshopper cocktail

Prep:5 mins No cook **Serves 1**

Ingredients

- ice
- 25ml crème de menthe
- 25ml white crème de cacao
- 25ml single cream
- To garnish
- mint sprig
- 25g melted chocolate (optional)

Method

STEP 1

Start by making the garnish. Take a sprig of mint, strip off the leaves at the base and dip the stalk in the melted chocolate, holding the upper leaves gently. Leave to set on a plate or tray.

STEP 2

Fill a cocktail shaker with ice then pour in the liqueurs and cream. Shake hard until the outside of the cocktail shaker is cold, then strain in to a cocktail glass or small coupe. Garnish with the chocolate-dipped sprig of mint.

Eyeball & hand fruit punch

Prep:10 mins plus overnight freezing, no cook **Serves 14-15**

Ingredients

- 425g can lychees
- 225g jar cocktail cherries
- 15 raisins
- 1 litre carton blueberry, blackberry or purple grape juice , chilled
- 1 litre carton cherry or cranberry juice , chilled
- 1 litre sparkling water , chilled
- You'll also need
- 2 pairs powder-free disposable gloves

Method

STEP 1

Rinse the disposable gloves and fill each with water. Tie a knot in the top of each as you would a balloon, or use a tight bag clip to hold the opening closed. Freeze overnight.

STEP 2

Drain the lychees and cocktail cherries, reserving the juices in a jug. Push a raisin into one end of each cherry, then push the cherries into the lychees to make 'eyeballs'.

STEP 3

Tip all of the juices, plus the reserved lychee and cherry juices, into a large bowl with the 'eyeballs'. Carefully peel the gloves from the ice hands, add to the punch, then top up with the sparkling water.

Halloween cupcakes recipe

Prep:25 mins **Cook:**20 mins plus cooling and decorating **Makes 22**

Ingredients

- 200g butter, softened
- 300g golden caster sugar
- 200g dark chocolate, melted
- 2 eggs
- 250g self raising flour
- ¼ tsp baking powder mixed with 100ml boiling water
- 50g cocoa powder
- 200ml milk
- 1-2 tsp black food colouring (optional)

For the buttercream

- 300g unsalted butter , softened
- 500g icing sugar
- 1 tsp vanilla extract
- black food colouring

For the decorations

- pack of Smarties
- black icing pen
- 1 pack mixed coloured fondant icing (you'll need pink, green, blue and white)
- liquorice and strawberry laces and other sweets such as jelly fangs and liquorice allsorts
- icing eyes (see tip, below)

Method

STEP 1

Heat oven to 180C/160C fan/gas 4. Line two 12-hole cupcake tins with cases. Beat the butter and sugar until the mixture is creamy. Beat in the chocolate and the eggs until combined, then stir in the flour and baking powder, cocoa powder, milk and food colouring, if using. Spoon the mixture evenly between the cupcake cases, levelling the tops.

STEP 2

Bake for 20 mins or until the cakes are risen and springy to the touch. Cool for 5 mins in the tin, then lift out onto a wire rack to cool completely.

STEP 3

To make the buttercream, beat the butter until soft, then stir in the icing sugar a little at a time. Beat in the vanilla and some black food colouring, then transfer to a piping bag fitted with a plain nozzle.

STEP 4

For the cat face, pipe the black buttercream in an even swirl onto the cupcake and smooth with a palette knife. Pipe two ears by making a blob for each and pulling the icing bag upwards to a point. Add two eyes on each with Smarties and use the black icing pen to paint a pupil onto each. Add a triangle nose made of pink fondant icing and create whiskers with sweets.

STEP 5

For the monster faces, cut circles of green and blue fondant to fit the tops of the cupcake and fix them in place with a little buttercream. Add eyes, noses and mouths made of sweets or use icing eyes (see tip, below). For skeletons, cut out shapes with white fondant and fix in place with the buttercream.

Candy apples

228

Ingredients

- 8 red apples
- 400g caster sugar
- 1 tsp lemon juice
- 4 tbsp golden syrup

- a few drops red food colouring (optional)
- You will also need
- 8 sticks , chopsticks or lolly sticks

Method

STEP 1

Remove the stalks from the apples, then put them in a heatproof bowl and pour over boiling water from the kettle to cover them and leave for 3-4 mins. Remove with a slotted spoon and pat dry. (This removes the protective wax from the skin and makes the toffee stick to the apples better.)

STEP 2

Push the sharpest end of each stick into the stalk-end of each apple, making sure it's firmly wedged in. Put a large piece of baking parchment on a board.

STEP 3

Tip the sugar into a large saucepan, add the lemon juice and 100ml water. Bring to a simmer and cook until the sugar has dissolved. Swirl the pan gently to move the sugar around, but don't stir. Add the golden syrup and simmer the mixture (be careful it doesn't boil over) until it reaches 'hard crack' stage or 150C on a sugar thermometer. If you don't have a thermometer, test the toffee by dropping a small amount into cold water. It should harden instantly and, when removed, be brittle. If it's soft, continue to boil. When it's ready, drip in some food colouring, if you like, and swirl to combine. Turn off the heat.

STEP 4

Working quickly, dip each apple into the toffee, tipping the pan to cover it fully. Lift out and allow any excess to drip off back into the pan before placing on the baking parchment. Repeat with the remaining apples. Gently heat the toffee again, if you need to. Leave to set. Best eaten on the same day.

Halloween cheeseboard with creepy crackers

Prep:20 mins **Cook:**15 mins plus cooling **Makes 30**

Ingredients

- selection of cheeses , including an orange one, blue-veined variety, white one, and if you can find it, a charcoal-coated cheese
- figs , black grapes and celery, to serve
- For the creepy crackers
- 2 tbsp olive oil

- 150g plain flour , plus extra for sprinkling
- 1 tsp sea salt flakes
- 1 tsp golden caster sugar
- 1 tbsp black sesame seeds , plus 1 tsp for sprinkling
- black food colouring

Method

STEP 1

Heat the oven to 220C/200C fan/gas 7. Mix the olive oil with 60ml water, then put in a bowl with the flour, salt, sugar, sesame seeds and a few drops of the food colouring. Mix with your hands until you have a rough dough. If it's too sticky, add a little more flour until it's smooth.

STEP 2

Sprinkle a non-stick baking mat or a sheet of baking parchment with some flour, roll the dough out to the thickness of a £1 coin, then use a pizza cutter or knife to cut it into skinny strips. Brush the strips with a little water and sprinkle with some salt and extra sesame seeds. Prick each strip with a fork.

STEP 3

Transfer the strips with the mat to a baking sheet, separating the strips with a palette knife, and bake for 12-15 mins, or until the crackers are firm and feel hard. Leave to cool. Will keep in an airtight container for up to two weeks. Arrange your selection of cheeses with the fruit and crackers on a serving board.

Healthy Halloween pizzas

Prep:20 mins **Cook:**10 mins **Serves 4**

Ingredients

- 200g strong white flour
- 200g strong wholewheat flour
- 1 tsp or 7g sachet easy-blend dried yeast
- 250ml warm water

For the topping

- 300g passata
- 1 garlic clove , crushed

- 1 tbsp olive or rapeseed oil
- 75g grated mozzarella
- 10 black olives
- handful cherry tomatoes , halved
- handful basil leaves , to serve

Method

STEP 1

Mix the flours and yeast with a pinch of salt in a food processor fitted with a dough blade, or combine in a bowl. Pour in the water and mix to a soft dough, then work for 1 min in a processor or 5 mins by hand. Remove the dough, divide into 4 pieces and roll out on a lightly floured surface to rounds about 15cm across. Lift onto heavily oiled baking sheets.

STEP 2

Mix the passata with the garlic, oil and a little seasoning. Spread over the dough to within 2cm of the edges. Scatter with the mozzarella. Halve the olives and tomatoes. Place an olive in the centre of each pizza to make the spider's body. Cut the rest into little legs and arrange them around the spider bodies. Dot the tomatoes here and there. Leave to rise for 20 mins. Heat oven to 240C/ fan 220C/gas 9 or the highest setting.

STEP 3

Bake the pizza for 10-12 mins until crisp and golden around the edges. Scatter with the basil to serve.

Devilled eggs

Prep:20 mins **Cook:**10 mins plus at least 3 hrs soaking **Makes 24 halves**

Ingredients

- 12 eggs
- red, orange, green or black food colouring , or a mixture
- 1-4 tbsp vinegar
- 3 tbsp mayonnaise , plus extra if the eggs are large
- 1 small red pepper , finely chopped
- a few tarragon sprigs , finely chopped (optional)
- paprika , for sprinkling

Method

STEP 1

Put the eggs in a single layer in a pan and add enough water to cover them by 2cm. Bring to the boil, then cover, turn off the heat and leave for 12 mins. Drain, cool completely in very cold water, then drain again.

STEP 2

Put the different food colourings into separate bowls or containers that will hold the eggs, using 1 tsp food colouring per bowl, plus 700ml water and 1 tbsp of the vinegar each. Gently tap the eggs all over using a spoon or knife to crack the shells without removing them. Divide the cracked eggs between the bowls with the food colourings, submerge them in the liquid and leave to soak for at least 3 hrs, or ideally overnight. If you can't submerge them fully, turn the eggs every hour so that they stain evenly.

STEP 3

Drain, rinse and peel the eggs, then halve them and pop the yolks into a bowl. Add the mayonnaise, adding a little more if you need to in order to create a slightly stiff paste, then mix in 3 tbsp of the chopped pepper and the tarragon, if using. Spoon the yolk mixture back into the whites, then sprinkle over the remaining pepper and the paprika.

Kiwi slime pies

Prep:25 mins **Cook:**30 mins plus cooling

Ingredients

- 320g shop-bought ready-rolled shortcrust pastry
- 4 egg yolks , plus 1 egg white (freeze the remaining whites to make meringues another day)
- 400ml milk
- 35g golden caster sugar
- 1 heaped tbsp plain flour
- 5 cubes green jelly
- 2-3 green and golden kiwi fruit , peeled and sliced

Method

STEP 1

Heat the oven to 190C/170C fan/gas 5. Divide the pastry into eight equal pieces. Roll each out until large enough to line deep 7-8cm fluted tartlet tins or eight holes of a large muffin tin. Line the tins with the pastry, leaving a little sticking up above the rims, then line with paper cases and baking beans. Put the tins on a baking tray and bake for 10 mins, then remove the paper and beans, brush with the egg white and bake for 5-10 mins more until crisp and golden. Leave to cool for 5 mins, then remove from the tins and leave to cool completely.

STEP 2

Put the milk in a pan and bring almost to the boil, then remove from the heat. Put the egg yolks, sugar and flour in a bowl and whisk with an electric whisk until pale and fluffy – it should leave a trail that stays on the surface momentarily when the whisk is lifted. Pour a third of the hot milk into the bowl, slowly whisking all the time, until it has all been mixed in. Whisk in the remaining milk.

STEP 3

Return the mixture to the pan, scraping it out using a rubber spatula. Bring slowly to the boil, stirring, until the custard is thick, smooth and glossy. At first, it will look a bit lumpy, but keep stirring and it will become smooth. Reduce the heat and simmer for 2 mins, stirring. Stir in the jelly until the cubes have dissolved. Leave the mixture to cool until just warm, then divide it between the baked tart cases. Top each with a slice of kiwi and leave to cool completely.

Spooky surprise truffles

Prep:20 mins **Cook:**5 mins plus 2 hrs chilling

Makes 20-25

Ingredients

- 100ml double cream
- 200g dark chocolate , chopped into small pieces
- 5 capers , drained, rinsed and patted dry
- 5 small sour fizzy sweets
- 1 olive , cut into 5 pieces
- cocoa powder or chocolate sprinkles, for rolling

Method

STEP 1

Pour the cream into a pan and bring just to the boil. Put the chocolate in a large bowl, then pour over the hot cream. Stir until the mixture is smooth and all the chocolate has melted. Leave to cool, then transfer to the fridge and chill for 2 hrs, or until solid.

STEP 2

Scoop out a teaspoonful of the mixture, poke a caper, sweet or piece of olive into the centre and roll into a walnut-size ball with your hands. Repeat with the remaining fillings, then roll the remaining mixture into balls without any filling. Roll the truffles in cocoa or sprinkles. Chill until ready to serve.

Black cat cake

Prep:50 mins **Cook:**1 hr and 40 mins Plus drying and cooling

Serves 16

Ingredients

- icing sugar , for dusting
- 100g each black and yellow or orange fondant icing
- 200g butter , cubed, plus extra for the tin
- 200g dark chocolate , chopped
- 1 tbsp instant coffee granules
- 170g plain flour

- ½ tsp bicarbonate of soda
- 400g golden caster sugar
- 30g cocoa powder
- 3 medium eggs
- 75ml milk
- 1 heart-shaped jelly sweet , plus Pocky sticks, Matchmakers or liquorice sticks

For the frosting

- 150g butter , very soft
- 330g icing sugar
- 60g cocoa powder
- 4 tbsp milk
- 100g dark chocolate

Method

STEP 1

Lightly dust your work surface with icing sugar, then roll out a quarter of the black fondant icing to the thickness of a £1 coin. Cut out two triangles for the ears and leave to dry overnight.

STEP 2

Heat oven to 160C/140C fan/gas 3. Butter and line a 20cm round cake tin (about 7.5cm deep). Put the dark chocolate in a medium pan with the butter. Mix 1 tbsp coffee granules into 125ml cold water and add to the pan. Warm over a low heat until just melted – don't let it boil. Alternatively, melt in the microwave for about 5 mins, stirring halfway through.

STEP 3

Mix the flour, bicarb and sugar with the cocoa powder. Beat the eggs with the milk. Pour the melted chocolate mixture and the egg mixture into the flour mixture and stir everything together to make a smooth batter.

STEP 4

Pour the batter into the tin and bake for 1 hr 25-1 hr 35 mins until a skewer inserted into the centre of the cake comes out clean and the top feels firm (don't worry if it cracks a bit). Leave to cool in the tin for 30 mins – the top may sink a little as it cools – then turn out onto a rack to cool completely. Cut the cake horizontally into three.

STEP 5

To make the frosting, put the butter in a bowl and beat until light and fluffy. Gradually beat in the icing sugar and cocoa powder, then stir in enough milk to make the icing fluffy and spreadable. Sandwich the layers of the cake together using a small amount of frosting. Melt the chocolate in a microwave or small bowl set over a pan of simmering water, then stir it into the remaining frosting. Use the mixture to cover the sides and the top of the cake.

STEP 6

Stick the black fondant ears into the top of the cake. Cut out two yellow or orange fondant circles to make the eyes and use the black fondant to make the pupils. Stick these onto the cake and add a heart-shaped jelly sweet for the nose. Use Pocky sticks, Matchmakers or liquorice cut into lengths for the whiskers.

Pastry snakes

Prep:27 mins **Cook:**14 mins

Serves 20

Ingredients

- 320g pack ready-rolled puff pastry
- 50g grated parmesan or vegetarian alternative
- flour , for dusting
- 1 egg , beaten
- poppy seeds , nigella seeds, sesame seeds or celery seeds, to decorate
- black or green peppercorns

Method

STEP 1

Heat the oven to 220C/200C fan/ gas 7. Unroll the pastry and top with a couple of handfuls of parmesan, then fold in half. On a lightly floured surface, roll the pastry out to a thickness of 2mm. Cut into 1cm strips, then twist each strip several times to form a snake.

STEP 2

Lay out the snakes on a baking sheet, then brush each one with egg and sprinkle with more cheese. To decorate, scatter over the seeds. Flatten one end of each snake and press in two peppercorns for eyes. Bake for 12-14 mins, or until golden. Leave to cool. Will keep for two days in an airtight container.

Chocolate-covered Halloween pretzels

Prep: 15 mins **Cook:** 5 mins Plus setting

Serves 15

Ingredients

- 100g white chocolate chips
- 100g dark chocolate chips
- 100g milk chocolate chips
- 200g giant pretzels
- edible eyes (available in the baking aisle, or make your own)

Method

STEP 1

Melt each batch of chocolate chips in separate bowls, either in the microwave or set over a pan of simmering water. If melting in the microwave, heat each batch on high in 30-second bursts. Leave to cool until thick.

STEP 2

Dip a third of the pretzels into the white chocolate, a third of the pretzels into the dark chocolate and the remaining pretzels into the milk chocolate, then lay them all out on a sheet of baking parchment.

STEP 3

Add edible eyes to each pretzel (three eyes looks extra spooky). Leave to set, then peel carefully off the paper. Will keep in an airtight container for up to a week.

Halloween biscuits

Prep: 45 mins **Cook:** 25 mins

Serves 7 - 8

Ingredients

For the biscuits

- 200g unsalted butter , softened
- 200g golden caster sugar
- 1 large egg
- ½ tsp vanilla extract
- 400g plain flour , plus extra for dusting
- 20g popping candy (or rainbow sprinkles for very young children)

For decoration

- White, black and grey sugar paste
- 100g icing sugar

Method

STEP 1

Heat oven to 200C/180C fan/gas 6 and line a baking sheet with baking parchment.

STEP 2

Put the butter in a bowl and beat with electric beaters until soft and creamy. Beat in the sugar, then the egg and vanilla, and finally the flour to make a dough. If the dough feels a bit sticky add a little more flour and knead it in. Wrap in cling film and put in the fridge for half an hour.

STEP 3

Heavily flour a surface and cut the pastry in half. Roll out one half to 5mm thickness. Using a cookie cutter in the shape of a ghost (or any spooky shaped cutter you like), cut out 12 ghost shapes, which will make 4 cookies. Put the cut shapes on a baking tray lined with baking paper and put back in the fridge. Repeat with the second half of the pastry. Swap into the fridge, taking the chilled ghost biscuits out.

STEP 4

Using a smaller cutter or a knife, cut a ghost-shaped hole in the middle of 4 of the biscuits on the tray, this is the space to store the surprise centre! Put these biscuits into the oven to bake for 10-12 mins, until pale but cooked through. Transfer to a wire rack to cool. Repeat with the other tray.

STEP 5

Once all the biscuits have cooled completely, they are ready to be assembled. Mix the icing sugar with 3 tbsp of water and mix well. It should be quite thick so add a little more icing sugar if the mixture is too runny. Take a biscuit without the centre missing, and spread or pipe a little icing around the edge. Press a biscuit with a centre missing on top, then sprinkle popping candy into the pocket that you have created (or rainbow sprinkles as an alternative, if you're serving to very young children). Spread icing on the edge of the second biscuit and press another whole biscuit on top. Set aside to firm up. Make sure you leave them for a while so they don't slide when you are finishing the decoration.

STEP 6

Once the biscuits feel firm and the icing has set, use the sugar paste to decorate them as you please, rolling it out, cutting it to shape and topping the biscuits. You may have to use a little of the icing to glue it down. Decorate with icing pens if you like.

Pumpkin hummus

Prep:10 mins **Cook:**50 mins

Serves 8

Ingredients

- 1 small pumpkin (about 500g)
- olive oil , for roasting
- 2 garlic cloves , peeled
- ½ lemon , juiced
- 2 tbsp tahini paste

- 400g can chickpeas , drained
- 1 red pepper , deseeded, and sliced
- 1 yellow pepper , deseeded, and sliced
- mini breadsticks and pitta chips, to serve

Method

STEP 1

Cut the top off the pumpkin, about two-thirds of the way up. Remove the pumpkin seeds, then scoop the flesh out of the bottom and the lid.

STEP 2

Heat oven to 200C/180C fan/gas 6. Cut the pumpkin flesh into pieces and put in a roasting tin with the garlic and a good glug of oil. Season, then bake for 45 mins until very tender. Leave to cool.

STEP 3

Tip the pumpkin into a food processor with any juices from the roasting tin and the garlic. Add the lemon juice, tahini paste and chickpeas. Season with salt and blend to a paste – add a little more oil if it's too thick. Scoop the hummus back into the pumpkin and serve with the peppers, breadsticks and pitta chips.

Healthy pumpkin pancakes

Prep:10 mins **Cook:**30 mins

Makes 9 large or 27 mini pancakes

Ingredients

- 200g plain flour
- ½ tsp baking powder
- 200ml milk

- 100g cooked butternut squash or pumpkin, mashed
- 1 egg , separated

Method

238

STEP 1

Tip the flour into a bowl and add the baking powder. Measure the milk into a jug and stir in the butternut squash, followed by the egg yolk.

STEP 2

Make a well in the centre of the flour and gradually add the milk mixture until you have a lump-free batter. Alternatively, tip everything into a blender and whizz it.

STEP 3

Whisk the egg white until stiff, then fold it into the batter.

STEP 4

Heat a non-stick pan and cook 1 large or 3 small pancakes at a time (if making small pancakes, use 1 tbsp for each). Wait until lots of bubbles have risen to the top and the surface has begun to dry out before turning them over, but keep an eye on the base to make sure it doesn't get too brown. Repeat with the remaining mixture.

Spider's web cake

Prep: 1 hr and 15 mins **Cook:** 40 mins

Serves 15

Ingredients

For the cake

- 110g unsalted butter , plus extra for greasing
- 3 tbsp cocoa powder
- 140ml chocolate stout (we used Young's Double Chocolate Stout, available from Tesco)
- 170g white caster sugar
- 170g light brown soft sugar
- 1 tsp vanilla extract
- 3 large eggs , lightly beaten
- 100g dark chocolate , melted and cooled
- 280g plain flour
- 2 tsp bicarbonate of soda

For the white chocolate buttercream

- 3 large egg whites
- 240g caster sugar
- 360g unsalted butter , room temperature
- 200g white chocolate , melted and cooled

To decorate

- 100g white mini marshmallows
- 25g black sugar paste

Method

STEP 1

Heat oven to 180C/160C fan/gas 4. Grease three 20cm round cake tins and line the bases with baking parchment. To make the cake, put the cocoa in a bowl, add 280ml boiling water and whisk until dissolved. Pour in the stout, mix, then set aside to cool.

STEP 2

In a stand mixer or a large bowl using an electric hand whisk, beat together the butter, both sugars and vanilla extract until light and fluffy (about 5 mins). Add the eggs little by little, mixing until fully incorporated before adding more. Once all the egg has been added, spoon in the melted chocolate and mix to combine.

STEP 3

In another bowl, mix the flour, bicarb and 1/2 tsp salt. Add this mixture to the butter mixture in three stages, alternating with the stout mixture (which will be very runny). Pour the batter equally between the prepared tins and bake for 25-30 mins until a skewer inserted into the cake comes out clean. Leave to cool in the tins for 10 mins, then turn out onto a wire rack to cool completely.

STEP 4

To make the buttercream, put the egg whites and sugar in a heatproof bowl and set over a pan of gently simmering water. Stir with a whisk until the sugar has dissolved and the mixture is warm to the touch. Remove the bowl from the heat and beat with an electric hand whisk on high speed until the mixture has tripled in volume and has cooled down. Slowly add the butter 1 tbsp at a time while continuing to whisk. Once all the butter has been added, the mixture should look glossy and thick – if it doesn't, keep whisking until it does, or if the bowl still feels warm, chill for 10 mins before whisking again. Once ready, mix in the melted white chocolate.

STEP 5

To assemble the cake, put one of the cake layers on a cake stand and top with a layer of buttercream. Repeat with the other two layers. Spread the remaining buttercream all over the cake, using a spatula or palette knife to smooth the sides. Chill for 1 hr or until the buttercream is firm (see tip, below).

STEP 6

To decorate, melt the marshmallows in a heatproof bowl set over a pan of simmering water, stirring from time to time. Remove from the heat and put to one side for a few mins until the mixture is cool enough to handle. Use your fingers to grab a small amount of the marshmallow and stretch it out to form long strands (dipping your fingers in vegetable or sunflower oil will help!) Drape the strands over the cake in a random pattern, so it's thoroughly covered. Create a spider using the sugar paste (roll two balls, one bigger than the other, for the body, and thin strands for the legs) and place on top of the cake. Will keep for up to three days in an airtight container.

Halloween punch

Prep:10 mins **Cook:**5 mins plus 4 hrs chilling

Serves 12

Ingredients

- 2l cherry juice
- peel from 3 oranges , pared with a vegetable peeler
- 1 thumb-sized red chilli , pierced a few times but left whole

- 3 cinnamon sticks
- 10 cloves
- 6 slices ginger
- Dracula's fangs sweets (available from sweet shops), to serve, optional

For an alcoholic punch (optional)

- 200ml vodka , or 25ml per glass

Method

STEP 1

Tip the cherry juice, orange peel, chilli, cinnamon sticks, cloves and ginger into a large saucepan. Simmer for 5 mins, then turn off the heat. Leave to cool, then chill for at least 4 hrs, or up to 2 days – the longer you leave it the more intense the flavours. If serving to young children, take the chilli out after a few hours.

STEP 2

When you're ready to serve, pour the juice into a jug. Serve in glass bottles or glasses and pop a straw in each. If you're adding vodka, do so at this stage. Dangle a fangs sweet from each glass.

Eyeball pasta

Prep:15 mins **Cook:**10 mins

Serves 4-6 children

Ingredients

- 100g cherry tomato

- 150g pack mini mozzarella balls, drained

- handful basil
- 400g green tagliatelle
- 350g jar tomato sauce
- 4 tbsp fresh pesto

Method

STEP 1

Halve the cherry tomatoes and use a small, sharp knife or a teaspoon to remove the seeds. Cut the mozzarella balls in half. Place one half inside each tomato, trimming the edges if necessary to fit it in. Either cut the smallest circles you can from a basil leaf or finely chop the leaves and scrunch into small circles. Place one at the centre of each mozzarella ball.

STEP 2

Boil the pasta. Meanwhile, heat through the tomato sauce. When the tagliatelle is cooked, drain and stir through the pesto and any remaining basil, chopped finely. Divide between 4-6 serving bowls. Spoon over some tomato sauce, then arrange the stuffed tomato eyeballs on top.

Healthy Halloween nachos

Prep:40 mins **Cook:**5 mins

Serves 4 - 6

Ingredients

For the guacamole

- 2 limes , juiced
- 2 small avocados , peeled and chopped
- 1 bunch coriander , finely chopped

For the sweetcorn salsa

- ½ a 160g can sweetcorn
- 200g cherry tomatoes , quartered
- 1 red pepper , finely chopped
- 2 spring onions , thinly sliced
- 3 sundried tomatoes , finely chopped
- 400g can black beans
- ½ tsp cumin
- ½ tsp coriander
- ½ tsp smoked paprika

For the bat-shaped nachos

- 4 wholewheat tortillas
- 1 ½ tsp oil
- 4 purple carrots , cut into sticks

Method

242

STEP 1

Start by making the guacamole. Pour the lime juice into a bowl and add the avocado. Mash well with a potato masher or the back of a fork until it's the consistency you like – we served ours fairly chunky. Add half of the chopped coriander, season to taste and spoon into a shallow bowl or serving dish.

STEP 2

Now mix all of the salsa ingredients together, along with the remaining chopped coriander. Season with salt and pepper. Arrange clumps of the salsa on top of the guacamole – this will allow guests to get a bit of everything with each scoop. Cover and chill for up to 30 mins while you make the bat nachos.

STEP 3

Lay a tortilla wrap out on your chopping board and brush with a little of the oil. Cut out bats (or other spooky shapes) using a cookie cutter, scissors or both. Cut them as close together as possible to minimise waste. You should be able to get about 8-10 from each wrap, depending on the size of your cutter.

STEP 4

Heat oven to 200C/180C fan/gas 6. Put all the tortilla shapes on 2 or 3 large baking sheets and bake for about 4-5 mins or until golden and crisp, then serve with the carrot sticks, guacamole and salsa plate.

Pumpkin spice scones

Prep: 15 mins **Cook:** 12 mins

Makes 25

Ingredients

- 450g self-raising flour , plus extra for rolling
- 100g cold butter
- 50g golden caster sugar
- 1-2 tsp pumpkin spice (or mix ½ tsp cinnamon, ¼ tsp ginger, a good grind of nutmeg and a pinch of allspice)
- 200g cooked pumpkin
- 80-100ml milk
- butter or cream cheese flavoured with a pinch of cinnamon, to serve

Method

STEP 1

Heat oven to 220C/200C fan/gas 7. Put the flour in a bowl and coarsely grate in the butter (dipping the butter into the flour can make it easier to grate; do this as often as you need). Use a butter knife to stir the butter into the flour, then mix in the sugar and spice.

STEP 2

Add the pumpkin and 80ml milk to the flour mixture and quickly stir everything together. Add more milk if you need to.

STEP 3

Tip the mixture onto a floured surface and lightly bring together with your hands a couple of times. Roll out until 4cm thick and stamp out rounds with a 7cm cutter. Re-shape the trimmings until all the dough has been used. Place the rounds on a lightly floured baking sheet and brush the tops with any remaining milk. Bake for 10-12 mins until risen and lightly browned.

Halloween biscuits

Prep:45 mins **Cook:**25 mins

Serves 7 - 8

Ingredients

For the biscuits

- 200g unsalted butter , softened
- 200g golden caster sugar
- 1 large egg
- ½ tsp vanilla extract

For decoration

- White, black and grey sugar paste
- 100g icing sugar

- 400g plain flour , plus extra for dusting
- 20g popping candy (or rainbow sprinkles for very young children)

Method

STEP 1

Heat oven to 200C/180C fan/gas 6 and line a baking sheet with baking parchment.

STEP 2

Put the butter in a bowl and beat with electric beaters until soft and creamy. Beat in the sugar, then the egg and vanilla, and finally the flour to make a dough. If the dough feels a bit sticky add a little more flour and knead it in. Wrap in cling film and put in the fridge for half an hour.

STEP 3

Heavily flour a surface and cut the pastry in half. Roll out one half to 5mm thickness. Using a cookie cutter in the shape of a ghost (or any spooky shaped cutter you like), cut out 12 ghost shapes, which will make 4 cookies. Put the cut shapes on a baking tray lined with baking paper and put back in the fridge. Repeat with the second half of the pastry. Swap into the fridge, taking the chilled ghost biscuits out.

STEP 4

Using a smaller cutter or a knife, cut a ghost-shaped hole in the middle of 4 of the biscuits on the tray, this is the space to store the surprise centre! Put these biscuits into the oven to bake for 10-12 mins, until pale but cooked through. Transfer to a wire rack to cool. Repeat with the other tray.

STEP 5

Once all the biscuits have cooled completely, they are ready to be assembled. Mix the icing sugar with 3 tbsp of water and mix well. It should be quite thick so add a little more icing sugar if the mixture is too runny. Take a biscuit without the centre missing, and spread or pipe a little icing around the edge. Press a biscuit with a centre missing on top, then sprinkle popping candy into the pocket that you have created (or rainbow sprinkles as an alternative, if you're serving to very young children). Spread icing on the edge of the second biscuit and press another whole biscuit on top. Set aside to firm up. Make sure you leave them for a while so they don't slide when you are finishing the decoration.

STEP 6

Once the biscuits feel firm and the icing has set, use the sugar paste to decorate them as you please, rolling it out, cutting it to shape and topping the biscuits. You may have to use a little of the icing to glue it down. Decorate with icing pens if you like.

Maggoty apples

Prep: 20 mins plus chilling, no cook

Serves 6

Ingredients

- 6 apples (we used Braeburn)
- juice 0.5 lemon
- 100g white chocolate
- 50g puffed rice
- jelly worm sweets (optional)

Method

STEP 1

Core the apples, starting at the base and trying to keep the stalk ends intact. Use a blunt table knife or melon baller to scoop out any remaining bits of seeds and core if you need to. You can also use a metal skewer to make 1 or 2 holes in the sides. Brush the cut parts of the apples with lemon juice and put on a plate or board.

STEP 2

Put the chocolate in a heatproof bowl over a pan of simmering water to melt. Once melted, stir in the puffed rice, then remove from the heat. Using a teaspoon, pack the chocolate and puffed rice mixture into the apples, sticking a few into the smaller holes and on the top to look like they're crawling out. Transfer the apples to the fridge for around 20 mins to set.

STEP 3

Spoon any remaining mixture into a mini muffin tin lined with paper petit four cases and put in the fridge to set along with the apples.

STEP 4

Once the chocolate has set, peel away the paper cases and put the 'maggot balls' around the apples. Add a few wriggly jelly worms too, if you dare.

Eyeball snot-tail

Prep:25 mins plus chilling, no cook

Serves 10 - 15

Ingredients

- 135g pack lime jelly
- 700ml apple & pear juice (we used Copella)
- 300ml lemonade
- 425g can lychees in syrup

- 10-15 cocktail cherries from a jar
- 10-15 raisins
- You will need
- 10-15 cocktail sticks

Method

STEP 1

Make the jelly following pack instructions and chill until set. Combine the apple & pear juice with the lemonade in a large jug and chill in the fridge.

STEP 2

To make the eyeballs, drain the lychees and poke a hole in each cherry with one of the cocktail sticks. Put the cherry inside the lychee, then push the raisin into the cherry. Press the eyeball onto the end of a cocktail stick and set aside until serving.

STEP 3

When the jelly has set, use a whisk to break it up into small chunks. Spoon into the cocktail glasses and top up with the apple juice mixture. Put an eyeball into each glass before serving.

Frozen banana ghosts

Prep:10 mins plus freezing, no cook

Makes 8 ghosts

Ingredients

- 200g bar white chocolate (supermarket own brand Belgian is good), broken into chunks
- 4 medium-large, ripe bananas
- 85g desiccated coconut (you won't use it all)
- handful dark chocolate drops

Method

STEP 1

In a small bowl, gently melt the chocolate either in the microwave – in short bursts on high or over a pan of simmering water (make sure the bowl isn't touching the water). Set aside for a moment while you get the bananas ready.

STEP 2

Peel the bananas, cut in half, and push a lolly stick into the middle of each piece. Spread the coconut out in a shallow bowl. Line a large baking tray with baking parchment, and make sure there is room for the tray in the freezer.

STEP 3

Using a pastry brush, coat a banana half in chocolate, letting excess drip away. Sprinkle with plenty of the coconut until coated, then set it on the prepared sheet. Now add two chocolate eyes and a mouth, and if you like, cut a few little eyebrows from the chocolate drops too. Freeze the lollies for at least 4 hrs, and up to a week.

Freaky finger red velvet cake

Prep: 1 hr **Cook:** 25 mins plus chilling

Serves 12 - 16

Ingredients

For the red velvet cake

- 175g soft butter , plus extra for greasing
- 225g white caster sugar
- 1 tsp vanilla extract
- 3 large eggs , at room temperature
- 1 tbsp red food colouring paste (we used Christmas red from Sugarflair)
- 200g plain flour
- 50g cocoa powder (we used Green & Black's)
- 1 ½ tsp bicarbonate of soda
- ½ tsp baking powder
- ¼ tsp salt
- 150g pot low-fat plain yogurt , loosened with 2 tbsp milk

For the fingers and frosting

- about 3 x 114g boxes white chocolate fingers (we found them in Tesco)
- 140g icing sugar
- 2 tsp milk
- small blob of red food colouring paste
- 100g soft butter
- 300g full-fat cream cheese , fridge cold (we used Philadelphia as it has the firmest texture)
- zest 1 orange (optional)

Method

STEP 1

Heat oven to 180C/160C fan/gas 4. For the cake, grease 2 x 20cm sandwich tins and line the bases with baking parchment. Cream together the butter, sugar and vanilla, then add the eggs, one at a time, beating well after each egg, until fluffy and light. Beat in the colouring.

STEP 2

Mix the dry ingredients for the cake, and sift half onto the creamed mix. Fold in with a spatula, followed by half of the thinned yogurt. Repeat, then spoon the smooth batter into the tins and level. Bake for 25 mins or until risen and springy when pressed lightly in the centre. Cool for 10 mins, then turn out onto a wire rack and cool completely.

STEP 3

For the fingers, line a baking tray with parchment. Cut one end from each chocolate finger. Mix 50g icing sugar, the milk and a small blob of colouring to make a thick, red icing. The icing needs to be thick to stay put; add a little more sugar if you need to. Dip the severed biscuit ends into the icing, let the

248

excess drip off, then paint a red fingernail on the other end, using a small paintbrush. Leave to dry on the parchment.

STEP 4

For the frosting, use an electric mixer to beat the butter well until very smooth, then beat in the cream cheese and the zest (if using) until even. Sift in the remaining icing sugar, then fold it into the cheese mixture using a spatula until smooth. Don't overbeat. Chill until needed.

STEP 5

Sandwich and cover the top and sides of the cake with the frosting – you will only need a thin layer on the sides of the cake to stick on the chocolate fingers. Stand the severed fingers around the cake in a neat collar, pressing them lightly into the frosting. You'll have a few left over to put on the top. Keep the cake in the fridge but enjoy it at room temperature.

Chocolate bat biscuits

Prep: 10 mins **Cook:** 10 mins plus firming and cooling

makes 25-30 biscuits, depending on cutter size

Ingredients

- 125g butter , softened
- 85g icing sugar
- 1 large egg yolk
- 1 tsp vanilla extract
- 1 tsp milk

- 175g plain flour , plus extra for rolling
- 1 tsp fine espresso-style powder coffee (I used Azeera)
- 50g cocoa powder
- ¼ tsp salt

To decorate

- 100g bar dark or milk chocolate
- chocolate hundreds and thousands
- coloured writing icing (or make your own with 100g icing sugar, 3-4 tsp water and some colouring)

Method

STEP 1

Heat oven to 180C/160C fan/gas 4 and line two baking sheets with baking parchment. Beat the butter and sugar together until creamy and pale, then beat in the yolk, the vanilla and milk. Sift the flour, coffee, cocoa and salt into the bowl, then mix together to make a soft dough. Shape the dough into a disc, wrap and chill for 15 mins.

STEP 2

Dust the dough all over with a little flour, then roll it between two large sheets of baking parchment, to the thickness of a £1 coin. Remove the top layer of the paper, stamp shapes with an 8cm bat (or other) cutter, and carefully lift to the lined sheets using a palette knife. Re-roll the trimmings. Cut a 1.5cm x 5mm notch at the base of each bat's body. This is about right to sit the bats on thick tumblers; if your glasses are finer-edged, make the notches thinner so that the bats stay put. Bake for 10 mins or until the biscuits feel sandy and smell rich and chocolatey. Cool on the sheets for 5 mins, then lift the cookies onto a wire rack and cool completely.

STEP 3

To decorate, melt the chocolate over a pan of simmering water or in the microwave. One biscuit at a time, brush chocolate over the bat ears and wings with a small paintbrush, then cover with chocolate sprinkles. Tap off the excess. Pipe faces and fangs onto your bats, then leave to dry. Keep in an airtight container for up to a week.

Halloween spider pizzas

Prep:20 mins **Cook:**12 mins Plus proving

Serves 8

Ingredients

- 1 pack pizza base mix
- plain flour , for dusting
- 120ml passata or tomato pasta sauce
- 1 garlic clove , crushed
- 150g grated mozzarella
- 25g-50g parmesan , grated
- 4 large pitted black olives
- 6 small slices salami or chorizo
- 8 small capers , drained

Method

STEP 1

Make the pizza dough following pack instructions. Tip the dough onto a floured surface, flour your hands, then gently knead the dough for about 2 mins until fairly even, soft and bouncy. Return the dough to the bowl, cover with oiled cling film, then let it rise in a warm place until doubled in size (about 1 hr). While the dough proves, mix the passata and garlic in a bowl.

STEP 2

Heat oven to 240C/220C fan/gas 9 or as hot as it will go. Dust two baking sheets with flour. Split the dough into eight, then roll four balls into thin, rough circles. Lift onto the floured sheets. Smear a thin layer of the tomato sauce on top of each and scatter over the mozzarella and parmesan.

STEP 3

Halve each olive and put four halves, cut-side down on four pizzas – these are the spider bodies. Cut the rest of the olive halves into thin strips, then arrange on either side of the bodies to look like legs.

STEP 4

Put four pieces of salami or chorizo on the four remaining pizza bases. Cut the other pieces of salami into thin strips and use them to make the legs of the spiders. Add 2 capers to each spider for the eyes.

STEP 5

Bake each tray for 12 mins or until golden and crisp and the cheese is starting to brown.

Haunted graveyard cake

Prep: 45 mins **Cook:** 2 hrs

Serves 10

Ingredients

To decorate

- 1 egg white
- 50g icing sugar
- 200ml single cream
- 200g dark chocolate , finely chopped

- 125g rich tea finger biscuits
- 100g double chocolate cookies
- 25g white chocolate
- silver balls , to decorate

For the cake

- 85g cocoa powder
- 200g self-raising flour
- 375g light brown muscovado sugar

- 4 eggs
- 200ml milk
- 175ml vegetable oil

Method

STEP 1

To make the ghosts, heat oven to 110C/90C fan/gas ¼. Whip the egg white in a clean bowl until stiff peaks form. Whisk in the sugar a tbsp at a time and keep whisking for a couple of mins until the mixture is thick and resembles shaving foam. Gently spoon the mixture into a large freezer bag, then cut a 1.5cm hole in one of the corners. Cover a baking sheet with some baking parchment. Carefully squeeze a small circle of whipped egg white out of the bag, pulling upwards as you do to make a ghost shape. Repeat until the mixture is used up – you should get about 15 ghosts. Bake for 1½ hrs until crisp. Can be stored in an airtight container for up to 2 days.

STEP 2

251

Now make the cake. Heat oven to 180C/160C fan/gas 4. Tip the cocoa powder, self-raising flour and sugar into a large bowl, breaking up any clumps of sugar. Mix together the eggs, milk and oil in a measuring cup or bowl, then pour over the dry ingredients and stir everything together until smooth. Grease and line a deep baking dish (20 x 30 x 5cm) with baking parchment. Pour in the cake mixture and bake for 30 mins. Leave to cool, then turn out onto a serving plate. Alternatively, wrap well and store for up to 2 days.

STEP 3

Finish decorating the cake: heat cream in a saucepan until just boiling. Place the dark chocolate in a large bowl and pour over the hot cream. Stir until the chocolate melts. Use a clean brush to paint a layer of chocolate over 7 rich tea finger biscuits, then set aside to cool. Pour the rest of the chocolate mixture over the cake and smooth over with a knife. Whizz the chocolate cookies, or bash in a freezer bag with a rolling pin, until small crumbs form. Sprinkle over the top of the cake.

STEP 4

Place the white chocolate in a small bowl, set over a pan of simmering water. Leave for 5 mins or until melted, then spoon into a small freezer bag. Wait for 10 mins so the mixture is not too runny, then cut a tiny hole in one corner of the bag. Pipe out 2 small blobs onto each ghost, place a silver ball on each to make eyes, then pipe out suitable words and shapes on the gravestones. Leave for 30 mins to set, then push the biscuit gravestones into the cake and arrange the ghosts around. To get the ghosts to 'fly', push a thin wire (you can get these from a florist shop – remember to remove before eating) into the bottom of the ghost, then place in the cake, hiding the wire behind a gravestone.

Spider web chocolate fudge muffins

Total time 45 mins Ready in 40-45 minutes

Makes 10

Ingredients

- 50g dark chocolate (55% cocoa solids is fine)
- 85g butter
- 1 tbsp milk , water or coffee
- 200g self-raising flour

- ½ tsp bicarbonate of soda
- 85g light muscovado sugar
- 50g golden caster sugar
- 1 egg
- 142ml carton soured cream

For the topping

- 100g dark chocolate (as above)
- 100g white chocolate

Method

252

STEP 1

Preheat the oven to fan 170C/ conventional 190C/gas 5 and line a muffin tin with 10 paper muffin cases. Break the chocolate into a heatproof bowl, add the butter and liquid. Melt in the microwave on Medium for 30-45 seconds (or set the bowl over a pan of gently simmering water). Stir and leave the mixture to cool.

STEP 2

Mix the flour, bicarbonate of soda and both sugars in a bowl. Beat the egg in another bowl and stir in the soured cream, then pour this on the flour mixture and add the cooled chocolate. Stir just to combine – don't overmix or it will get tough.

STEP 3

Spoon the mixture into the cases to about three quarters full. Bake for 20 minutes until well risen. Loosen the edges with a round-bladed knife, let them sit in the tins for a few minutes, then lift out and cool on a wire rack.

STEP 4

For the topping, make two piping bags out of greaseproof paper (or cut the ends off two clean plastic bags). Break the dark and white chocolate into separate bowls and melt in the microwave on Medium for 2 minutes (or over a pan as in step 1). Put 2 spoonfuls of dark chocolate in one bag and the same of white chocolate in the other.

STEP 5

Working with one muffin at a time, spread with dark chocolate from the bowl, letting it run down a bit, then pipe four concentric circles of white chocolate on top. Using a small skewer, drag through the circles at regular intervals, from the centre to the edge, to create a cobweb effect. Repeat with four more muffins. On the remaining five, spread over the white chocolate and decorate with the dark. Best eaten the day they're made – even better while the chocolate's soft.

Healthy Halloween stuffed peppers

Prep:25 mins **Cook:**35 mins

Serves 4

Ingredients

- 4 small peppers (a mix of orange, red and yellow looks nice)
- 25g pine nuts
- 1 tbsp olive or rapeseed oil

- 1 red onion , chopped
- 2 fat garlic cloves , crushed
- 1 small aubergine , chopped into small pieces

- 200g pouch mixed grains (we used bulghur wheat and quinoa)
- 2 tbsp sundried tomato paste

- zest of 1 lemon
- bunch basil , chopped

Method

STEP 1

Cut the tops off the peppers (keeping the tops to one side) and remove the seeds and any white flesh from inside. Use a small sharp knife to carve spooky Halloween faces into the sides. Chop any offcuts into small pieces and set aside.

STEP 2

Toast the pine nuts in a dry pan for a few mins until golden, and set aside. Heat the oil in the pan, and heat the oven to 200C/180C fan/gas 6. Cook the onion in the oil for 8-10 mins until softened. Stir in the garlic, pepper offcuts and aubergine and cook for another 10 mins, until the veggies are soft. Add a splash of water if the pan looks dry. Season.

STEP 3

Squeeze the pouch of grains to break them up, then tip into the pan with the tomato paste. Stir for a minute or two to warm through, then remove from the heat and add the lemon zest, basil and pine nuts.

STEP 4

Fill each pepper with the grain mixture. Replace the lids, using cocktail sticks to secure them in place, and put the peppers in a deep roasting tin with the carved faces facing upwards. Cover with foil and bake for 35 mins, uncovered for the final 10. The peppers should be soft and the filling piping hot.

Funny face cookies

Prep: 10 mins **Cook:** 12 mins plus chilling and decorating, cooking time is per batch

Makes about 20

Ingredients

For the cookies

- 175g soft butter , plus extra for greasing
- 100g golden caster sugar
- 1 large egg yolk
- ½ tsp vanilla extract

- zest 1 lemon
- 250g plain flour , plus extra for dusting
- ½ tsp salt

To decorate

- cake pops or lolly sticks

- 200g icing sugar

- 1 large egg white
- pink and brown food colouring pastes
- pink and gold edible glitter (optional)

Method

STEP 1

Beat together the butter and sugar until pale and creamy, then beat in the yolk, vanilla and zest. Sift the flour and salt into the bowl, then stir in to make a soft dough. Split into two flat discs, then wrap in cling film and chill for 30 mins, or until firm but not rock hard. Meanwhile, heat oven to 180C/160C fan/gas 4. Line two baking sheets with baking parchment.

STEP 2

Flour the work surface, then roll the dough to 5mm thick. Stamp the dough with an 8cm round cutter, then re-rolling any trimmings. Using the same cutter, cut a crescent moon and a pointy oval shape from each circle. Pinch the corners of the oval and indent the top and bottom to make lips. For moustaches, shape the half moon, pressing a dent into the top of the curve, then tweak and pinch the ends to make a moustache.

STEP 3

Chill for 10 mins, or until firm, then poke cake pop sticks carefully into the dough. I find putting one hand on top of the dough as I insert the stick with the other prevents the stick from popping through the surface of the dough.

STEP 4

Bake for 12 mins, one tray at a time, until pale golden. Leave on the tray for 5 mins before lifting to a wire rack (use a palette knife rather than the sticks) and cooling completely. Make the icing by beating the egg white and the sugar until thick and smooth. Divide into four batches and colour them two shades of pink and two of brown. Spoon the darker icings into disposable piping bags and snip off the tips (or use a number 2 nozzle).

STEP 5

Pipe moustache and lip outlines onto the cookies. Dry for a few mins. Now loosen the paler icings with a few drops of water until runny. Spoon a little onto each cookie and let it flood to the outline, nudging it up to the edge if needed, using a cocktail stick or tip of a teaspoon. Dry for 10 mins, then pipe a darker mouth line onto the lips, and zig-zagged lines over the moustaches. Sprinkle with glitter if using, and leave to set.

Sausage mummy dippers

Prep: 15 mins **Cook:** 20 mins

Makes 12

Ingredients

- oil , for greasing
- 1 tbsp honey
- 1 tbsp ketchup
- 2 tsp French's yellow mustard , plus a little extra to decorate
- 12 chipolatas
- tube of 6 ready-to-roll croissant (look in the chiller cabinets near the pastry in the supermarkets)

Method

STEP 1

Heat oven to 200C/180C fan/gas 6 and brush 2 baking trays with a little oil. Mix the honey, ketchup and mustard together in a bowl, then brush over the chipolata sausages.

STEP 2

Unroll the croissant dough and divide into 3 rectangles. Pinch together the diagonal perforated seams, then cut into long thin strips – you should get about 16 per rectangle.

STEP 3

Wind the little croissant strips around the chipolatas, leaving a little gap at one end to make a slit for the eyes. Place on baking trays and bake for 20 mins. Cool a little, then, using the mustard, dot a pair of little yellow eyes on to each mummy. Serve warm with glow-in-the-dark goo (see goes well with, below) and/or your favourite dip.

Witch's cauldron with glow-in-the-dark goo

Prep:35 mins **Cook:**25 mins

Makes enough for 12 with other nibbles

Ingredients

- 1 large round loaf of bread
- 1 egg , beaten
- 100g bag poppy seed
- 1kg butternut squash chunks
- 1 onion , roughly chopped
- 2 garlic cloves , peeled
- 400g can cream of tomato soup
- 1 tsp ground cumin
- 1 tsp ground coriander
- 2 tbsp chilli sauce , we used Lingham's
- extra toasted pitta bread , Sausage mummies (see goes well with) and cucumber sticks, to dip

Method

STEP 1

Slice the top off the loaf, then scoop out the soft bread from the middle of the base, leaving the crust about 2.5cm thick all the way round. Slice the bread out in chunks for toasting to serve, or simply get the kids to pull it out with their fingers.

STEP 2

Heat oven to 200C/180C fan/gas 6. Brush the outside of the large 'cauldron' and lid all over with beaten egg, then roll the crust of the cauldron and lid in poppy seeds to coat – tipping them onto a big dinner plate first makes this easier. Sit on baking sheets, poppy seed-sides up, and bake for 10 mins. Set aside until you are ready to party.

STEP 3

Bring a large pan of salted water to the boil, add the butternut squash, onion and garlic, then simmer until the squash and onion are tender. Drain really well, then tip into a food processor or blender with the soup, spices, chilli sauce and some seasoning and whizz to a smooth purée (or put back in the saucepan and whizz with a stick-blender). Set aside.

STEP 4

Just before the guests are due to arrive, heat the dip in a microwave or saucepan – it should be nice and hot. Spoon into the bread cauldron, pop on the lid and carry to the party table, ready for dunking in the Sausage mummies (see goes well with), cucumber sticks and more toasted bread. And as the dip disappears, you can start to eat the cauldron, too!

Blood beetroot cocktails

Prep: 15 mins plus chilling, no cook

Serves 6

Ingredients

For the beetroot lemonade

- 200g raw beetroot , grated
- juice 8 lemons
- 200g golden caster sugar
- For the cocktail

- 300ml Aperol
- ice
- 750ml prosecco , chilled

Method

STEP 1

First, make the beetroot lemonade. In a bowl, stir together the beetroot, lemon juice and sugar. Steep in the fridge for at least 1 hr, stirring occasionally to dissolve the sugar. Pour the mixture through a sieve into a large jug to get rid of the pulp.

STEP 2

To make the cocktail, pour 25ml of the beetroot lemonade into each glass, followed by 50ml of Aperol and a few ice cubes. Top with Prosecco and serve.

Scary Halloween jelly

Prep:25 mins Plus chilling

Serves 8

Ingredients

- 2 x 135g packs strawberry or raspberry jelly
- 425g can lychee in syrup
- 12-14 small seedless green grapes
- 12-14 dark coloured jelly beans

- 80g white marzipan
- 6-8 whole blanched almonds
- red piping gel or red icing in a tube

Method

STEP 1

Cut the jelly into cubes with scissors and place in a bowl. Add 400ml boiling water and stir continuously until dissolved.

STEP 2

Drain the lychees, reserving the juice. Put the juice in a measuring jug and make up to 400ml with cold water. Add to the dissolved jelly.

STEP 3

Pour about a quarter of the jelly into a clear glass dish and place in the fridge to set.

STEP 4

Take a grape and gently push a jelly bean into the centre, using the hole where the stalk has been. Then gently push the grape into a lychee. Repeat with the remaining grapes and lychees to make eyeballs.

STEP 5

To make the spooky fingers, divide the marzipan into 6 and shape into sausages the size of a finger. Pipe a little red gel at one end and attach an almond to represent a fingernail. Using a small knife mark three or four lines half way down the finger to make a knuckle.

STEP 6

When the jelly is set, arrange half the eyeballs over the surface, add more jelly and return to the fridge.

STEP 7

When this has set, arrange the remaining eyeballs over the jelly. Place the spooky fingers against the side of the bowl. Pour over the remaining jelly and place in the fridge to set. Serve in the bowl.

Orange pumpkin face cookies

Total time55 mins Takes 45-55 minutes, plus 1 hour chilling

Makes 12

Ingredients

- 140g butter , softened
- 175g plain flour
- 50g icing sugar
- finely grated zest 1 medium orange

For the filling

- 100g mascarpone
- 1 tsp icing sugar
- 25g plain chocolate (55% cocoa solids is fine), melted

For the glaze

- 50g icing sugar
- about 1 tbsp orange juice

Method

STEP 1

Preheat the oven to fan 160C/ conventional 180C/gas 4. Put the butter in a bowl and beat with a wooden spoon until smooth. Add the flour, icing sugar and orange zest and beat together to make a softish dough. Knead into a ball and wrap in cling film. Chill for 1 hour.

STEP 2

Roll the dough out on a lightly floured surface to a thickness of about 3mm. Cut 24 circles with a 7.5 cm round plain cutter. Put them on a couple of baking sheets.

STEP 3

259

Using a small sharp knife, cut out Hallowe'en faces on 12 of the circles. Gather up the spare biscuit dough and press into pumpkin stem shapes, trimming with a sharp knife. Press to the top of each biscuit with a knife to join. Make lines on the face biscuits with the back of a roundbladed knife, to look like the markings on a pumpkin. Bake all the biscuits for about 15 minutes until pale golden. Leave to set for a while, then cool completely on a wire rack.

STEP 4

Mix the glaze ingredients to make a smooth, runny icing, adding a bit more juice if needed, then set aside. For the filling, beat the mascarpone with the icing sugar, then stir in the cooled melted chocolate.

STEP 5

Spread the filling over the cooled plain biscuits, then press the 'face' ones on top – do this just before you want to eat them, otherwise they go soft. Brush with the glaze, using a clean paint brush or pastry brush. Eat the same day.

Frankenstein cupcakes

Prep: 1 hr **Cook:** 20 mins plus cooling, chilling and setting

Makes 12

Ingredients

For the cupcakes

- 200g soft butter
- 175g golden caster sugar
- 250g self-raising flour
- 1 tsp baking powder

- ¼ tsp salt
- 3 large eggs , at room temperature
- ½ tsp vanilla extract
- 100ml milk , at room temperature

To decorate

- 300g icing sugar , sifted
- 2-3 tbsp milk
- green food colouring paste (we used Party Green from Sugarflair)

- 36 mini marshmallows , 12 snipped in half (for the eyes)
- tube of black piping icing or gel

Method

STEP 1

Heat oven to 180C/160C fan/gas 4 and line a 12-hole muffin tin with deep muffin cases. Cream the butter with the sugar until pale and fluffy. Add the remaining cake ingredients and beat until smooth. Spoon into the muffin cases and bake for 20 mins or until golden and a skewer inserted into one of the middle cakes comes out clean. Cool for 5 mins in the tin, then completely on a wire rack.

260

STEP 2

Using a small, sharp serrated knife, cut a semi-circle piece of cake from the left and right of each cake, to make stepped edges, level with the cupcake case. Next, make a widthways cut about 3cm from the top of the cake, about 1cm deep. Slice a 5mm piece off the surface of the cake to meet this cut, to make a flat, raised face and prominent forehead. Chill for 10 mins to firm the crumbs.

STEP 3

Mix the icing sugar, milk and green colouring to make a very thick icing that flows slowly from the spoon. Spoon 1 tbsp onto a cake and let it begin to spread itself over the cut shape. Ease it here and there with a palette knife to coat. Add marshmallow neck bolts and eyes. Repeat for each cupcake. Leave to set, then pipe on the faces and hair.

Chocolate spider cookies

Prep:30 mins **Cook:**5 mins

Makes 14

Ingredients

- 200g dark or milk chocolate , broken into chunks
- 113g pack liquorice Catherine wheels (we used Barratts)
- 2 x 154g packs Oreo cookies
- white and black icing pens

Method

STEP 1

Melt the chocolate in a heatproof bowl over a pan of barely simmering water. Once melted, turn off the heat and leave the chocolate in the bowl to keep warm while you assemble the spiders.

STEP 2

Unroll some of the liquorice wheels and cut into 2-3cm lengths to use as the Chocolate spiders' legs.

STEP 3

Splodge a small tsp of chocolate onto half of the cookies. Arrange eight liquorice legs on top, then sandwich with another cookie. Spread some more chocolate on top of the second cookie to cover, then put somewhere cool to set.

STEP 4

Use the icing pens to add eyes, by first blobbing two big dots of white icing on each, topped with two smaller dots of black icing.

Spooky spider cakes

Prep:40 mins **Cook:**25 mins

Makes 12

Ingredients

- 200g butter , at room temperature
- 200g golden caster sugar
- 200g self-raising flour
- 4 eggs

- ½ tsp baking powder
- 1 tsp vanilla extract
- 6 tbsp chocolate chips or chopped chocolate

To decorate

- 2 packs liquorice Catherine wheels
- 12 tbsp Nutella or other chocolate spread
- liquorice allsorts (the black ones with the white centre)

- tube black writing icing
- 1 length red bootlace

Method

STEP 1

Heat oven to 180C/fan 160C/gas 4 and line a muffin tin with 12 cases, preferably brown ones. Put the butter, sugar and flour in a mixing bowl. Break the eggs into a smaller bowl, taking care not to get any shell into it, then tip on top of the butter mixture.

STEP 2

Add the baking powder and vanilla to the larger bowl, then beat with an electric hand whisk until smooth and creamy. Stir in the chocolate drops or chocolate. Spoon the cake mixture evenly into the cases and bake for 20-25 mins until golden – a cocktail stick pushed into the middle of one of the cakes should come out clean. Cool on a wire rack.

STEP 3

To decorate the cakes, unravel the liquorice wheels and cut into lengths with scissors to make dangly legs. Stick 8 into the top of each cake, making small cuts with the tip of a sharp knife so they push in really securely.

STEP 4

Spoon the chocolate spread on top and spread lightly within the liquorice legs to make a round spider's body. Now cut the Allsorts to make eyes and the red bootlaces to make mouths, then stick them onto the cakes and dot on the icing to make eyeballs. Will keep for up to 2 days in a cool place.

Caption cookies

Prep:10 mins **Cook:**12 mins plus chilling and decorating, cooking time is per batch

Makes about 24

Ingredients

For the cookies

- 175g soft butter , plus extra for greasing
- 100g golden caster sugar
- 1 large egg yolk
- ½ tsp vanilla extract
- zest 1 lemon
- 250g plain flour , plus extra for rolling
- ½ tsp salt

To decorate

- cake pop sticks
- 200g icing sugar , sifted
- 1 large egg white
- food colouring of your choice, we used orange and pink

Method

STEP 1

Beat together the butter and sugar until pale and creamy, then beat in the yolk, vanilla and zest. Sift the flour and salt into the bowl, then stir in to make a soft dough. Split into two flat discs, then wrap in cling film and chill for 30 mins, or until firm but not rock hard. Meanwhile, heat oven to 180C/160C fan/gas 4. Line two baking sheets with baking parchment.

STEP 2

Flour the work surface, then roll the dough to the thickness of 2 x £2 coins. Stamp circles with an 8cm cutter and re-roll the trimmings. If you like, pinch a speech bubble point into the bottom of each round. Chill for 10 mins, or until firm, then poke cake pop sticks carefully into the dough. (I find putting one hand on top of the dough as I insert the stick with the other prevents the stick from popping through the surface of the dough.)

STEP 3

Bake for 12 mins, until pale golden. Leave on the tray for 5 mins before lifting to a wire rack (use a palette knife rather than the sticks) and cooling completely. Make the icing by beating sugar and egg white until thick and smooth. Remove half to another bowl, colour it, then spoon into a disposable piping bag and snip off the tip (or use a number 2 nozzle). Pipe a speech bubble border around each cookie and leave to set for a few mins.

STEP 4

Now loosen the white icing with a few drops of water until runny. Spoon a little onto each cookie and let it flood to the outline, nudging it up to the edge if needed using a cocktail stick or tip of a teaspoon. Dry for 10 mins, then pipe captions on top. Leave to dry. Keep the cookies in an airtight tin for up to 3 days.

Hooting Halloween owls

Total time35 mins Ready in 30-35 mins, plus cooling and decorating

Makes 12

Ingredients

- 280g butter , softened
- 280g golden caster sugar
- 200g self-raising flour , minus 1 rounded tbsp

- 1 rounded tbsp cocoa powder
- 6 medium eggs

For icing and decoration

- 200g butter , softened
- 280g icing sugar , sifted
- 1 tube orange ready-to-use icing
- 1 small bag Maltesers

- 1 tube choco M&Ms minis (use just the brown sweets) or Cadbury's mini buttons
- 1 tub jelly diamonds (just the orange ones)

Method

STEP 1

Heat oven to 190C/fan 170C/gas 5. Line a 12-cup muffin tin with brown muffin cases. Beat the first 5 ingredients to a smooth batter and spoon between the cases, almost filling them to the top. You may have a little left over. Bake for 20-25 mins until risen and spongy. Cool on a rack.

STEP 2

Beat the butter and icing sugar until smooth. Slice off the very tops of the cakes and cut each piece in half. Spread a generous layer of icing over each cake.

STEP 3

264

Working on one cake at a time, squirt a pea-sized blob of orange icing onto two Maltesers and use to fix a brown M&M on each. Sit the eyes, two pieces of cake top (curved edge up) and a jelly diamond on the icing to make an owl.

Halloween treats & drinks

Prep:30 mins **Cook:**20 mins

Serves 10

Ingredients

Freaky fingers

- 100g caster sugar
- 100g butter
- 1 egg yolk
- 200g plain flour

Brainballs

- 85g popping corn
- 1 tbsp vegetable oil , plus extra for shaping
- 25g butter
- 85g marshmallows

Bloodthirsty squash

- 1l lemonade
- 1l cranberry juice
- juice 3-4 limes

- ½ tsp vanilla extract
- 20 blanched almonds
- red food colouring , paste is best (optional)

Method

STEP 1

For the freaky fingers, place the first five ingredients and a pinch of salt in a food processor and whizz just until a ball of dough forms. Tear off a golfball-size piece of dough and use your hands to roll into finger-size cylinders – you should get about 20. Place on a baking sheet lined with baking parchment – a little apart as they will spread during baking. Use a knife to make a few cuts, close together, for the knuckles. Place an almond at the end of each finger and trim away excess pastry around the edge to neaten. Place in the fridge for 30 mins, heat oven to 180C/ 160C fan/ gas 4, then bake for 10-12 mins just until firm. Leave to cool a little, then paint the almond with food colouring, if you like. Makes 20.

STEP 2

For the brainballs, place the popping corn and vegetable oil in a large pan set over a medium heat. Stir the kernels around the pan to coat in the oil. When the kernels starts to pop, place a lid firmly on top and turn the heat down to low. Cook, shaking the pan often to stop the popcorn burning or sticking, until the corn has stopped popping, about 5 mins. Tip into a bowl, discarding any unopened kernels. Heat butter and marshmallows over a low heat until melted. Pour over popcorn and mix well until coated. Lightly rub oil over your hands and shape the popcorn into small balls. Set aside on a tray lined with baking parchment and leave to set. Makes 10.

STEP 3

For the bloodthirsty squash, fill up a kitchen glove with water, secure the end with a freezer clip or rubber band and place in the freezer overnight. When ready to serve, stir together 1 litre each lemonade and cranberry juice with the juice 3-4 limes. Pour into a punch bowl. Remove the hand from the freezer and use scissors to carefully take off the glove. Place in the punch bowl and serve. Serves 10.

Hubble bubble pumpkin pot

Total time 45 mins Ready in 35-45 minutes

Serves 4 hungry trick or treaters

Ingredients

- 2 leeks , thickly sliced and washed to remove any grit
- 8 rashers smoked bacon , chopped
- 350g/12oz pumpkin flesh, cut into chunks (or use butternut squash)

- 50g butter
- 1 chicken stock cube
- 250g long grain rice

Method

STEP 1

Hubble. Toss the leeks, bacon and pumpkin together in a large microwaveable bowl. Dot the butter on top and cover the bowl with cling film or a plate. Pierce the cling film a couple of times if using and microwave on High for 5 minutes until everything's hot and starting to cook.

STEP 2

Bubble. While the veg is cooking, bring a kettleful of water to the boil and make 700ml/1 1/4 pints stock using the cube. Carefully remove the bowl from the microwave and uncover, watching out for the hot steam. Tip in the rice and season with salt and pepper, then pour in the stock and stir to mix.

STEP 3

Worth the trouble. Cover the bowl with a fresh piece of cling film or the same plate and microwave on High for 10 minutes. Uncover and give it a stir, then microwave for 5-10 minutes until the rice is cooked. Leave to stand for 5 minutes before giving everything a final stir. Serve scooped straight from the bowl.

Creamy pumpkin & lentil soup

Prep: 15 mins **Cook:** 35 mins

Serves 4

Ingredients

- 1 tbsp olive oil, plus 1 tsp
- 2 onions, chopped
- 2 garlic cloves, chopped
- approx 800g chopped pumpkin flesh, plus the seeds
- 100g split red lentil
- ½ small pack thyme, leaves picked, plus extra to serve
- 1l hot vegetable stock
- pinch of salt and sugar
- 50g crème fraîche, plus extra to serve

Method

STEP 1

Heat the oil in a large pan. Fry the onions until softened and starting to turn golden. Stir in the garlic, pumpkin flesh, lentils and thyme, then pour in the hot stock. Season, cover and simmer for 20-25 mins until the lentils and vegetables are tender.

STEP 2

Meanwhile, wash the pumpkin seeds. Remove any flesh still clinging to them, then dry them with kitchen paper. Heat the 1 tsp oil in a non-stick pan and fry the seeds until they start to jump and pop. Stir frequently, but cover the pan in between to keep them in it. When the seeds look nutty and toasted, add a sprinkling of salt and a pinch of sugar, and stir well.

STEP 3

Whizz the cooked pumpkin mixture with a hand blender or in a food processor until smooth, then add the crème fraîche and whizz again. Taste for seasoning.

STEP 4

Serve with a spoonful of crème fraîche, a few thyme leaves and the toasted seeds scattered on top.

Meatballs with vine tomato sauce

Total time1 hr and 45 mins Ready in 1¾ hours**Serve 4 children and 2 adults**

Ingredients

- 500g lean minced beef
- 1 small onion , finely chopped
- 1 eating apple , peeled and finely chopped (or grated)

- 1 red pepper , cored, seeded and finely chopped
- leaves from 2 sprigs oregano or 1 tsp dried
- plain flour for coating
- olive oil , for frying

For the sauce

- 1 small onion , finely chopped
- 2 tbsp olive oil
- 4 x packs cherry tomatoes on the vine, halved

- dash of Worcestershire sauce
- dash of soy sauce
- handful of fresh basil leaves

Method

STEP 1

Mash the meat in a bowl with a spoon, then tip in the onion, apple, red pepper and oregano (and seasoning if you want to). Mash again to mix everything together. Now mix well with your hands until the mixture is sticky and divide into 16 smallish balls. Chill in the fridge while you make the sauce. You can make them up to this stage 2 days ahead, or freeze them.

STEP 2

Make the sauce. Soften the onion in a medium saucepan with the oil. Tip in the tomatoes and simmer very gently, uncovered, for about 20 mins. Add the rest of the ingredients except the basil and slow cook for another 15-20 mins. Add the basil and a splash of water from the kettle. Tip the contents of the pan into the food processor and whizz until smooth.

STEP 3

Heat oven to 190C/fan 170C/gas 5. Gently roll the meatballs in flour. Heat a spoonful of oil in an ovenproof non-stick frying pan, wipe out with kitchen paper, then add the meatballs and fry gently and slowly over a low heat for 10 mins, turning them over once with tongs. (You may need to do this in batches if your pan is not very big.) Drain off any excess fat, pour in the sauce and finish off cooking in the oven for 15 mins. Serve with pumpkin mash.

Pumpkin risotto

Prep:30 mins **Cook:**1 hr

Serves 4

Ingredients

- 1 small pumpkin or butternut squash- after peeling and scraping out the seeds, you need about 400g/14oz
- 1 tbsp olive oil, plus a drizzle for the pumpkin
- 2 garlic cloves
- 8 spring onions
- 25g butter

- 200g risotto rice
- 2 tsp ground cumin
- 1l hot vegetable stock, plus extra splash if needed
- 50g grated parmesan (or vegetarian alternative)
- small handful coriander, roughly chopped

Method

STEP 1

Heat oven to 180C/160C fan/ gas 4. Chop up the pumpkin or squash into 1.5cm cubes (kids- ask for help if it's slippery). Put it on a baking tray, drizzle over some oil, then roast for 30 mins.

STEP 2

While the pumpkin is roasting, you can make the risotto. Put the garlic in a sandwich bag, then bash lightly with a rolling pin until it's crushed.

STEP 3

Cut up the spring onions with your scissors.

STEP 4

Heat 1 tbsp oil with the butter in your pan over a medium heat – not too hot. Add the spring onions and garlic. Once the onions are soft but not getting brown, add the rice and cumin. Stir well to coat in the buttery mix for about 1 min.

STEP 5

Now add half a cup of the stock, and stir every now and then until it has all disappeared into the rice. Carry on adding and stirring in a large splash of stock at a time, until you have used up all the stock – this will take about 20 mins.

STEP 6

Check the rice is cooked. If it isn't, add a splash more stock, and carry on cooking for a bit. Once the rice is soft enough to eat, gently stir in the grated cheese, chopped coriander and roasted pumpkin.

Pumpkin soup

Prep: 20 mins **Cook:** 25 mins

Serves 6

Ingredients

- 2 tbsp olive oil
- 2 onions, finely chopped
- 1kg pumpkin or squash (try kabocha), peeled, deseeded and chopped into chunks

For the croutons

- 2 tbsp olive oil
- 4 slices wholemeal seeded bread, crusts removed
- handful pumpkin seeds

- 700ml vegetable stock or chicken stock
- 150ml double cream

Method

STEP 1

Heat 2 tbsp olive oil in a large saucepan, then gently cook 2 finely chopped onions for 5 mins, until soft but not coloured.

STEP 2

Add 1kg pumpkin or squash, cut into chunks, to the pan, then carry on cooking for 8-10 mins, stirring occasionally until it starts to soften and turn golden.

STEP 3

Pour 700ml vegetable or chicken stock into the pan and season with salt and pepper. Bring to the boil, then simmer for 10 mins until the squash is very soft.

STEP 4

Pour 150ml double cream into the pan, bring back to the boil, then purée with a hand blender. For an extra-velvety consistency you can pour the soup through a fine sieve. The soup can now be frozen for up to 2 months.

STEP 5

To make the croutons: cut 4 slices wholemeal seeded bread into small squares.

STEP 6

Heat 2 tbsp olive oil in a frying pan, then fry the bread until it starts to become crisp.

STEP 7

Add a handful of pumpkin seeds to the pan, then cook for a few mins more until they are toasted. These can be made a day ahead and stored in an airtight container.

STEP 8

Reheat the soup if needed, taste for seasoning, then serve scattered with croutons and seeds and drizzled with more olive oil, if you want.

Toffee apple cookies

Prep: 10 mins - 15 mins **Cook:** 12 mins Plus cooling time

Makes 24 cookies

Ingredients

- 175g unsalted butter , at room temperature
- 140g golden caster sugar
- 2 egg yolks
- 50g ground almond
- 85g chewy toffees , roughly chopped
- 85g/3oz ready-to-eat dried apple chunks, roughly chopped
- 225g self-raising flour
- 2 tbsp milk

Method

STEP 1

Preheat the oven to fan 170C/conventional 190C/gas 5. Using an electric whisk, beat together the butter and sugar until pale and creamy.

STEP 2

Stir in the egg yolks, ground almonds, toffees, dried apple and flour. Mix well together then roll into walnut-sized balls.

STEP 3

Place well apart on two non-stick or lined baking sheets and flatten slightly with your hand. Brush with milk and bake for 8-12 minutes until golden. Leave to firm up for 5 minutes, then transfer to a wire rack and leave to cool completely.

Sticky hot dog jackets

Prep: 15 mins **Cook:** 1 hr

Serves 4

Ingredients

- 4 baking potatoes , each weighing about 225g/8oz
- olive oil for brushing
- For the sausages and glaze
- 2 tbsp maple syrup or clear honey

For the mayo

- 8 tbsp mayonnaise
- 2 tsp wholegrain mustard
- 3 tbsp snipped chives or finely chopped spring onion

- 1 tbsp balsamic vinegar
- 2 tsp wholegrain mustard
- 1 tsp tomato purée
- 8 pork sausages

Method

STEP 1

Rub the potatoes with a little oil, then sprinkle generously with salt (preferably flakes) and black pepper. Wrap each one in double-thickness foil and cook on the barbecue for 1 hour, turning frequently, until cooked. Or bake unwrapped in the oven at fan 180C/ conventional 200C/gas 6 for the same amount of time.

STEP 2

Mix the maple syrup, vinegar, mustard and tomato purée to make a glaze. Brush over the sausages and cook on the barbecue, turning and basting often, for 10 minutes until cooked and sticky. Meanwhile, mix the mayo ingredients in a small bowl.

STEP 3

Unwrap the potatoes and split down the middle. Add mayo and sausages (like a hot dog). Serve with a leafy salad.

Spiced roasted apples & blackberries

Prep:10 mins **Cook:**50 mins Ready in about an hour

Serves 4

Ingredients

- 4medium Bramley apples , each weighing about 200g/8oz
- 4 tbsp clear honey

- ½ tsp ground cinnamon
- finely grated zest and juice of 1 large orange
- 250g blackberry

Method

STEP 1

Preheat the oven to 180C/gas 4/fan 160C. Core the apples so you have a hole the size of a pound coin in each one. Make a cut just into the skin around the middle of each apple.

STEP 2

Stand the apples in a shallow baking dish large enough to take all four. Mix together the honey, cinnamon and orange zest, put an equal amount into the cavity of each apple, then pour the orange juice into the dish.

STEP 3

Roast the apples for about 40 minutes, spooning the juices over them occasionally. Then, when the apples are almost ready, spoon the blackberries around and over the top of each apple. Return to the oven for 10 minutes or until the juices start to run. Spoon the blackberries and juices over the apples to serve.

Sausage & pumpkin roast

Prep:5 mins **Cook:**25 mins

Serves 4

Ingredients

- 450g pack pork sausages (or 8 large sausages)
- 800g pumpkin wedge, peeled and cut into finger-thick moon-shaped chunks
- 2 red onions , peeled and cut into wedges

- 2 tbsp olive oil
- 2 tsp caraway seeds
- 300g tub fresh beef gravy from the chiller cabinet

Method

STEP 1

Heat oven to 220C/fan 200C/gas 7. Put the first five ingredients into a large non-stick roasting pan, toss to coat in the oil and roast for 20 mins until the sausages are browned and the pumpkin softened and starting to crisp at the edges.

STEP 2

Tip the gravy into the pan and gently stir around the pumpkin and sausages with a wooden spoon, scraping up any sticky or crispy bits as you go. Return to the oven for another 2 mins until the gravy starts to bubble. Season to taste and serve with greens or beans.

Baked apples with prunes, cinnamon & ginger

Prep:10 mins **Cook:**40 mins

Serves 4

Ingredients

- 4 cooking apples , cored but left whole
- 2 stem ginger balls, finely chopped
- ½ tsp ground cinnamon
- 4 prunes , chopped

- 50g light muscovado sugar
- 1 tbsp butter
- 4 big scoops good quality vanilla ice cream , to serve

Method

STEP 1

Heat oven to 200C/fan 180C/gas 6. Using a sharp knife, score a line around the equator of each apple. Put them into a baking dish with a small splash of water in the bottom.

STEP 2

In a bowl, combine the ginger, cinnamon, prunes and sugar. Stuff the mixture into the apples so that they are well packed. Top each with a knob of butter and bake for 35-40 mins, or until cooked through. To test, pierce with a sharp knife – it should slide straight through. The apples can be cooked up to a day ahead, then warmed through in the oven or microwave before eating.

STEP 3

Remove from the oven and baste the apples with the liquid left in the dish. Serve hot or warm with the ice cream.

Garlicky pumpkin risotto

Total time1 hr and 30 mins Ready in about 1½ hrs plus cooling time

Serves 6

Ingredients

For the pesto

- large bunch basil , leaves and stalks torn
- 3 garlic cloves , roughly chopped
- 3 tbsp pine nuts , toasted
- olive oil
- 50g parmesan , finely grated

For the risotto

- 6 garlic cloves , peeled
- 1.4l hot chicken stock
- 85g unsalted butter
- 400g/14oz piece pumpkin (unpeeled weight), peeled, seeded and cut into 1cm cubes
- 2 tbsp olive oil
- 1small onion , finely chopped
- 400g arborio rice
- 100g pecorino , finely grated
- 50g parmesan , finely grated

For the crispy shallots

- 50g shallots , finely chopped
- 100g plain flour , seasoned with salt and pepper
- vegetable oil , for shallow frying

Method

STEP 1

Make the pesto. Pulse the basil, garlic and pine nuts in a food processor to a coarse paste, adding enough olive oil to produce a loose-textured purée. Pour into a bowl and fold in the parmesan.

STEP 2

Blanch remaining garlic in boiling water for 3 mins, until slightly softened. Drain, return to the pan with 200ml/7fl oz of the chicken stock and half the butter. Simmer for about 15 mins until the garlic is soft and coated in the syrupy stock. Remove from the heat. You can do this up to 4 hrs in advance.

STEP 3

Heat oven to 200C/fan 180C/gas 6. Toss the pumpkin cubes with the olive oil in a roasting tin, and roast for 10-15 mins until the flesh is just tender.

STEP 4

Make the crispy shallots. Dust them in the flour and shake off excess. Heat 2cm oil in a large pan and fry until light golden brown. Drain and keep warm.

STEP 5

Sweat the onion in the remaining butter in a large shallow pan until soft, about 5 mins. Tip in the rice, raise the heat and toast until translucent. Lower the heat and add the remaining stock a ladleful at a time, stirring well until the stock is completely absorbed before you add the next ladleful.

STEP 6

Once the rice is al dente, fold in the 2 cheeses, garlic cloves and pumpkin and cook for 2 mins. Serve with a drizzle of pesto and the shallots on top.

Slime bug cups

Prep: 25 mins plus setting

Makes 12

Ingredients

- 4 x 135g packs lime jelly
- a selection of animal and bug sweets (see tips, below, for our selection)
- 2 x 154g packs Oreo biscuits

Method

STEP 1

Make up the jelly following pack instructions. Pour a third of the mixture into 12 small glasses or plastic pots. Add a couple of bugs to each pot, then leave to set in the fridge, keeping remaining jelly at room temperature.

STEP 2

Once set, add more bugs to each container (lean some against edges, so they stick out the top). Pour over a third of the jelly and leave to set in the fridge. Repeat with remaining bugs and jelly.

STEP 3

For the soil topping, place cookies in a plastic bag and, using a rolling pin, bash into crumbs, then tip onto a plate.

STEP 4

Just before serving, sprinkle a layer of soil over each set jelly, then top with a mushroom, a slug and some ants or your choice of creepy crawlies.

Pumpkin cupcakes

Prep: 15 mins **Cook:** 25 mins

Makes 12

Ingredients

- 175ml sunflower oil
- 175g light muscovado sugar
- 3 large eggs
- 1 tsp vanilla extract
- 200g coarsely grated pumpkin or butternut squash flesh

- 100g sultanas
- grated zest 1 orange
- 2 tsp ground cinnamon
- 200g self-raising flour
- 1 tsp bicarbonate of soda

For the frosting

- 200g tub full-fat cream cheese
- 85g icing sugar
- toasted chopped pecans to decorate (optional)

Method

STEP 1

Heat oven to 180C/160C fan/gas 4. Line a 12-hole muffin tray with paper cases. Pour the oil into a large bowl and add the sugar, eggs and vanilla. Beat together, then add the grated pumpkin, sultanas and orange zest.

STEP 2

Stir in the cinnamon, flour and bicarbonate of soda, the mixture will be quite wet. Spoon into the cases. Bake for 25 mins until firm and springy to the touch and a skewer inserted in the centre of a cupcake comes out clean. Cool completely on a wire rack. At this stage you can freeze the cakes for 4 months.

STEP 3

To make the frosting, beat the cream cheese and sugar together until smooth then spread on top of the cupcakes. Leave plain or decorate with toasted pecans. Store in the fridge, but return to room temperature to serve for the best flavour and texture.

Homemade Butterfingers

YIELDS:24 servings PREP TIME:1 hour 0 mins COOK TIME:0 hours 0 mins TOTAL TIME:1 hour 0 mins

Ingredients

- 1/2 c. Roasted, Salted Peanuts
- 1/2 c. Smooth Peanut Butter (Not All-natural)
- 3 c. Candy Corn
- 1 c. Cornflakes
- 2 packages (10 To 12 Oz. Size) Milk Chocolate Melting Wafers

Directions

1. Grease an 8x8 pan with shortening. Line with two pieces of parchment, one in each direction, greasing in between.
2. Place peanuts in a food processor and pulse until ground into fine pieces.
3. Heat peanut butter in the microwave for 20 seconds on 50% power to warm. Stir.
4. In another bowl, melt candy corn in 30- to 40-second increments on 50% power. Stir between each heating. Once melted, stir in peanut butter.
5. Immediately turn out onto a sheet of parchment paper. Form into a rectangle a little larger than the pan. No need to be exact. Press the peanuts into the mixture. Fold into thirds, like a letter.
6. Use a rolling pin to roll into a rectangle of about the same size as before. Press cornflakes on top, crushing them as you do. Fold into thirds in the same manner. Roll flat. Fold into thirds again.
7. Once more, roll flat into a square about the size of the pan. Press into the pan, smoothing with your hands. Let the mixture set up about 15 minutes.
8. Lift out of the pan and cut into pieces. Place on a wire rack and let cool completely.
9. Once cool, melt chocolate wafers as directed on the package. Dip and place on a waxed paper-lined cookie sheet. Let chocolate set up before storing or packaging. Store at room temperature in an airtight container.

Concession Stand Crackers

YIELDS:45 PREP TIME:0 hours 15 mins COOK TIME:0 hours 15 mins TOTAL TIME:0 hours 30 mins

Ingredients

- 1 c. chocolate melting wafers
- 2 heaping tablespoons chocolate-hazelnut spread (such as Nutella)
- 1 sleeve Saltine crackers (about 45)
- 3 c. chopped candy, such as Sno-Caps, M&Ms, Reese's Pieces and/or Whoppers

Directions

1. Combine the chocolate and chocolate-hazelnut spread in a microwave-safe bowl and microwave until melted, stirring every 30 seconds.
2. Line a baking sheet with wax paper. Dip the crackers partway in the chocolate and let the excess drip back into the bowl. Lay on the baking sheet and sprinkle with the chopped candy. Let set, 15 minutes.

Reese's Bats

YIELDS:10 PREP TIME:0 HOURS 15 MINS TOTAL TIME:0 HOURS 15 MINS

INGREDIENTS

- 10 mini Reese's cups
- 5 oreos
- 20 Candy eyes
- 1 tbsp. peanut butter

DIRECTIONS

1. Cut all Oreo cookies in half and gently remove the cream. Cut each half in half to create the wings.
2. Using a toothpick or a small spoon, apply a small dab of peanut butter to one end of each Oreo. Press onto the Reese's cup to make wings.
3. Next, place a small dab of peanut butter onto the back of two candy eyes and place on top of the edge of the wings. Serve.

Halloween Layer Cake

YIELDS:16 SERVINGS PREP TIME:0 HOURS 30 MINS TOTAL TIME:2 HOURS 0 MINS

INGREDIENTS

FOR THE CAKE

- Cooking spray, for pans
- 1 box Devil's Food cake mix, plus ingredients called for on box
- 1 box vanilla cake mix, plus ingredients called for on box

FOR THE FROSTING

- 2 c. (4 sticks) butter, softened
- 7 c. powdered sugar, divided
- 1/2 c. whole milk
- 2 tsp. pure vanilla extract
- 2 tsp. pumpkin spice
- Orange food coloring

FOR THE GANACHE AND ASSEMBLY

- 1 1/2 c. semisweet chocolate chips
- 3/4 c. heavy cream
- Ghost Peeps
- Milano cookies
- Oreos, crushed
- Candy corn
- Candy pumpkins
- Sprinkles
- Candy eyeballs

DIRECTIONS

1. Preheat oven to 350° and spray four 9" cake pans with cooking spray. In two large bowls using a hand mixer, prepare both chocolate and vanilla cake batter.
2. Divide batter among prepared pans, two chocolate and two vanilla, and bake until a toothpick comes out clean, 30 minutes. Transfer to a wire rack to cool completely.
3. Make frosting: In another large bowl using a hand mixer, beat together butter and half of the powdered sugar until smooth. Beat in the milk, vanilla, pumpkin spice, and the rest of the powdered sugar until light and fluffy. Stir in food coloring until frosting is a bright, jack-o-lantern orange.
4. Make ganache: In a small saucepan over low heat, heat heavy cream just until it bubbles. Place chocolate chips in a medium, heatproof bowl and pour over hot heavy cream. Let sit 2 minutes, then whisk until smooth.
5. Assemble the cake: Level cake layers with a large serrated knife. Place a dab of frosting on a cake plate or serving platter and top with the first vanilla cake layer.
6. Top cake with 1 cup frosting and smooth into an even layer. Add the first chocolate cake on top of that, frost with another cup of frosting, then repeat with remaining vanilla and chocolate layers. Frost outside of cake with remaining frosting.
7. Drip ganache down the sides of the cake, then pour the rest on top of cake and smooth out with an offset spatula.
8. Decorate the cake: Create a graveyard scene by placing ghost peeps on skewers to stick out of cake, break Milanos in half and place on cake like graves, surrounded by Oreo "dirt", sprinkles, candy corn and pumpkins, and candy eyeballs.

Dracula Dentures

YIELDS:12 PREP TIME:0 HOURS **10** MINS **TOTAL TIME:0** HOURS **30** MINS

INGREDIENTS

- 1 tube chocolate chip cookie dough
- 1 can vanilla frosting
- red food coloring
- mini marshmallows
- slivered almonds

DIRECTIONS

1. Preheat oven to 350°. Line two large baking sheets with parchment paper. Roll cookie dough into 1 ½" balls and place on baking sheets. Bake until golden, about 12 minutes. Let cool completely then cut in half.
2. Add a few drops of red food coloring into vanilla frosting and stir until smooth. Spread a thin layer of red frosting onto each cookie half.
3. Place mini marshmallows around the round edges of half of the halves. Place the remaining halves on top, then stick a slivered almond on each side to create fangs.

Spooky Ghost Cookies

YIELDS:24 PREP TIME:0 HOURS **10** MINS **TOTAL TIME:2** HOURS **0** MINS

INGREDIENTS

FOR THE COOKIE DOUGH

- 3 c. all-purpose flour, plus more for surface
- 1 tsp. baking powder
- 1/2 tsp. kosher salt
- 1 c. (2 sticks) butter, softened
- 1 c. granulated sugar
- 1 large egg
- 1 tbsp. milk
- 1 tsp. pure vanilla extract

FOR ROYAL ICING

- 3 c. powdered sugar
- 1/4 c. light corn syrup
- 1/4 c. milk, plus more for thinning
- 1/4 tsp. almond (or vanilla) extract
- Black food coloring

DIRECTIONS

1. In a large bowl, whisk together flour, baking powder, and salt.

281

2. In another large bowl, beat butter and sugar together. Add egg, milk, and vanilla and beat until combined, then add flour mixture gradually until just combined. Shape into a disk and wrap in plastic. Refrigerate 1 hour.

3. When ready to roll, preheat oven to 350º and line two large baking sheets with parchment. Lightly flour a clean work surface and roll out dough until 1/8" thick. Using a ghost cookie cutter, cut out cookies. Re-roll scraps and cut out more cookies. Transfer to prepared baking sheets and freeze for 10 minutes.

4. Bake until edges are lightly golden, 8 to 10 minutes. Place on a wire cooling rack and let cool completely.

5. Meanwhile, make icing: In a medium bowl, combine powdered sugar, corn syrup, milk, and almond extract.

6. Place about 1/4 of icing into a small bowl and dye black with black food coloring.

7. Place about half the white icing in a piping bag fitted with a small round tip and pipe edges around cookies.

8. Thin remaining white icing by adding 1 teaspoon milk at a time until icing runs easily on cookies, but isn't water thin. Place icing in another piping bag with a small round tip and fill in centers of cookies. Use a toothpick to pop any air bubbles and to spread icing to help fill any gaps. Let cookies dry until icing is set, 15 minutes.

9. Place black icing in a piping bag with a small round tip and pipe eyes and mouths onto cookies.

Candy Apples with Gummy Worms

YIELDS:**4** servings TOTAL TIME:**0** hours **35** mins

INGREDIENTS

- 4 Grammy Smith apples
- Wooden sticks
- 3/4 c. praline crunch ice cream topping
- 1 c. sugar
- 1/2 c. water
- Pinch cream of tartar
- Green food coloring
- 4 gummy worms

DIRECTIONS

1. Wash and dry apples. Insert the wooden sticks into tops of apples.

2. Line a baking sheet with foil. Sprinkle 1/2 cup of the praline crunch topping over foil.

3. In a medium saucepan, combine sugar, water, and cream of tartar. Bring to a boil, cover, and boil for 3 minutes. Uncover and cook until a candy thermometer reaches 300°F or hard-crack stage, approximately 3 minutes. Remove pan from stove and place in a bowl of hot water. Tint green if desired with a few drops of food coloring.

4. Dip apples, one at a time, into candy to coat. Allow excess candy to drip off then place on prepared sheet. Sprinkle with remaining praline crunch and add gummy worms. Repeat with remaining apples and ingredients. Let apples cool completely before peeling from the foil.

Candy Corn Cupcakes

YIELDS:**24** servings TOTAL TIME:**1** hour **5** mins

INGREDIENTS

FOR CUPCAKES

- 1 16.5-oz box white cake mix
- 3 large eggs
- 1 cup water
- 1/4 c. vegetable oil

- 2 tsp. pure vanilla extract
- 1 tbsp. yellow food coloring
- 1 tbsp. orange food coloring
- Candy corn, for topping

FOR CREAMY MARSHMALLOW FROSTING

- 1 8-oz package cream cheese, softened
- 1 c. confectioners' sugar
- 1 tsp. pure vanilla extract

- 1 7-oz container marshmallow créme
- 1 8-oz container frozen whipped topping, thawed

DIRECTIONS

MAKE CUPCAKES

1. Preheat oven to 350°F. Line two 12-cup muffin pans with paper liners; set aside.
2. In a large bowl, beat cake mix, eggs, water, oil, and vanilla with an electric mixer on medium speed for 1 minute. Increase mixer speed to high and beat for 2 minutes. Place half of batter in a separate bowl. To one bowl, add yellow food coloring; mix well. To the other bowl, add orange food coloring; mix well.
3. Evenly divide yellow batter among muffin cups, then top with orange batter. Bake until a wooden pick inserted in the centers comes out clean, about 18 to 22 minutes. Remove from oven and cool in pan for 10 minutes. Remove to wire racks to cool completely.
4. Place Creamy Marshmallow Frosting in a pastry bag fitted with a large round tip. Pipe frosting onto cupcakes. Garnish with candy corn if desired. Store covered in refrigerator for up to 3 days.

MAKE CREAMY MARSHMALLOW FROSTING

1. In a large bowl, beat cream cheese until smooth, about 3 minutes. Add confectioners' sugar and vanilla and beat until combined. Add marshmallow crème and beat until creamy, about 2 minutes. Add whipped topping and beat until combined. Use immediately, or store covered in refrigerator for up to 3 days. If refrigerated, allow to come to room temperature for 30 minutes and beat with an electric mixer until smooth and creamy.

Cheesy Spiders

YIELDS:**24** servings TOTAL TIME:**0** hours **10** mins

INGREDIENTS

- 1 8-oz package cream cheese, softened
- 1 16-oz package shredded cheese
- Black paste food coloring
- 1 3.5-oz package round rice crunch crackers (or 24 of any round cracker)
- 1 cup chow mein noodles

DIRECTIONS

2. Mix 2 tablespoons softened cream cheese with food coloring to tint black. Spoon into a resealable bag; set aside.
3. Beat remaining cream cheese with all but 1 cup of the shredded cheese until blended. Shape mixture into 1 1/4-inch balls.
4. Place remaining shredded cheese in a shallow bowl. Roll balls in cheese to coat. Place one ball on a cracker. Insert 8 chow mein noodles into each ball as legs of the spider. Snip a very small corner from the bag with black cream cheese., then pipe eyes on each spider.

Chocolate Apple Cat Faces

YIELDS:**4** servings TOTAL TIME:**0** hours **25** mins

INGREDIENTS

- 4 Granny Smith apples
- Wooden sticks
- 1 12-oz bag semisweet chocolate chips
- 1 tbsp. shortening
- 1 c. chocolate sprinkles

- 1 chocolate wafer cookie, cut into eights with a serrated knife
- 8 yellow banana-shaped candies (Runts)
- 4 pink heart-shaped candies (Runts)
- 1 tube each pink and white decorating frosting

DIRECTIONS

1. Wash and dry apples. Insert the wooden sticks into tops of each apple. Line a baking pan with wax paper.
2. In a saucepan, melt chocolate chips and shortening on low heat, stirring constantly until completely melted.
3. Put sprinkles in a medium bowl. Working with one apple at a time, dip apple into melted chocolate to cover completely. Allow excess to drip off. Coat apple in sprinkles and place on prepared baking pan; Refrigerate until chocolate is set.
4. Spoon remaining melted chocolate into a resealable bag. Snip a small corner from the bag and use chocolate to attach chocolate wafer pieces as ears, yellow candies as eyes, and red candies as noses. Use chocolate to pipe on mouths.

5. Pipe on pink frosting ears and white frosting whiskers.

Crude-Ités with Green Slime Dip

YIELDS:**12** servings TOTAL TIME:**0** hours **25** mins

INGREDIENTS

DIP

- 1 c. packed basil leaves
- 1/4 c. packed parsley leaves
- 1 clove garlic
- 2 scallions, chopped

- 1/2 c. sour cream
- 1/2 c. mayonnaise
- Kosher salt and pepper
- Green food coloring (optional)

CRUDE-ITÉS

- 1 bunch celery
- 1 head Belgian endive, separated into leaves
- 1 head radicchio
- 1 lb. carrots, cut into sticks
- 1 seedless cucumber, cut into sticks

- 1 each red, yellow, and orange peppers, cut into strips
- 1 c. green beans, stem ends snipped and boiled to crisp-tender

DIRECTIONS

1. Make dip: Combine basil, parsley, garlic, scallions, and sour cream in a blender. Blend until creamy, scraping down side as necessary. Pour mixture into a bowl. Whisk in mayonnaise and season with salt and pepper. Tint a brighter green with food coloring if desired. (Cover and refrigerate overnight if desired.)
2. To assemble: Arrange vegetables in a serving bowl so they stand up. Cover with moist paper towels and refrigerate until ready to serve with dip.

Decorated Cookies

YIELDS:**42** servings TOTAL TIME:**1** hour **10** mins

INGREDIENTS

- 2 rolls (18 oz each) refrigerated sugar cookie dough
- 1 1/3 c. flour
- 2 batches royal icing

- Orange, yellow, gray, brown, black, purple, light green, and red food paste coloring
- Black, brown, red, green, white, and orange decorating sugars (optional)

DIRECTIONS

285

1. Preheat oven to 350°F. Coat four baking sheets with cooking spray.
2. Knead cookie dough with flour on a clean work surface until smooth.
3. Divide dough into quarters. Working with one piece at a time (keep remaining dough refrigerated) roll out dough on a lightly floured work surface to a scant 1/4-in. thickness. Use floured cutters to cut out as many shapes as possible; transfer shapes with an offset spatula to prepared pans. Re-roll the scraps.
4. Bake until cookies are golden around edges, about 10 to 12 minutes. Transfer to a wire rack and cool completely. Repeat with remaining dough.
5. Make royal icing and divide into nine bowls. Using food paste coloring, tint each portion a different color, leaving one white. Keep the bowls covered with plastic wrap to prevent frosting from drying out while not in use. Spoon half of each color into a small piping bag. Thin the remaining half of each color with 1 tsp of water until it has the texture of slightly whipped cream. Spoon each thinned color into separate piping bags.
6. Use the thicker icing to pipe outlines of designs on cookies as shown. Use the thinned icing (called flooding) to fill in outlined areas. Allow cookies to dry for at least an hour.
7. Use the thicker icing to pipe details on top of dry cookies. Sprinkle with colored sugars while still wet if desired.

Ghost Cupcakes

YIELDS:**24** servings TOTAL TIME:**1** hour **5** mins

INGREDIENTS

FOR CUPCAKES

- 1 16.5-oz box white cake mix
- 3 large eggs
- 1 c. water
- 1/4 c. vegetable oil
- 2 tsp. pure vanilla extract
- 1 tbsp. orange coloring

FOR CREAMY MARSHMALLOW FROSTING

- 1 8-oz package cream cheese, softened
- 1 c. confectioners' sugar
- 1 tsp. pure vanilla extract
- 1 7-oz container marshmallow crème
- 1 8-oz container frozen whipped topping, thawed

FOR DECORATING

1. Confectioners' sugar, for the surface
2. 1/2 5-lb. box white rolled fondant
3. Black gel icing

DIRECTIONS

MAKE CUPCAKES

1. Preheat oven to 350°F. Line two 12-cup muffin pans with paper liners; set aside.
2. In a large bowl, beat cake mix, eggs, water, oil, and vanilla extract with an electric mixer on medium speed for 1 minute. Increase mixer speed to high and beat for 2 minutes. Add food coloring; mix well. Evenly divide batter among muffin cups.
3. Bake until a wooden pick inserted near the center comes out clean, about 18 to 22 minutes. Remove from oven and cool in pan for 10 minutes, then remove to wire rack to cool completely.
4. Place Creamy Marshmallow Frosting in a pastry bag fitted with a large round tip. Pipe frosting onto cupcakes. Garnish with fondant ghost. Store covered in refrigerator for up to 3 days.

MAKE CREAMY MARSHMALLOW FROSTING

1. In a large bowl, beat cream cheese until smooth, about 3 minutes. Add confectioners' sugar and vanilla and beat until combined. Add marshmallow crème and beat until creamy, about 2 minutes. Add whipped topping and beat until combined. Use immediately or store covered in refrigerator for up to 3 days. If refrigerated, allow to come to room temperature for 30 minutes and beat with an electric mixer until smooth and creamy.

MAKE FONDANT GHOSTS

2. Lightly dust a work surface with confectioners' sugar. Roll out fondant to 1/8-inch thickness.
3. Using a 2-inch round cutter, cut rounds from fondant.
4. Roll out fondant circles smoothly into oval shapes.
5. Using your index finger, mold oval over finger, creating a ghost form.
6. Using your fingers, shred or tear the ends of the ghost. Set on parchment paper to dry, at least 4 hours.
7. Pipe eyes with black gel icing; allow 30 minutes to dry.

Cheese-Stuffed Jalapeño Poppers

YIELDS:**12** PREP TIME:**0** hours **20** mins TOTAL TIME:**0** hours **40** mins

INGREDIENTS

- 4 oz. cream cheese, at room temperature
- 2 oz. extra-sharp Cheddar, coarsely grated
- 1 scallion, finely chopped
- Dash hot sauce
- 6 small jalapeños
- 1 sheet refrigerated crescent roll dough
- 24 frozen peas, thawed, or tiny pieces of roasted red pepper, or a combination

DIRECTIONS

1. Heat oven to 375 degrees F. Line a large rimmed baking sheet with nonstick foil or parchment paper.
2. In a medium bowl, combine the cream cheese, Cheddar, scallion, and hot sauce. Spoon into a resealable plastic bag and snip off one corner.

287

3. Cut the jalapeños in half lengthwise, then remove and discard the seeds. Pipe the cheese mixture into the pepper halves.
4. Unroll the crescent dough and cut into 1⁄4" strips. Wrap 2 strips around each filled jalapeño half to create a mummy-like pattern. Transfer the halves to the prepared baking sheet and bake until golden brown, 15 minutes.
5. Let the mummies cool for 5 minutes, then place two peas or pieces of pepper on each one for eyes. Transfer to a platter and serve warm or at room temperature.

Cereal Treat Eyeballs

YIELDS:16 PREP TIME:0 hours 30 mins TOTAL TIME:0 hours 30 mins

Ingredients

- 1/2 batch Rice Krispies Treats
- Green candy melts, melted
- Candy eyeballs

Directions

1. Make a half batch of Rice Krispies Treats using your favorite recipe. Form into 2-inch balls and let set.
2. Spoon some melted green candy melts onto each and top with a candy eyeball.

Halloween Bark

YIELDS:16 servings PREP TIME:0 hours 20 mins COOK TIME:0 hours 10 mins TOTAL TIME:0 hours 30 mins

Ingredients

- 1 package White Almond Bark
- 16 whole Graham Crackers
- Pretzel Sticks, Broken In Half
- Oreo's, Chopped
- Reese's Pieces
- Chopped Pistachios

- Mini Chocolate Chips
- Other Misc Ingredients: Mini Marshmallows, Candy Corns, M & M's, Colored Sprinkled, Different Nuts, Broken Chocolate Bars

Directions

1. Melt the almond bark over a double boiler (I use a glass bowl over a saucepan of simmering water.) Stir until smooth and allow to cool slightly.

2. Arrange whole graham crackers together on a rimmed baking sheet so that they're butted up against one another. Pour the melted almond bark over the top and use an offset spatula to spread it evenly over the surface.

3. Sprinkle on pistachios, chocolate chips, pretzels, and Reese's Pieces (along with anything else you'd like to add.) Lightly press all the ingredients with the palm of your hand to make sure they're all anchored on.

4. Place the pan in the fridge and allow it to set completely. Break the bark into smaller pieces. Serve on a platter or package in small cellophane bags.

Cookie Skulls and Pumpkin Sugar Cookie

YIELDS:**40** servings TOTAL TIME:**1** hour **0** mins

INGREDIENTS

- 2 3/4 c. all-purpose flour
- 1/2 tsp. baking powder
- 1/4 tsp. kosher salt
- 1 c. (2 sticks) unsalted butter, at room temp
- 3/4 c. sugar
- 1 large egg

- 1 1/2 tsp. pure vanilla extract
- Skull and pumpkin cookie cutters
- Royal icing, gel food coloring, and candy-coated sunflower seeds, for decorating
- Jelly beans for serving plates (optional)

DIRECTIONS

1. In a large bowl, whisk together flour, baking powder, and salt. Using an electric mixer, beat butter and sugar until combined. Beat in egg, then vanilla. Reduce mixer speed to low and gradually add flour mixture, mixing just until incorporated.

2. Roll dough between sheets of waxed paper or parchment paper to 1/8 inch thick. Refrigerate until firm, at least 30 minutes.

3. Heat oven to 350°F. Line baking sheets with parchment paper. Using floured cookie cutters, cut out cookies. Place on prepared sheets, spacing 2 inches apart. Reroll, chill, and cut scraps. Bake, rotating the sheets halfway through, until cookies are lightly golden brown around edges, 10 to 12 minutes. Let cool on sheets 5 minutes before transferring to wire racks to cool completely.

4. Once cool, tint royal icing with desired colors and transfer half of each color to piping bags fitted with size 1.5 tips. Using a little water, loosen remaining icing to flood consistency and transfer to piping bags fitted with size 2 tips.

5. **For skulls:** Outline each cookie with thicker icing, then fill in with flooding icing and let dry slightly. Decorate with additional royal icing colors and sunflower seeds as desired.

6. **For pumpkins:** Outline each cookie with thicker icing; fill in with flooding icing and let dry slightly. Using royal icing, pipe straight lines or circles; then, using a toothpick, gently drag to create patterns. Serve on platters lined with jelly beans if desired.

Enchanted Brooms

YIELDS:**6** PREP TIME:**0** hours **45** mins TOTAL TIME:**0** hours **45** mins

INGREDIENTS

- 30 gummy peach rings
- 6 pretzel rods
- 9 grape fruit rolls
- cornstarch

- 6 bite-size banana or lime Tootsie Fruit Rolls or taffy
- Colored decorating sugar

DIRECTIONS

1. Stretch 5 gummy rings, one at a time, onto one end of a pretzel rod, keeping rings close together, so that the pretzel will stand up straight. Repeat with remaining gummy rings and pretzels.
2. Unroll 3 fruit rolls into flat circles, leaving them attached to the plastic backing. With a pizza wheel, cut each circle in half. For each broom, peel half of the fruit circle off backing; line up the straight edge with bottom of peach ring stack and wrap around stack and pretzel, gently pressing fruit roll to adhere. This is the broom base to which broom bristles will be attached.
3. Working with one broom at a time, unroll another fruit roll into a flat circle; remove from its backing. Lightly rub both sides of the fruit roll with cornstarch. Using the pizza wheel, cut a 4 x 6-in. rectangle out of the circle. With a long side facing you, cut several parallel narrow strips in the rectangle, to within 1/2 in. of the opposite long side (like making a grass skirt). Wrap the row of broom bristles around the broom base, pressing gently to adhere.
4. With rolling pin, flatten and roll out Tootsie Rolls until very thin. Cut out 3-in. long x 1/4-in.-wide bands; wrap around top of broom base, cutting to fit.
5. To serve: Put colored decorating sugar on a large platter. Using a dry pastry brush, sweep sugar in decorative swirls on platter to create broom tracks. Stand brooms in tracks.

Spider Bite Cupcake

YIELDS:**24**

INGREDIENTS

- 24 cupcakes
- 1 1/2 can Vanilla Frosting
- 24 chocolate-covered marshmallow cookies (such as Mallomars)

- 48 Tootsie Roll Midgees
- Brown tube icing
- Regular M&M's and mini M&M's

DIRECTIONS

1. Frost cupcakes with vanilla frosting, reserving 1 Tbsp. Place cookies on top.

2. Cut Tootsie Roll Midgees into 4 pieces each. Using the palm of your hand, roll each piece into a 3-in. rope. Press into rope with tines of a fork to make texture lines. Press 8 ropes onto each frosted cupcake for legs.
3. Pipe small dots of tube icing onto cookies for eyes and nose; press on M&M's for eyes and mini M&M for nose. With a toothpick, dot eyes with reserved white frosting.

Black Cat, Bat, Spider, and Mice Doughnuts

YIELDS:**28** servings TOTAL TIME:**0** hours **25** mins

INGREDIENTS

- 6 oz. semisweet chocolate, finely chopped
- 3/4 c. heavy cream
- Black gel food coloring
- 8 doughnuts (we used Entenmann's Frosted)
- 20 doughnut holes

- Candy corn, candy eyeballs, licorice, yellow and orange M&M's, banana and heart Runts, chocolate wafer cookies, Pocky sticks, and royal icing, for decorating

DIRECTIONS

1. Line a large baking sheet with parchment paper and place a wire rack on top.
2. Place chocolate in a medium bowl. In a small saucepan, heat cream until hot but not boiling. Pour over chocolate, let sit 2 minutes, then stir until melted and smooth. Stir in a few drops of food coloring to tint black.
3. Using 2 forks, dip each doughnut in chocolate, tapping off any excess, then transfer to a wire rack to set. Decorate using candies, cookies, and royal icing as desired.

Mini-Cauldrons

YIELDS:**6** PREP TIME:**0** hours **35** mins TOTAL TIME:**1** hour **45** mins

INGREDIENTS

- Mini–fluted bundt pan (6-cavity)
- 1 box pumpkin bread mix
- 1 1/2 tsp. ground cinnamon
- 1/2 c. cranberry Raisinets
- 1/2 c. walnuts
- 1 can chocolate frosting
- 1/2 can Vanilla or white frosting
- Black and red pouches of decorating icing

- Toothpick
- green gel food color
- White gumballs
- Sour or Gummi Worms
- Green miniature marshmallows
- Chocolate sticks
- cranberry Raisinets
- Orange and red gumdrops

DIRECTIONS

1. Heat oven to 400°F. Coat pan with nonstick spray.
2. Prepare bread mix as package directs, stirring in cinnamon, Raisinets and nuts. Spoon ½ cup batter into each mini bundt.
3. Bake 20 minutes or until wooden pick inserted comes out clean. Let cakes cool in pan 10 minutes. Invert onto wire rack. Cool completely.
4. Microwave chocolate frosting in glass bowl in 5- to 10-second intervals, stirring, until frosting melts and can coat a spoon. Place wire rack over baking sheet. Spoon melted frosting over cakes to cover; let set.
5. Tint vanilla frosting green. Pipe black frosting on gumballs for a pupil. Pipe red frosting on a sheet of wax paper. Dip a toothpick into frosting and drag onto gumball to make veins; let dry. With rolling pin, flatten gumdrops on a sugared surface; cut with scissors into flame shapes.
6. Spoon green marshmallows into hollow center of the bundt cakes. Microwave green frosting; spoon over marshmallows, letting some drip down side. Insert chocolate stick into center. Decorate with worms and eyeballs. Place cakes on additional Raisinets on serving plates. Arrange orange and red flames around cakes.

Candy Apples

CAL/SERV:**298** YIELDS:**12** PREP TIME:**0** hours **45** mins TOTAL TIME:**1** hour **30** mins

INGREDIENTS

- 12 very small Red Delicious apples (from bagged apples)
- 12 clean twigs
- 2 c. sugar
- 1 c. each light corn syrup and hot water
- 1/2 c. red cinnamon candies (like Red Hots)
- 1/4 tsp. liquid red food color

DIRECTIONS

1. Line a large baking sheet with nonstick foil or parchment paper.
2. Wash and thoroughly dry apples; remove stems. Insert twigs firmly into stem ends.
3. Combine sugar, corn syrup and water in a medium saucepan over medium-high heat; stir until sugar dissolves. Attach a candy thermometer to side of pan. Continue to cook, without stirring, until mixture reaches 250°F (wipe down sides of pan with a wet pastry brush occasionally to prevent crystallization).
4. When mixture reaches 250°F, add cinnamon candies and stir just to blend. Continue to cook until 300°F, about 15 to 20 minutes. Remove syrup from heat and swirl in food color, tilting saucepan, until blended. Let mixture settle for a minute until bubbles slow down.
5. Holding an apple by the twig and tilting pan, dip and swirl apple until coated. Lift apple and gently twirl over saucepan, letting excess drip back into pan. Place on prepared baking sheet, twig up. Repeat with remaining apples.
6. Allow apples to stand at room temperature until candy coating hardens, about 1 hour. Candy apples can be made up to 1 day ahead and stored at room temperature.

Halloween Cat Cake

YIELDS:**12** servings TOTAL TIME:**2** hours **0** mins

INGREDIENTS

FOR THE CAKE

- Oil, for the pan
- 3 c. all-purpose flour
- 1 c. unsweetened cocoa powder
- 1 tsp. kosher salt
- 1 tsp. baking powder
- 1/2 tsp. baking soda
- 1 c. sour cream
- 1 tsp. pure vanilla extract

- 1 tsp. pure almond extract
- 1 c. (2 sticks) unsalted butter, at room temperature
- 1 1/2 c. granulated sugar
- 1/2 c. dark brown sugar
- 2 large eggs
- 1 c. whole milk

FOR THE GANACHE

- 12 oz. bittersweet chocolate, finely chopped
- 1 1/2 c. heavy cream
- Black gel food coloring

FOR THE FILLING

- Buttercream frosting

FOR DECORATING

- Orange cotton candy
- Black, white, and orange fondant
- Black food-safe marker

DIRECTIONS

MAKE CAKE

1. Heat oven to 350°F. Oil two 10-inch round cake pans and line with parchment paper; oil parchment.
2. In a medium bowl, whisk together flour, cocoa, salt, baking powder, and baking soda.In a second bowl, combine sour cream and extracts.
3. Using a food processor, pulse together butter and sugars until combined, about 1 minute. Add eggs 1 at a time, pulsing until incorporated before adding the next. Add sour cream mixture.
4. Pulse in flour mixture in 3 parts, alternating with milk until just incorporated. Divide batter among the prepared cake pans and bake until a wooden pick inserted into the center comes out clean, 25 to 30 minutes.

5. Transfer cakes to a wire rack and let cool in the pans 10 minutes, then invert onto the rack to cool completely.

MAKE GANACHE

1. Place chocolate in a large bowl. In a small saucepan, heat cream until hot but not boiling. Pour over chocolate, let sit 3 minutes, then stir until melted and smooth. Let cool until slightly thickened. Stir in a few drops of food coloring to tint black.

DECORATE CAKE

2. Use a 3 1/2-inch round cutter to stamp out the middle round of each cake (being sure they line up). Reserve rounds.
3. Sandwich cake layers together with 2 cups buttercream frosting. Use ¼ cup buttercream frosting to sandwich together the two rounds. Cut the bottom third off the sandwiched cake and reserve for another use. Turn cake to stand on cut sides and place pieces of cut cardboard under cut ends. Use a plastic straw to attach the small round to one side of the cake for head.
4. Freeze cake until very cold, about 30 minutes. Cover cake in a thin layer of chocolate ganache, scraping away any excess to make very smooth. Return to freezer or refrigerator for at least 10 minutes to set. Cover cake in a second layer of ganache and freeze again. Repeat a third time.
5. Wrap cotton candy around a skewer and press into back of cake for tail. Cut 2 triangles from black fondant for ears and adhere to head using a little leftover ganache. Roll white fondant and cut out bones, skull, and insides of ears. Roll orange fondant and cut circles to serve as eyes and toes. Use a little water and a brush to adhere to cake. Using a food-safe marker, draw cat whiskers and mouth.
6.

Frankenstein and His Bride Cupcakes

YIELDS:**12** servings TOTAL TIME:**0** hours **30** mins

INGREDIENTS

- 3 c. buttercream frosting, half dyed green and half dyed brown
- 12 cupcakes
- 18 mini chocolate-covered doughnuts (we used Entenmann's; 2 per Frankenstein, 1 per bride)
- Chocolate sprinkles and finely shredded coconut, for decorating
- Black licorice (we used Twizzlers)
- 1 batch royal icing, one-third kept white, one-third dyed black, one-third dyed red
- 24 brown M&M's
- 6 wafer ice cream cones

DIRECTIONS

FOR FRANKENSTEIN

1. Working 1 at a time, spread a small amount of green buttercream all over surface of a cupcake. Top with a doughnut, then use a dab of frosting to act as glue and sandwich with another doughnut. Cover doughnuts with green buttercream. Sprinkle top of frosted doughnuts with chocolate sprinkles for hair.
2. Place 2 licorice pieces on sides of head for neck knobs. Using black and red royal icing, pipe on mouth, bangs, and scar. Pipe 2 large dots of white royal frosting for eyes and press in 2 M&M's.

FOR THE BRIDE

1. Cover ice cream cones in brown buttercream and immediately coat with chocolate sprinkles. Use white royal frosting to create white streaks in hair and sprinkle with coconut.
2. Working 1 at a time, spread a small amount of green buttercream all over surface of a cupcake. Top with a doughnut and cover in green buttercream, then place a cone on top of each doughnut. Using red royal icing, pipe on mouth. Pipe 2 large dots of white royal frosting for eyes and press in 2 M&M's.

Banana Mummies

CAL/SERV:**398** YIELDS:**8** PREP TIME:**0** hours **25** mins TOTAL TIME:**0** hours **25** mins

INGREDIENTS

- 4 bananas
- 1 lb. white chocolate
- 4 oz. white chocolate
- 16 mini m&m's
- 4 oz. milk chocolate chips
- 8 Lollipop sticks

DIRECTIONS

1. Line a large baking sheet with parchment paper. Skewer each banana half with a lollipop stick and freeze until firm, at least 2 hours.
2. In a large microwave-safe measuring cup, melt 1 pound white chocolate in the microwave according to package directions. One at a time, dip the bananas into the chocolate to coat, shaking off any excess. Return to the baking sheet and immediately place two M&M candies near the top for eyes.
3. Melt the remaining white chocolate in the microwave according to package directions and fill a small piping bag fitted with a small, round nozzle tip. Pipe zigzags over the banana to form bandages. Repeat this step with the milk chocolate, if using. Chill or freeze until ready to serve.

Candy Corn Fudge

CAL/SERV:**105** YIELDS:**64** PREP TIME:**0** hours **25** mins TOTAL TIME:**2** hours **25** mins

INGREDIENTS

- 8 oz. cream cheese at room temperature
- 2 c. confectioners' sugar

- 2 tsp. pure vanilla extract
- 3 c. white chocolate chips (about 18 oz)
- 2 c. mini pretzels or broken pretzel pieces
- 1 c. dried cherries
- 1 c. candy corn

DIRECTIONS

1. Line an 8- or 9-in. square pan with 2 sheets of parchment paper, leaving an overhang on all sides.
2. Using an electric mixer, beat the cream cheese and sugar in a large bowl until smooth, about 2 minutes; beat in the vanilla.
3. Meanwhile, melt the chocolate in the microwave according to package directions.
4. Add the melted chocolate to the cream cheese mixture and beat until smooth, 1 to 2 minutes. Fold in the pretzels and cherries. Transfer the mixture to the prepared pan and top with the candy corn. Refrigerate until firm, at least 2 hours and up to 2 days.
5. Using the overhangs, transfer the fudge to a cutting board and cut into 1-in. pieces. Serve in mini cupcake liners, if desired.

Spooky Spinach Dip in Bread Bowl Cauldron

YIELDS:**6** PREP TIME:**0** hours **30** mins TOTAL TIME:**2** hours **0** mins

INGREDIENTS

- 1 c. sour cream
- 1/2 c. mayonnaise
- 1 tsp. dried basil
- 1/2 tsp. black pepper
- 1/2 tsp. garlic powder
- 1/2 tsp. salt
- 1 package frozen chopped spinach
- 1/2 c. chopped scallions
- 1/4 c. shredded carrots
- Wilton leaf green icing color (optional)
- 2 refrigerated breadsticks (from an 11-oz can)
- Wilton Black Icing Color
- 1 round loaf pumpernickel bread
- 1 package cream cheese

DIRECTIONS

1. In medium bowl, combine sour cream, mayonnaise, basil, black pepper, garlic powder and salt; mix well. Stir in spinach, scallions and carrots; blend well. Tint green with icing color if desired. Cover and refrigerate 2 hours or overnight for flavors to develop.
2. Heat oven to 350°F. Unroll 2 attached breadsticks from package of refrigerated breadsticks. Twist and form into handle shape. Insert toothpick into each end and bake as package directs. (You can bake the remaining breadsticks as well and serve them as an accompaniment to dip. Make sure to bake them immediately after opening the package.)
3. Remove to rack to cool completely. Paint handle with black icing color. Cut top off bread and hollow out to form a bowl. Insert handle into top of bread bowl.

4. In a small bowl, tint cream cheese black with icing color. Transfer to ziptop bag. Snip 1/2-in. hole from one corner of bag. Pipe around top of cauldron. Spoon dip into top of cauldron. Serve with Pumpkin-Shaped Tortilla Dippers and raw vegetables.

Halloween Cheese Balls

YIELDS:**12** PREP TIME:**0** hours **25** mins TOTAL TIME:**0** hours **25** mins

INGREDIENTS

- 4 large green tortillas or wraps
- 2 c. Cheetos, finely crushed into crumbs
- 2 tbsp. black sesame seeds
- 2 tbsp. poppy seeds
- 1 (8-oz.) package cream cheese, at room temperature

- 1 (4-oz.) package goat cheese, at room temperature
- black pepper
- black and green olives

DIRECTIONS

1. Heat oven to 375 degrees F. Cut the tortillas into 24 bat-shaped wings. Place on a large rimmed baking sheet and bake until dry and crisp, but not browned, about 15 minutes; let cool. Line a second large rimmed baking sheet with parchment paper.
2. Place the Cheetos crumbs and seeds in separate small bowls.
3. In a medium bowl, combine the cream cheese, goat cheese and pepper to taste. Using a 1-ounce cookie scoop, scoop balls of cheese and round out, gently molding with your hands.
4. Coat the cheese balls in the crumbs or seeds. Transfer to the prepared baking sheet, then refrigerate until ready to serve.
5. Once the tortilla wings are cool, gently press into the sides of each cheese ball. Thinly slice olives and place on the top of each ball for eyes.

Saucy Spider with Hairy Leg Sticks

CAL/SERV:**223** YIELDS:**12** PREP TIME:**0** hours **40** mins TOTAL TIME:**1** hour **30** mins

INGREDIENTS

- 2 balls pizza dough (thawed if frozen)
- 1 large egg
- 1/4 c. grated Parmesan (1 oz)

- 2 tbsp. grated Parmesan (1 oz)
- 1 large pitted black olive
- 2 c. marinara sauce

DIRECTIONS

1. Heat oven to 375°F. Line 2 large baking sheets with parchment paper.

2. Make the spider: Cut 1 ball of dough in half. Shape one half into a 5-in. ball to make the spider body. Cut a 1 1/2-in. strip from the remaining half and shape into a 2 1/2-in. ball to make the head. Cut the remaining dough into 8 strips and roll each strip into a 6-in. rope to make the legs.
3. Arrange the body, legs and head on one of the prepared baking sheets to resemble a spider, gently pressing all of the pieces of dough together. Brush the entire spider with some of the egg. Sprinkle the legs with 2 Tbsp Parmesan. Place 2 of the olive slices on the top of the head for eyes and 2 on the bottom for pincers. Bake until golden brown, 25 to 30 minutes (covering the legs with foil if browning too quickly).
4. Meanwhile, make the spider leg sticks: Cut the remaining ball of dough into 8 pieces. Roll each piece into a 3/4-in.-thick rope. Cut each rope into various lengths. Taper one end of each piece and slightly bend the other to resemble legs. Place on the second baking sheet. Brush with the remaining egg and sprinkle with the remaining 1/4 cup Parmesan. Bake until golden brown, 15 to 20 minutes.
5. Meanwhile warm the marinara sauce. Using a knife, hollow out the body of the spider and fill with the warm sauce. Serve with the leg sticks.

Halloween Spider Bark

YIELDS:**20** servings TOTAL TIME:**0** hours **20** mins

INGREDIENTS

- 5 oz. Pretzel sticks (about 3 cups)
- or 35 Oreos
- 1 1/4 lb. white chocolate, chopped
- 2 oz. semisweet chocolate, chopped

- small and large chocolate covered malt balls, halved
- black royal icing

DIRECTIONS

1. Line a 9 x 13-in. pan with parchment paper, leaving at least 1 in. of overhang on the two long sides.
2. Arrange pretzels or cookies on bottom of the pan to cover it completely.
3. Place white chocolate in a medium microwave-safe bowl and melt on 50 percent power in 30-second increments until smooth. Carefully pour white chocolate over pretzels or cookies and spread with a small offset spatula to evenly cover.
4. Place semisweet chocolate in a small microwave-safe bowl and melt on 50 percent power in 30-second increments until smooth. Let sit at room temperature for 5 minutes, then transfer to a small resealable bag, cut off a small corner, and use to pipe webs.
5. To make spiders, place small and large malt balls cut side down on white chocolate while still wet, then pipe black royal icing eyes and legs.

Coffin Cake

YIELDS:**2** TOTAL TIME:**1** hour **50** mins

INGREDIENTS

- Oil, for the pans
- 3 c. all-purpose flour
- 2 tsp. baking powder
- 1 tsp. baking soda
- 1/2 tsp. freshly ground nutmeg
- 1/2 tsp. kosher salt

FOR THE FROSTING

- 1 8-oz. package cream cheese, at room temperature
- 4 tbsp. unsalted butter, at room temperature
- 2 c. confectioners' sugar

- 2 c. sugar
- 1 c. (2 sticks) unsalted butter, melted
- 3 large eggs
- 1 15-oz. can pumpkin
- 1 tsp. pure vanilla extract
- 1/2 c. buttermilk

- 1/4 c. heavy cream
- 1/2 tsp. pure vanilla extract
- 4 candy eyeballs for serving

DIRECTIONS

1. Heat oven to 350°F. Lightly oil two 8½ x 4½-in. loaf pans and line the bottoms with parchment paper, leaving at least 1 in. of overhang on the two long sides.
2. In a large bowl, whisk together flour, baking powder, baking soda, nutmeg, and salt.
3. In a second large bowl, beat together sugar, butter, eggs, pumpkin, and vanilla. Add flour mixture in 3 additions, alternating with buttermilk and mixing in between addition to combine.
4. Divide mixture between the prepared loaf pans and bake, rotating the pans halfway through, until a wooden pick inserted into the center comes out clean, 65 to 70 minutes. Transfer the pans to a wire rack to cool for 10 minutes before using the parchment overhangs to remove cakes to a rack to cool completely.
5. Using an electric mixer, beat cream cheese and butter in a large bowl on low speed until smooth. Add sugar, beating until just combined. Add heavy cream and vanilla and beat until soft peaks form, about 2 minutes. Spread a thin layer of frosting (about ¼ cup) over the top of each cake. Transfer remaining frosting to a large piping bag fitted with a large flat tip, then pipe lines back and forth on a diagonal to create mummy bandages. Place two candy eyeballs at one end of each cake.

Bite-Size Eyeballs

YIELDS:**40** TOTAL TIME:**1** hour **0** mins

INGREDIENTS

- 1/2 c. (1 stick) Unsalted butter
- Kosher salt and pepper
- 1 c. all-purpose flour
- 4 large eggs
- 4 oz. Guryère cheese, coarsely grated

- Cream cheese, Persian cucumbers, and pimiento-stuffed olives, for decorating
- Sriacha or ketchup, for decorating

DIRECTIONS

1. Heat oven to 425°F. Line 2 large baking sheets with parchment paper.
2. Place butter, 1 cup water, and ½ tsp salt in a medium saucepan and bring to a boil over medium heat. Add flour and stir vigorously until mixture comes together and looks smooth and shiny, about 1 minute. Continue stirring for 1 minute, then transfer mixture to a large bowl and let sit until no longer hot to the touch, about 15 minutes.
3. Add eggs, 1 at a time, and beat, using a wooden spoon, until mixture comes back together and is smooth. Add ¼ tsp pepper and cheese.
4. Using a 1-Tbsp cookie scoop, drop small balls 2 in. apart on prepared baking sheet. Bake for 10 minutes, then rotate the pans top to bottom and front to back. Reduce heat to 350°F and continue baking until light golden brown and set, 12 to 17 minutes more. Transfer to a wire rack to cool.
5. To make eyeballs, use cream cheese as glue to place slices of cucumber and olives on top of each puff. Squeeze sriacha or ketchup into lines around the sides.

Cheese Pumpkins

YIELDS:**15** PREP TIME:**0** hours **20** mins TOTAL TIME:**0** hours **20** mins

INGREDIENTS

- 3 3/4 c. shredded cheddar
- 3 package cream cheese
- 1 1/2 tsp. garlic salt
- 1 tsp. dry mustard
- Garnish: parsley sprigs
- Accompaniments: toasted pumpernickel bread or crackers
- You will need: Wilton Dimensions Multi-Cavity Mini Pumpkins Pan

DIRECTIONS

1. Put Cheddar, cream cheese, garlic salt and mustard in a food processor and process until smooth.
2. Coat pan with nonstick spray. Spoon cheese mixture into cavities, pressing with back of spoon to pack mixture tightly into pan. Cover with plastic wrap. Chill overnight.
3. To unmold, briefly dip bottom of pan into a larger pan filled with hot water. Tap pan firmly on flat surface to loosen, then unmold.
4. Press matching halves of pumpkins together to attach. Garnish tops of pumpkins with parsley sprigs. Serve with accompaniments.

Jack-o'-Lantern Tamale Bake

YIELDS:**12** PREP TIME:**0** hours **30** mins TOTAL TIME:**0** hours **55** mins

INGREDIENTS

- 1 1/4 lb. Lean Ground Beef
- 1 jar chunky salsa
- 1 can corn
- 1 can sliced black olives
- 1 1/2 tsp. chili powder
- 1 tsp. salt
- 1/4 tsp. Pepper
- 1 c. shredded Cheddar cheese

- 4 box cornbread mix
- Green bell pepper, scallions or chives, roasted red peppers, olive tapenade
- Sour cream, chopped scallions or tomatoes, guacamole
- You will need: Wilton Iridescents! Jack-O-Lantern Pan

DIRECTIONS

1. Heat oven to 400°F. Coat pan with nonstick cooking spray.
2. In a large nonstick skillet, brown ground beef; drain. Stir in salsa, corn, olives, chili powder, salt, and pepper; heat 5 minutes, stirring occasionally. Remove skillet from heat; stir in cheese. Keep filling hot.
3. Prepare two boxes cornbread mix according to directions. Spread batter evenly on bottom of pan; spoon in filling to approximately 1-in. from edge of pan. Prepare remaining boxes of mix. Spread batter evenly over filling making sure batter flows into edges of pan.
4. Bake 20 to 25 minutes or until top crust is golden brown and firm to the touch. Remove from oven to wire rack to cool 15 minutes. If cornbread has baked over edge of pan, loosen edges from pan. Place serving plate on top and turn over to release.
5. Cut bell pepper into stem, scallions into strips for hair and roasted peppers into triangles for eyes and nose. Arrange on Tamale Bake. Spread olive tapenade into mouth shape.

Bewitching Brownies

YIELDS:**14** PREP TIME:**1** hour **0** mins TOTAL TIME:**1** hour **0** mins

INGREDIENTS

- 1 box brownie mix
- Violet, red and white tube decorating icing
- 1 can Vanilla Frosting
- 1 can dark chocolate frosting

- Wilton jumbo confetti and Halloween confetti sprinkles
- White fondant

DIRECTIONS

1. Cut prepared and cooled brownies into eight coffin shapes, using a 3-in. coffin-shaped cookie cutter. Using a 2 1/2-in. round cookie cutter, cut six brownies into rounds for vampire faces.

2. Pipe on rim of coffins with violet and red decorating icing. Pipe "RIP" using white decorating icing.
3. Spread top of circles with vanilla frosting. Pipe on hair and eyebrows using the chocolate frosting in a pastry bag fitted with a #3 tip. Use jumbo confetti sprinkles for eyes and Halloween confetti sprinkles for pupils. (You can also pipe on the pupils with some of the chocolate frosting.) Using fingers, form fondant into ears, nose, and fang shapes; attach to face. Pipe on mouths using red decorating icing.

Severed Toes in Bandages

YIELDS:**36** PREP TIME:**0** hours **30** mins TOTAL TIME:**0** hours **30** mins

INGREDIENTS

- 1 box refrigerated pie crusts
- 1 package beef cocktail franks
- 36 almond slices
- 1 large egg
- Ketchup, for serving

DIRECTIONS

1. Heat oven to 450°F. Line a large baking sheet with nonstick foil. On work surface, unroll a pie crust and, using a pizza wheel, cut crust into 3/8-in. strips.
2. Working with 1 frank at a time, wrap one-half to two-thirds of the cocktail frank with a dough strip (like a bandage), cutting the dough to fit. Repeat with remaining franks. Arrange on prepared baking sheet.
3. Using a small paring knife, make a horizontal slit on the unwrapped end of each frank, and insert an almond slice into the slit to resemble a toenail. Brush dough bandages with egg wash.
4. Bake 10 minutes, or until pastry is light golden brown. Serve immediately with ketchup.
5.

Creepy Cookie Stacks

YIELDS:**10** PREP TIME:**0** hours **30** mins TOTAL TIME:**1** hour **0** mins

INGREDIENTS

- 1/2 c. all-purpose flour
- 2 tubes refrigerated sugar cookie dough
- Wilton Meringue Powder
- Orange, green, yellow, black, red, white, and purple Wilton Icing colors
- You will need: Wilton Stackable! Halloween Cookie Cutter Set

DIRECTIONS

1. Heat oven to 350°F. Have baking sheets ready.
2. Knead flour into sugar cookie dough. Roll out dough on lightly floured surface to 3/16-in. thickness. Cut out cookies using cutter set. Place 1-in. apart on baking sheets.
3. Bake 8 to 14 minutes until lightly browned around edges. Remove baking sheets to wire rack to cool 5 minutes, then remove cookies to rack to cool completely.
4. Prepare Royal Icing according to directions included with meringue powder. To decorate jack-o'-lanterns, use icing tinted orange, green and yellow. Spread orange icing on pumpkin-shaped cookie. Spread green on stem. Spread yellow on eyes, noses, and mouths. Let stand at room temperature to set. When set, stack eyes, noses and mouths on pumpkin bases.
5. To decorate spider webs, use icing tinted green, black, orange, red and white. Spread webs with green icing and spider body with black icing. Let set at room temperature. Meanwhile, pipe on spider legs using black icing in a pastry bag fitted with a #2 tip. Let set at room temperature. Pipe white web using white icing in a pastry bag fitted with a #2 tip. Pipe face and details on spider using red, orange and green icing. Let set at room temperature. When dry, set spiders on top of webs.
6. To decorate bats and moons, use icing tinted yellow, black, purple, orange, white and red. Spread yellow icing on moon-shaped cookies. Spread black icing on bat body. Outline wings in black. Let stand at room temperature to set. When set, spread purple icing on bat body and wings, pipe face on bat using orange, white, and red icing in pastry bags fitted with #2 tips. Let set at room temperature. When dry, set wings on top of moons and bat bodies on top of wings.

Guacamoldy Eyeballs

CAL/SERV:**29** YIELDS:**20** PREP TIME:**0** hours **20** mins TOTAL TIME:**0** hours **40** mins

INGREDIENTS

- 10 large eggs
- 1/4 c. lowfat sour cream
- 2 tbsp. smooth taco sauce (without chunks)
- 2 tsp. chili powder

- 1 large avocado (or 1 1/2 small)
- 2 tbsp. fresh lemon juice
- Kosher salt and pepper
- 4 medium pimiento-stuffed olives

DIRECTIONS

1. Place the eggs in a large saucepan, add enough cold water to reach 2 in. above submerged eggs, and bring to a boil. Remove from heat, cover the saucepan and let stand for 12 minutes.
2. Meanwhile, in a small bowl, whisk together the sour cream, taco sauce and chili powder. Place in a pastry bag fitted with a fine writing tip.
3. In a second small bowl, mash the avocado with the lemon juice and 1/4 tsp each salt and pepper. Transfer to a resealable plastic bag and cut off the tip to create a 1/2-in. opening.
4. Drain the eggs and return them to the saucepan. Gently shake the saucepan to crack the eggs all over. Run under cold water to cool, then peel the eggs. Cut the eggs in half lengthwise. Remove the yolks and save for another use.

5. Using the sour cream mixture, pipe thin squiggly lines on each egg white half so they resemble bloodshot eyes. Pipe the avocado mixture into each white and place a slice of olive on top.

Marshmallow Heads

CAL/SERV:**84** YIELDS:**28** PREP TIME:**1** hour **0** mins TOTAL TIME:**2** hours **0** mins

INGREDIENTS

- 28 marshmallows
- 28 Lollipop sticks
- 1 bag white chocolate chips
- Green or orange gel or paste food color
- canola oil

- Vanilla or white frosting
- Green and red gel or paste food color
- chocolate frosting
- 4 pastry bags fitted with couplers and fine writing tips

DIRECTIONS

1. Place a marshmallow onto each lollipop stick with the flat sides facing out. One exception: If making Frankenstein's monster, place the marshmallows on the sticks with the flat sides facing up and down.
2. In a microwave-safe bowl, melt the white chocolate according to package directions.
3. To make Draculas or mummies, dip one marshmallow at a time into the melted chocolate, tapping gently on the edge of the bowl to shake off any excess. Place the sticks upright into florist's foam or a large bowl filled with granulated sugar or crushed chocolate cookies. Let stand at room temperature until set, 30 minutes.
4. To make Frankenstein's monsters or jack-o'-lanterns, tint the chocolate with green or orange food color (you will need to mix in 3 to 5 tsp of oil for every 1/2 cup melted chocolate to keep it from stiffening). Dip as directed above.
5. Tint 1/2 cup of the white frosting green and 1/2 cup red. Place the red, green, remaining white and chocolate frostings in the pastry bags and decorate, following the directions. Let set for 30 minutes before serving.

Mummy Meat Loaves

CAL/SERV:**152** YIELDS:**12** PREP TIME:**0** hours **30** mins TOTAL TIME:**0** hours **40** mins

INGREDIENTS

- 3/4 lb. white or yellow potatoes
- Kosher salt and pepper
- 2 large eggs
- 2 tbsp. Ketchup
- 2 tsp. Worcestershire sauce

- 1/2 c. panko or plain bread crumbs
- 2 clove garlic
- 1 medium carrot
- 3/4 lb. ground beef
- 1/2 lb. ground pork

- 12 grape tomatoes
- 3/4 c. lowfat sour cream

- 24 oz. peas

DIRECTIONS

1. Heat oven to 375°F. Line a 12-cup muffin tin with foil liners. Place the potatoes in a pot, add enough cold water to cover and bring to a boil. Add 1 tsp salt, reduce heat and simmer until just tender, 15 to 18 minutes.
2. Meanwhile, in a bowl, combine the eggs, ketchup, Worcestershire, 1/2 tsp salt and 1/4 tsp pepper; stir in the bread crumbs. Add the garlic and carrot and mix to combine. Add the beef and pork and mix just until incorporated. Divide the meat mixture among the foil liners and push a tomato into the center of each one. Transfer to the oven and roast until a thermometer inserted into the meat registers 155°F, 14 to 16 minutes.
3. Drain the potatoes and return them to the pot. Add the sour cream and 1/4 tsp salt and mash until very smooth. Transfer to a pastry bag fitted with a 1/2-in. ribbon tip (Wilton 104). Transfer the meat loaves to a platter and pipe the potatoes back and forth over each top to resemble a mummy's wrapping. Place 2 peas on each for eyes.

Nerdy Popcorn Balls

YIELDS:**16** PREP TIME:**0** hours **15** mins TOTAL TIME:**0** hours **15** mins

INGREDIENTS

- 3 tbsp. unsalted butter
- 1 package Mini Marshmallows
- 10 c. air-popped popcorn
- c. Nerds candies
- 16 Lollipop sticks

DIRECTIONS

1. Melt unsalted butter and mini marshmallows in a large pot over low heat, stirring frequently until combined and smooth. Fold in popcorn. Let cool for 5 minutes, then fold in Nerds (keep colors separate, if desired).
2. With wet hands, form the popcorn mixture into 16 balls and transfer to a wax paper–lined rimmed baking sheet. If desired, insert lollipop sticks into each ball.

Skulls and Monsters

YIELDS:**8** PREP TIME:**0** hours **20** mins TOTAL TIME:**0** hours **30** mins

INGREDIENTS

- 1 box Rice Krispies Treats
- 1 can whipped fluffy white frosting
- Green and yellow paste or gel food colors*
- Chocolate mini M&M's candies or M&M's mini baking bits
- Chocolate sprinkles (jimmies)
- Lime Tic Tacs
- 1/4 c. semisweet chocolate chips
- 1 tub red decorating gel

DIRECTIONS

1. Shape 4 Krispies Treats into skulls. Place on a wire rack over wax paper. Divide frosting between 2 microwave-safe bowls. Microwave 1 bowl, stirring every 10 seconds, until frosting is pourable. Spoon over skulls to cover. Pour rest into a small ziptop bag; reserve. Put M&M's in place for eyes and noses.
2. Put remaining Treats on rack. Using food colors, tint frosting in other bowl to match Tic Tacs. Microwave until pourable. Spoon over Treats. Add sprinkles for hair and Tic Tacs for eyelids and bolts. Refrigerate to set.
3. Cut a tip off corner of ziptop bag; pipe eyes on Monsters. Melt chocolate chips, stirring until smooth. Spoon into another ziptop bag and cut tip off corner; pipe eyes and mouths on Monsters, mouths on Skulls. With red gel, pipe scars on Monsters. Refrigerate until serving.

Spiderweb Cookies

YIELDS:**10** PREP TIME:**0** hours **20** mins TOTAL TIME:**0** hours **30** mins

INGREDIENTS

- 1 can whipped fluffy white frosting
- Orange paste or gel food color
- 1 can whipped fluffy chocolate frosting
- 1 package soft 3 1/4-in. oatmeal cookies
- Regular M&M's and mini M&M's candies or M&M's mini baking bits

DIRECTIONS

1. Tint white frosting orange and frost 5 cookies. Frost remaining cookies with chocolate frosting. Put remaining orange and chocolate frosting in separate small ziptop bags. Cut a tip off 1 corner of each bag and pipe a web on opposite-color frosted cookies.
2. To make spiders: Place an M&M on each web; lean a mini M&M of the same color slightly against larger candy. With chocolate frosting, pipe legs on both sides of each "body." Pipe orange or chocolate eyes. Refrigerate until set.

Bloodshot Eyeballs

YIELDS:**24** PREP TIME:**0** hours **20** mins TOTAL TIME:**0** hours **30** mins

INGREDIENTS

- 24 doughnut holes
- 1 can whipped fluffy white frosting
- 24 blue or brown M&M's
- c. seedless raspberry jam
- Red paste or gel food color

DIRECTIONS

1. Cut a thin slice off 1 side of each doughnut hole. Place trimmed side down on a wire rack over wax paper.
2. Microwave frosting, stirring every 10 seconds, until pourable. Spoon over doughnut holes to coat. Put M&M's on center of each. Refrigerate until set.
3. Stir jam and red food coloring until blended; spoon into a small ziptop bag. Cut a tip off 1 corner of bag; pipe veins on eyeballs. Refrigerate until serving.

Mummy Cakes

YIELDS:**8** PREP TIME:**0** hours **20** mins TOTAL TIME:**0** hours **30** mins

INGREDIENTS

- 8 Twinkies Snack Cakes (from a 15-oz box)
- 1 can whipped fluffy white frosting
- Assorted mini M&M's candies or M&M's mini baking bits
- You also need: pastry bag fitted with a 1/4-in. ribbon piping tip*

DIRECTIONS

1. Unwrap cakes; place on foil-lined baking sheet.
2. Place frosting in pastry bag; pipe mummy wrapping to cover each cake.
3. Place candies on cakes for eyes.
4. Refrigerate until serving, then transfer to serving platter.*Paste and gel food colors, pastry bags and piping tips can be found in cake-decorating, party-supply and crafts stores.

Bats Flying Across the Moon Cookies

YIELDS:**8** PREP TIME:**0** hours **45** mins TOTAL TIME:**1** hour **30** mins

INGREDIENTS

- 1 package soft-baked sugar cookies (8 cookies)
- 1/2 can lemon frosting
- Yellow and black gel food color
- 1/2 can dark chocolate frosting
- Jumbo orange nonpareil candies

DIRECTIONS

1. Using a 2 1/2-in. round cookie cutter, cut out a crescent moon from each cookie. From the remaining cookie scraps, using a 2-in. bat cookie cutter, cut out 8 bats. Place moon cookies and bat cookies on separate wire racks set over wax paper.
2. Spoon lemon frosting into a microwave-safe bowl; tint a shade or two deeper with yellow food color. Microwave on high 10 to 15 seconds, stirring once, until a pourable glaze consistency. Pour glaze over moon cookies to cover, letting excess frosting drip onto wax paper; let set at room temperature until dry (or refrigerate to speed up the process).
3. Spoon chocolate frosting into a microwave-safe bowl; tint black with the black food color. Microwave on high 10 to 15 seconds, stirring once, until a pourable glaze consistency. Pour glaze over bat cookies to cover, letting excess frosting drip onto wax paper. While frosting is still wet, add nonpareil eyes; let set at room temperature until dry (or refrigerate to speed up the process).
4. Spread undersides of bat cookies with a dab of the remaining lemon frosting, and attach to moon cookies.

Witchy Fingers

YIELDS:**48** PREP TIME:**0** hours **20** mins TOTAL TIME:**0** hours **28** mins

INGREDIENTS

- 1 tube refrigerated breadstick dough
- 1/2 stick butter
- 2 tbsp. cinnamon-sugar
- 1 large egg
- 48 slice natural (with skin) almonds

DIRECTIONS

1. Heat oven to 375°F.
2. Crumple 4 large pieces of foil; shape each into a 15 x 2-in. log. Place on a baking sheet.
3. Unroll dough. Cut each of the rectangles crosswise in half, then lengthwise into 2 strips. Cut 1 end of each into a fingertip.
4. Roll strips in butter and drape over foil logs; sprinkle with cinnamon-sugar. Brush fingertips with beaten egg; press an almond slice "nail" on each. Bake 8 minutes until golden. Serve, or wrap around cups of Monster Munch (see recipe in Woman's Day).

Haystack Creatures

YIELDS:**9** PREP TIME:**0** hours **30** mins TOTAL TIME:**1** hour **0** mins

INGREDIENTS

- 1 5-oz. can thin chow mein noodles (such as La Choy)
- 8 oz. bittersweet chocolate, finely chopped
- 1/2 c. vanilla frosting, tinted desired colors

- Candy eyes or jelly beans
- Toasted coconut, for serving

DIRECTIONS

1. Line a large baking sheet with parchment paper
2. Melt chocolate in microwave according to package directions
3. Place chow mein noodles in a large bowl, pour chocolate over top and gently toss until noodles are evenly coated
4. Drop 10 heaping spoonful's (about 1/4 cup each) onto prepared baking sheet. Refrigerate until firm, 20 to 30 minutes.
5. Transfer frosting to a resealable plastic bag(s). Snip off a tiny corner and use as glue to stick the eyes on creatures, then pipe on an additional pupil. Serve on toasted coconut, if desired.

Monster Munch

YIELDS:**4** PREP TIME:**0** hours **5** mins TOTAL TIME:**0** hours **10** mins

INGREDIENTS

- 1 box caramel popcorn-nut mixture
- 2 tbsp. semisweet chocolate chips
- 1/2 c. candy corn
- 1/2 c. Reese's Pieces candies
- 1 c. Halloween gummy candies

DIRECTIONS

1. Spread popcorn mix on a baking sheet. Melt chocolate; spoon into a small ziptop bag. Snip a tip off 1 corner of bag; drizzle over popcorn. Refrigerate to set.
2. Mix popcorn mixture with remaining ingredients. Serve in paper cups.

Large Sno Ball Spiders

YIELDS:**12** PREP TIME:**1** hour **0** mins TOTAL TIME:**1** hour **0** mins

INGREDIENTS

- Chocolate stick candies
- Wilton Dark Cocoa Candy Melts
- 12 Hostess Sno Ball cakes
- Wilton Color Mist food color spray
- Wilton Sparkle Gel
- Gum drops
- Red decorating frosting or gel
- Chocolate-covered sunflower seeds

DIRECTIONS

1. Cut chocolate stick candies to desired lengths for top and bottom of legs. Line a baking sheet with wax paper. Melt candy melts as package directs and transfer to a small ziptop bag. Snip a small hole

in one corner of bag. Attach bottoms and tops of legs with a drop of candy melts. Place on pan and refrigerate 5 to 10 minutes, until set.

2. Spray Sno Ball cakes with food color spray. Let dry. Poke holes in top of cakes with toothpick and insert legs. Decorate top of cake with sparkle gel.

3. To make heads, slightly flatten gum drops. Using red decorating frosting, attach chocolate-covered sunflower seeds for eyes and pipe on mouths. Attach heads to bodies with candy melts. Return to pan and refrigerate until set.

4.

Ghost Toasts

YIELDS:**12** PREP TIME:**0** hours **20** mins TOTAL TIME:**0** hours **40** mins

INGREDIENTS

- 1 package pita bread
- salt (optional)
- Favorite herbs and spices, fresh or dried (optional)

DIRECTIONS

1. Heat oven to 375°F.
2. Split pita breads in half through pocket. Cut into ghost shapes with 3-in. ghost-shaped cookie cutter, three cutouts per half. Arrange on baking sheet(s). Coat with nonstick spray. Sprinkle with salt, herbs and spices, if desired.
3. Bake 5 to 8 minutes or until lightly browned and crisp. Let cool slightly on wire rack.
4.

Skeleton Cupcakes

YIELDS:**18** PREP TIME:**0** hours **45** mins TOTAL TIME:**1** hour **30** mins

INGREDIENTS

CUPCAKES

- 1 box white cake mix
- 4 large egg whites
- 1 c. milk

- c. canola oil
- 2 can Vanilla Frosting

DECORATIONS

- 18 marshmallows
- 4-inch lollipop sticks

- Black food color
- Decorating pen

310

- Black writing gel
- 72 yogurt-covered mini-pretzels

DIRECTIONS

1. Heat oven to 350 degrees F. Line 18 regular size muffin cups with white liners.

2. Beat cake mix, egg whites, milk and oil in large bowl with mixer on low speed 1 minute until blended; increase speed to medium and continue to beat 2 minutes or until batter is smooth. Divide batter among muffin cups, filling each 2/3 full.

3. Bake 20 to 22 minutes until a wooden toothpick inserted in centers comes out clean. Cool in pans on wire rack 10 minutes before removing cupcakes to rack to cool completely. Frost cupcakes with vanilla frosting.

4. To decorate: Slightly flatten marshmallows with palm of your hand. Insert a lollipop stick into each marshmallow. With the black decorating pen, using photo as a guide, draw the skeleton mouth along the bottom of each marshmallow. Draw 2 nostrils above the middle of the mouth, as shown. Make the eyes with dabs of the black writing gel.

5. For each skeleton, carefully thread the stick end of the marshmallow head through the small hole of a pretzel, slowly twisting the pretzel from side to side as you push it up toward the head, stopping about 1/2 inch below the head. Secure the pretzel in position with a dab of frosting. Add 2 more pretzels, lining them up, to resemble the rib cage, securing with dabs of frosting. Stick the skeleton into the top of a cupcake. To make the arms, carefully cut a pretzel in half with a serrated knife and attach to the top rib with frosting as shown. Repeat with remaining skeletons.

Made in the USA
Monee, IL
10 October 2020